Errata

Pg. 102, para. 3:
The sentence 'The Executive Director... is "divine".' should be replaced by 'The President of the organisation's international wing, Soka Gakkai International (SGI), is Daisaku Ikeda. His followers, to be found around the world, call him "sensei" (a title given to someone regarded with great respect, as the Japanese do to teachers and doctors) and some members even assert that Ikeda is "divine".'

Pg. 102, para. 4, l. 1:
'director' should be replaced by 'President'.

Pg. 103, caption:
'Executive Director' should be replaced by 'President'.

Pg. 104, para. 2, l. 1:
'reaching "God' should be replaced by 'changing one's destiny'.

Pg. 104, para. 2:
The last two sentences, 'The "God"... her call.', should be deleted.

Pg. 105, l. 7:
'his God' should be replaced by 'the Dai Gohonzon'.

Pg. 105, ll. 10 & 11:
'the Goddess of Mercy' should be replaced by 'spiritual strength'.

JAPAN
BETWEEN MYTH AND REALITY

Lee Khoon Choy

World Scientific
Singapore • New Jersey • London • Hong Kong

Distributed by

World Scientific Publishing Co Pte Ltd
P O Box 128, Farrer Road, Singapore 9128
USA office: Suite 1B, 1060 Main Street, River Edge, NJ 07661
UK office: 57 Shelton Street, Covent Garden, London WC2H 9HE

British Library Cataloguing-in-Publication Data.
A catalogue record for this book is available from the British Library.

JAPAN — BETWEEN MYTH AND REALITY

ISBN 981-02-1865-6

Printed in Singapore.

Acknowledgement

I would like to thank Mr. Dennis Bloodworth for having taken the trouble to read the manuscript, and for giving his critical and valuable suggestions and comments. I am also indebted to Mrs. Elizabeth Su for spending so much time polishing up the book for better reading.

I would also like to thank all the Japanese political leaders, bureaucrats and businessmen mentioned in this book who have freely expressed their views and comments which have made it possible to me to write the chapter on Corriders of Power. I am also grateful to the Japan Imperial Palace Protocol Department and the Ministry of Foreign Affairs for having kindly arranged for the special luncheon with the Royal Highness Emperor Hirohito which makes the chapter on Emperor Hirohito more personalised. The Imperial Household and the Ministry of Foreign Affairs were most helpful during my stay in Japan. They organised visits to the Kokugaikan (the sumo stadium) to watch sumo wrestling as well as outings for ambassadors to see cormorant fishing in Gifu, the Imperial Palace riding ground to see Japanese traditional horse riding and the Imperial stock farms in Tochigi prefecture. All these activities enabled us to have a deeper understanding of Japanese culture.

Thanks should also be given to religious leaders of Shinto shrines, Buddhist temples including the Soka Gakai and Christian churches for their assistance when visiting the religious institutions which enabled the writing of the chapter on The Ultilitarian "Gods".

It is not possible for me to name the numerous professors and lecturers at Japanese universities whose conversations, frank views and opinions have enabled me to have a deeper understanding of the Japanese society, including the Japanese language.

I enjoyed the conversations I had with so many friends of mine — artisits, musicians, sumo wrestlers, restaurant owners, company managers, shopkeepers and peoples from all walks of life and strata of society. Their frank views and expressions enriched my life during my stay in Japan. I would like to thank them for their frankness, which enabled me to have a better glimpse of Japanese society.

Last but not least, I am grateful to the Kyodo News Service for allowing me to use most of the photographs contained in this book, particularly the photographs of politicians in Chapter 8 "Corridors of Power" and other historical pictures.

Contents

Introduction

It was mid 1984 when I decided to resign from politics and hand over my responsibilities to a younger generation. I was suddenly approached by the then Foreign Minister Dhanabalam to assume the post of Ambassador to Japan. I had served as the Singaporean Ambassador to Egypt, Lebanon, Yugoslavia and Ethiopia, and as High Commissioner to Pakistan in 1968, and then Ambassador to Indonesia from 1970–74. Why should I want to serve again as Ambassador to Japan?

I thought of the advantages of serving in Japan. First of all, it is the most technologically advanced country in Asia and the relations between Singapore and Japan were good. I had so far only served in developing countries, such as Egypt and Indonesia, whose relationships with Singapore were rather strained. A lot of my time and energy was expended on re-establishing good relations. Japan would be a more comfortable posting and I could learn something from an advanced country.

Two other factors led to my decision to accept the job as Singapore's Ambassador to Japan. Firstly, Japan had once conquered China and Southeast Asia, including Malaya and Singapore. The atrocities committed by the Japanese Imperial Army were well-known to the outside world. I saw the Japanese troops marching into Butterworth, my hometown, and I suffered three years of loneliness and hardship during the Japanese Occupation because I had to hide in the Bukit Brapit jungle and work as a farmer. I had to run away because I was deeply involved in anti-Japanese campaigns to raise funds to fight the Japanese. In pre-war days, all the Chinese educated were anti-Japanese because Japan had invaded and occupied a large part of the Chinese territories. I witnessed the cruel acts of the Japanese against the Chinese in Malaya when they occupied the country. I saw the Kempeitai Chief in Butterworth slash off the head of a Chinese in a huge playing field and then display the head in front of a Mohammedan rice shop for three days.

I very much wanted to know why the Japanese could be so cruel. What had made them decide to conquer Asia and challenge the world? There must be something in the Japanese character and psyche that accounted for this darker side of humanity, this extremism of risk taking and adventurism. What was the historical and psychological background that led to the venture?

The second reason why I accepted the post was my desire to know how a defeated and devastated Japan could rise again from the ashes of ruins to become a world economic giant, all within the short space of 40 years. What made the Japanese succeed in the post-war economic miracle? I thought there was much we could learn from the Japanese.

For four years and two months I stayed in Japan, in the Embassy, working with a skeleton staff — the smallest among Asean countries — and I spent my leisure hours digging into libraries, filing up newspaper cuttings and interviewing Japanese of high ranking as well as low ranking status. I had the advantage of knowing the top political and business hierarchy, as well as leaders of social organisations — those in charge of music, fine arts and sports. I became acquainted with Prime Minister Yasukiro Nakasone, and later Takeshita. As Cabinet changes were fast, I came into contact with three Foreign Ministers — first Shintaro Abe, then Kuranari, and then Uno, who later became Prime Minister and had to resign over a scandal with a "geisha" girl. I met many "Dietmen"(parliamentarians), both from the ruling Liberal Democratic Party, and the opposition parties — the Japan Socialist Party, the Democratic Socialist Party, the Komeito and the Japan Communist Party.

I had a good glimpse of Japanese politics, as well as the economic set-up and social organisations.

I observed the behaviour and manners of Japanese, always trying to fathom the meaning and motive of each move. I visited religious organisations, churches, Shinto shrines, innumerable Buddhist temples, and talked to a great number of religious leaders.

I was particularly interested in Sumo, a sport which the Japanese claim to be their own. I enjoyed watching the Sumo and began digging into its past.

I decided to call this book *Japan — Between Myth and Reality* because I found many things in the country hanging between myth and reality. For instance, Japan is a rich country, but the quality of life of most people is poor. Most salaried workers have to wake up early in the morning, cram into packed trains or Shinkansen, and journey for two hours before they arrive at the office. As discipline is rigid, they work quietly for the whole day and after work spend their time in bars or pachinko (pinball machine) parlours because it would bring shame to their wives' faces if they went home too early. It would mean that they are useless in the company. The amenities and quality of life of the ordinary Japanese are indeed poor compared to Western countries or even Singapore. Housing facilities are inadequate and food prices are exhorbitantly expensive. The Japanese generally lead a miserable life in terms of the quality of life.

The myth that they are descendants of the Sun Goddess still prevails, despite the fact that recent archaeological discoveries in the Nara area have put those who supported the theory of a clear-cut blue-blood Japanese Emperor descendancy into an embarrassing position. The number of Korean, Korean-like or even Chinese artifacts in the tombs have raised fears of what may be discovered when the coffins are opened. The authorities decided to postpone the actual opening of the stone coffins for fear that the Japanese ancestors were Koreans or Chinese after all.

Was it a myth that Emperor Hirohito was a "cultured biologist" who left the management of his realm to generals and admirals, and devoted all his energy to pottering about with fungi and small wormlike marine organisms? In reality, could he have been a person described by David Bergamani, an expert on Japan and author of *Japan's Imperial Conspiracy*, as "a formidable war leader, a tireless, dedicated, meticulous, clever and patient man who inherited from his great grandfather a mission which was to rid Asia of white men"?

Was Shintoism, an original native religion of Japan, a myth? Or was it brought into Japan by Xu Fu, who landed in Japan 2,000 years ago with 3,000 boys and girls to look for "the elixir of life" for Emperor Qin Xi Huang, the greatest and most powerful Emperor in Chinese history?

Did Sumo wrestling originate in Japan? Or is it again another myth? Long before the Japanese were civilised, Sumo was already practised in the Warring Period and the Han dynasty. Wall carvings dating from the Han dynasty show the existence of Sumo wrestling.

The Japanese are fond of myths. Having failed to unite the people under Buddhism and the rule of the "Man-God" Emperor — an image promoted by the fascist warlords to make all Japanese obey a single person in the name of the Emperor — they have also decided to make the Nihongo (Japanese language) a myth, the only myth left to unite the Japanese, as many younger Japanese have been disillusioned by the so-called mighty Emperor "Man-God". As they failed to achieve their objective of conquering the world with bullets, they now try to conquer the world with Nihongo.

But, the Japanese language itself is a myth. The Japanese think and believe that the Nihongo is the most superior language in the world. But, it is only a myth. Take away the Chinese Kanji, take away the Katagana, which they use to absorb Western vocabulary, particularly English, and the language is left with only Hiragana, which is an extract from 48 Kanji words. The language with only Hiragana is unintelligible.

The Japanese ruling party — the Liberal Democratic Party (LDP) — is a myth. Although the LDP ruled Japan, the reality is that it is ruled by five factions which constitute the party. The five factions are formal political entities with their own headquarters, regular factional meetings, an established structure and a firm discipline of their own. The factions are in fact parties within a party. LDP activities do not make sense unless the interests of the factions are taken into account.

Japanese behaviour is also a myth. What ordinary people see in the Japanese reaction is "tatamae", the face they show without inner feelings to outsiders. They will only show their faces with inner feelings to those who are close to them and who understand them. They call this behaviour "honne". In my four year stay in Japan, I regret to say I did not see too many "honne" faces because I did not have time to drink and talk to Japanese to cultivate their personal friendships.

Japanese politeness is again a myth. They are polite to strangers who are their customers and clients. They bow to one another because it is a custom to bow. It is only a form. When a Japanese bows, it does not mean he respects or likes you. I have seen Japanese behaving rudely on many occasions on buses and trains. They jostled and pushed strangers whom they do not know and to whom they are not obliged to be kind.

The problem with the Japanese is that once they embark on something, they do not know when to stop. They are followers and normally dislike thinking and making decisions. It took Commodore Perry's shelling at Japanese ports to wake them from the slumber of isolation and myth. The reality dawned on them that they were after all vulnerable and weak. When they copied Western technology, they became so strong that they did not know when to stop. They wanted to be the master race of Asia and went on to invade China and Southeast Asia, and also challenge the United States. Even before the days of Hideyoshi, the Japanese leaders had dreamt of more worlds to conquer. Hideyoshi sent 160,000 troops to Korea in 1592. He failed but tried again in 1597. The soldiers who matched into Malaya in 1941 had the same samurai spirit as those soldiers who had invaded Korea in 1592. The Japanese preserve the national orthodoxy of "land of the Gods" and believe that they are a unique people. Japan's uniqueness became a justification for invading other countries. They have a crude belief that Japan is a God-favoured country and the Japanese are a superior race in the context of Asia.

A term "Co-Prosperity Sphere" was used by Japanese militarists to describe Asia under their control as a sphere of mutual prosperity. This myth of "Co-Prosperity Sphere" lingered on until the atom bomb dropped on Hiroshima and Nagasaki, and reality again dawned on them that they were after all not that mighty.

Japanese believe in myths and they want their future generations to continue to live in myths. They will not allow the younger generation to know what went wrong in World War II and have kept them in the dark as to what their ancestors did. They never learnt from history. They want to continue with the myth that they are the strongest and most united people on earth. So long as they continue to believe that they are descendants of the Sun Goddess — a pure superior race — and refuse to face the realities and learn from history, they may continue to make further mistakes in the future. The younger generations are more likely to commit the same mistakes as their forefathers if they are not aware of what their forefathers have done.

The Japanese have been dangerous and may be militarily dangerous again. In the intensity to compete with the world for supremacy, they have no knowledge of where they are being led and how it will all end.

The trouble with the Japanese who believe in myths is that they do not know how and when to stop until something catastrophic happens to them.

History may repeat itself.

CHAPTER 1

Xu Fu and the Bittersweet Sino-Japanese Relations

When I was at school, I learnt from Chinese history textbooks the story of Xu Fu, who led 3,000 boys and girls from China's shores to Japan in search of the elixir of life for Emperor Qin Xi Huang. Emperor Qin was dictatorial and wanted to live forever. He had conquered all the warring states and had united China for the first time as a nation. He also formulated the Chinese script which united the different writing systems in various states. He unified the measurement of weights, built the Great Wall of China and was notorious for burying alive hundreds of Confucianist scholars whom he thought were superstitious.

Emperor Qin's reign was one of the shortest in Chinese history. Before he died he went to Langya port to look for Chinese medical scholars who were well-known for their research in prolonging life. He found Xu Fu, the most prominent scholar in the Qi Kingdom. He consulted Xu Fu and requested him to look for herbs that would make him live forever. The wise Xu Fu promised the Emperor that he would carry out his mission if he could be provided with 3,000 boys and girls and all the necessary food and logistics, including technicians, doctors and medicines. The Emperor provided him with fifty ships and all that he had asked for. The convoy of ships sailed towards the east for Japan. When the ships arrived at Japan, they saw the rising sun and named the country "Nation of the Rising Sun". Xu Fu never returned to China. Perhaps he could not get the "elixir herbs" that could make life permanent, or maybe he wanted to avoid the atrocities of Qin Xi Huang.

In my younger days, I thought the story was only a legend and that Xu Fu was a legendary figure. But, today, scholars from both China and Japan are still collecting evidence and doing serious research to convince the world of the existence of Xu Fu and his journey to Japan. In the city of Xuzhou, near Yangzhou, there is a Xu Fu Research Institute, attached to Xuzhou Teachers College, doing research on Xu Fu. The person in charge of the research is Professor Loh Zhiziang, who invited me to attend a seminar in Xuzhou in April 1987 while I was Ambassador to Japan, after he was informed that I was interested in Xu Fu. Scholars from Beijing, Shanghai, Tienjin, Xian, Manchuria and other cities were present at the seminar. All scholastic information confirmed that Xu Fu existed and even managed to identify his 71st descendant. During the seminar, the Japanese Mayor of Shingu, the place where Xu Fu landed when he arrived in Japan, also sent a congratulatory message.

I visited Shingu in 1987 because I was interested in seeing the place where Xu Fu had landed. The Shingu city is situated in the prefecture of Wakayama. I met the Mayor of Shingu, who also took a personal interest in Xu Fu. He took me to the place where Xu Fu had landed — a beautiful sea beach. There was a reddish Shinto shrine there and the place was quiet and serene. We found traces of the herbs which Xu Fu had discovered and which were supposed to make man live forever. The Mayor explained that the herbs were good for people suffering from kidney trouble. People with strong kidneys can normally live longer. The Mayor also took me to see the gravestone of Xu Fu which was erected near the city. It was a sheet of stoneslab carved with Chinese characters telling the story of how Xu Fu came to Japan to look for longevity herbs and why he decided to stay. The gravestone was erected in 1834. The words "Xu Fu's gravestone" were written by a Korean calligrapher and the poem by a Japanese sinologist.

The Mayor told me that every year, on 28th November, the people of Wakayama gather in front of the grave and organise a grand celebration. In 1980, the Wakayamas celebrated Xu Fu's 2,200th anniversary. In 1915 the Wakayaman people formed a committee to preserve the remains of Xu Fu. In 1931, they formed the Xu Fu Culture Preservation Committee and in 1955 they finally formed the Association of Xu Fu.

Near Xu Fu's gravestone are also seven graves believed to be the nearest disciples of Xu Fu. Nobody knows the whereabouts of the 3,000 boys and girls Xu Fu brought to Japan.

In various parts of Japan, particularly Kyushu, there are relics of Xu Fu. When I first visited Fukuoka, I asked a top Japanese official whether he knew of Xu Fu. He was a little puzzled for he had not heard of the name. I gave him some information about the man and the next day he gave me a book called *China in the Centre of Kyushu* which contained articles about Xu Fu and other Chinese connections in Kyushu.

The Japanese all over Japan pay high respect to Xu Fu. In the village of Kinryo of Jogata city, Kyushu, Xu Fu is one of the gods worshipped by the people. Xu Fu is worshipped as a god of knowledge and medicine. The other gods are the god of water and the god of agriculture. The villagers named Xu Fu "Mr. Kinryo". There is an old painting describing the arrival of Xu Fu and his connection with the town of Kinryo. It was painted by an artist during the 17th century and has become a treasure in the Kinryo temple.

In Kinryo, in the city of Saga, whenever there is a drought, the villagers go to the Kinryo temple, put Xu Fu's portrait into a mikoshi (portable shrine) and parade around the town praying for rain. When the mikoshi is paraded, it is always followed by a 36 metres long dragon weighing two tons, made of straw and bamboo leaves. The whole festival is called Sunerori-no-Amagoi Gyoji and is celebrated on August 8th once every four or five years. This is a noisy festival for the participants who would be hitting drums to appeal to heaven for rain. In 1724, there was a serious drought in Chibu, near Kiknryho. After the festival was performed a thunderstorm swept the city.

Japanese people believe that when Xu Fu went to Chibu to look for longevity herbs, he succeeded with the help of villagers. There is even a story that he fell in love with a Japanese girl in Chibu.

I also visited the seafront of Shingu and saw some debris of broken walls here and there stretching to about 20 miles long. They were piled up about 1.5 metres high. The Japanese there believe that Xu Fu had built a great wall, a miniature of the Great Wall of China. During the Edo period (AD 1600–1861) there were records of repairs to the Great Wall. Some scholars believe that Xu Fu had built the great wall to prevent Emperor Qin Xi Huang from attacking Japan to capture him. In Edo times, it was unimaginable that anyone could have built a wall so long without strong mass support of labour, as it would have cost a fortune.

The place where Xu Fu landed was exactly the same place where Japanese legendary figure Jimmu Tenno had landed. One Taiwanese author, Wei Teng Sen, wrote a book called *Xu Fu and Japan* in 1970 and claimed that Japan's first Emperor was in fact Xu Fu. He based his speculations on the timing of the landing of the Japanese first Emperor and that of Xu Fu, which incidentally coincided. The book claims that from the graves of prominent Japanese royalty who lived during Amaterasu's period, a Qin dynasty bronze mirror and a huge fighting knife used during the Qin dynasty were found. How could there be such relics in Japan had it not been for Xu Fu's visit? When Xu Fu arrived in Japan over 2,000 years ago, Japan was still in the stone age and they could not have produced such relics. The book said the evidence pointed to the fact that Xu Fu was in fact Japan's first Emperor.

The author was motivated by the fear that if the Japanese continued to believe that they were descendants of God without going deeper into scientific history, history might repeat itself, because they believe that they belong to a superior race. Japan's history is shrouded in mythology. Most Japanese still believe that they are descendants of God, as related in the two earliest chronicles — the Kojiki (ancient tales) and the Nihonshoki (chronicles of Japan). According to the chronicles, Emperor Jimmu, their first Emperor, ascended the throne in 660 BC. But since neither chronicle was compiled until the beginning of the 8th century, what was written could not be entirely reliable. Mystery further surrounds these two historical documents, which were written in classic Chinese.

The Taiwanese author was strongly criticised by many Japanese scholars who described his book as "baseless" and "nonsense".

Sometime in 1987, I met a Japanese scholar who has made an extensive study of Xu Fu. His name is Ino Okifu. He studied at the Waseda University and after the war emigrated to the United States and Latin America because Japan was occupied by the Allied Forces. He told me that he left the country to find out why Japan had committed so many atrocities in Asia and why Japan had decided to take on the world. He stayed away from Japan for 25 years and only returned ten years ago.

Ino was apologetic when he spoke of Japanese atrocities in Asia and Southeast Asia. He felt ashamed that the Japanese had committed so many inhuman things. Ino believes that during the Qin dynasty, Xu Fu was a prominent leader in the Chi kingdom, which was famous for medical research in prolonging life. Emperor Qin wanted to get rid of Xu Fu because he presented a threat to him, and he had asked Xu Fu to look for the herbs knowing that it was an impossible task. Xu Fu knew that if he were to return to China, he would be killed by Emperor Qin. That was why he refused to return to China.

Ino said that Xu Fu brought with him a store of Chinese knowledge and wisdom, including Taoism. Ino thinks that Xu Fu was the real founder of Japanese Shintoism. He said during the Warring period, the Kingdom of Chi took religion seriously. Everyone who went to a Taoist temple had to cleanse themselves and there would be a special room for people to cleanse their souls. In every Shinto shrine there is still a room for prayers for cleansing. This room is named "the chi room" — chi derives from the chi kingdom.

I doubted Ino's claim and started to visit Shinto shrines to find out the truth whenever I visited the prefectures. When I visited a Shinto shrine, I would ask the question, "Do you have a chi room to cleanse the soul of prayers?" The attendant of the shrine, who normally wears a white flowing gown, always looked at me with surprise, for no visitor had asked the question. The answer is always "Yes, we have a chi room and everyone who visits the shrine to pray has first to cleanse himself or herself in the chi room." I asked the attendants whether they knew the origin of the chi room and they apparently had no knowledge. I came to the conclusion that Ino's statement makes sense.

Ino came out with more surprising conclusions in his research. He said Xu Fu and his entourage who had stayed behind in Japan left behind millions of descendants. He said if I were to see any Japanese with eyes of "yellow tea colour" they would be the descendant of the chi tribe — the same tribe Xu Fu belonged to. Many of these Japanese would carry the surname of Saito, meaning chi in Chinese. He said Confucius and LaoTse both had chi origins. The descendants of Xu Fu's entourage carried different surnames. Many of them had the surname of Qin, the surname of the Qin Emperor. In the Yamaguchi prefecture, there was once the kingdom of Qin which was established about 1,300 years ago. When the Emperor of Sui sent his mission to Japan, he was told that the people in Yamaguchi had similar faces, customs and manners as those from China, and that they were descendants of Xu Fu's mission. In Ino's estimation, at least 30 percent of the Japanese have Chinese blood and are descendants of Xu Fu's entourage.

"If we Japanese knew that we are after all blood brothers of the Chinese, we would not have committed the atrocities in Chinese cities during the Second World War. We might not even have invaded China," said Ino. He added, "I have not been to China, because I am ashamed of what we did to the Chinese people during the last war. I must get over this feeling before I visit China."

Ino said that the theory that Japanese were descendants of God was dangerous and that history might repeat itself if the Japanese continued to believe that they were descendants of God. Hence, he was planning to write a book to enlighten the Japanese as to their origins.

In Japan, the most tightly guarded "secrets" are the graves of Japanese ancestors. Nobody is supposed to touch them, not to mention excavate them for research purposes, without the permission of the royal family. If the Japanese allow the tombs of their ancestors to be excavated and researched, the history of Japan might have to be rewritten. What if they discover that their ancestors were in fact Chinese or Koreans? It is better to leave history alone and believe in mythology.

After all, Japan is a country of myth and the Japanese too are fond of myths.

Xu Fu was perhaps the first Chinese to set foot in Japan and his entourage of 3,000 children made an impact on the Japanese society, which was then in the stone age. It is useless to argue whether Xu Fu was Japan's first Emperor. One thing is certain: he was the first Chinese to arrive in Japan and can be considered the pioneer of Sino-Japanese relations.

When Xu Fu arrived in Japan, most Japanese had long hair with a knot tied over their heads and a piece of white cloth tied over their foreheads. Even today, Japanese are fond of tying white cloth over their foreheads at a festival. Their clothing was simply a piece of cloth covering the whole body and they were barefooted.

The significant thing about the Japanese was that they were tattooed. As most of them were fishermen, it is believed that they were tattooed because they had to dive into the sea to catch fish and the tattoo could be a means of deceiving the fish.

The ladies only wore a piece of cloth, with a hole around the neck like a Mexican poncho. They were very tolerant and not jealous. There was polygamy and Japanese men normally married four or five wives. They loved wine. They used their hands to eat, like Malays, Indians and other Polynesians. Since there was no meat, they usually ate fish, vegetables and rice. Xu Fu taught them to catch whales and they started to learn to eat whale-flesh.

Xu Fu found most Japanese had lived a long life, reaching the age of 80–90 and some were even over 100.

Xu Fu was the first Chinese to introduce ancient Chinese culture and civilisation to the Japanese. He taught them magic, divination, astrology and geomancy, as well as rice planting and whale catching.

Since Xu Fu's arrival in Japan, there have been many waves of contact between Japan and China. The first official contact which China made with Japan was in the Han dynasty (57 BC) when Emperor Kuang We presented a gold seal as a token of appreciation to a Japanese envoy who visited Loh Yang. This gold seal was lost for 2,000 years until it was discovered by a farmer in 1784 in Kyushu. The gold seal can be viewed in a museum in Fukuoka.

Many things that the Japanese use in their daily life came from China. For instance, the custom of sitting on the floor on low tables to eat, the lacquer dish holders containing Japanese food, the lacquered clogs or "geta"

A sketch of Xu Fu.

An antique lacquer tray modernly used by Japanese, found in the grave of a famous military general Choo Ran in Anhei Province, 1984.

which Japanese ladies wear and the common use of name cards were all borrowed from China. In June 1984, in the Chinese province of Anhei, archaeologists discovered an old grave belonging to a famous military general called Choo Ran of the Wu Kingdom (the three kingdoms were Wu, Wei and Yeh). They found 140 pieces of various types of vessels. Among them were low tables, used for the people to lean against when they squatted on the floor. They also found lacquered clogs and name cards made of wood.

Japan started to introduce Chinese civilisation seriously from the Tang dynasty onwards by sending embassies, monks and other missions to China, which was unquestionably the richest, strongest and most advanced state in the world. Japan has demonstrated a passion for learning, the insatiable thirst for knowledge as well as an aptitude for choosing, adopting and adapting to their own uses the ideas and techniques of foreign countries. Buddhism, laws, the family system, city planning, Chinese characters, Confucianism, art, as well as new industries were introduced into Japan from Tang China.

Japan borrowed much from Chinese culture, just as England, France and Germany borrowed from ancient Greece and Rome. The difference is, however, that ancient Greece and Rome have disappeared, while the Chinese state, based on the traditional culture, still stands today.

The Japanese began to fear China when the Mongolians, after destroying the Sung dynasty, went on to invade Japan. Khublai Khan, whose army overran much of Asia and part of Europe, had incorporated Korea into their empire and demanded Japan's submission in 1266. In 1274, Khublai despatched a 30,000 strong navy of a mixed Mongol and Korean force from Korean ports to Hakata Bay in North Kyushu. In 1281, they staged another attack with 140,000, a mixture of Mongolians, Chinese and Koreans, from both the ports of China and Korea. It was probably the greatest overseas expedition the world had seen. The Japanese had erected a wall around Hakata Bay and this managed to contain the invaders for almost two months, while smaller, more mobile Japanese boats played havoc with the Mongolian junks.

God was however on the side of the Japanese. A typhoon, which the Japanese described as a Kamikaze, struck, destroying much of the Mongol fleet and forcing the remaining Mongolian force to withdraw. This kamikaze confirmed the Japanese belief that the country was unique and "divine".

These abortive invasions of the Mongolians left two significant and countervailing impressions on the Japanese minds: a sense of a potential threat from China and at the same time, a conviction that Japan was invincible.

Japan's physical isolation, coupled with good relations with its giant and venerable neighbour, gave birth to the unique national characteristics of Japan during the Kamakura period onwards. Among them, the development of a highly homogeneous race, a certain sense of inferiority and insecurity, nationalism and fraternal feelings toward China are some of the striking features.

There was a standstill in Sino-Japanese relations during the Yuan dynasty because of the Mongolian invasion. By the Ming and Ching dynasties Japan had virtually stopped sending scholars and missions to China to study from the Chinese. Mainland China became politically weak due to internal strife and inner power struggles, and European countries gradually moved in to carve out the Chinese territories into different spheres of influence. There was nothing new which the Chinese could teach the Japanese.

By then, the Portuguese had found their way to Japan and it was the beginning of European influence in the region. The great and most lasting European influence in Japan at that time was Western military technology and Western political organisation. The aruebuses of the Portuguese were the first firearms the Japanese had encountered and they made a tremendous impact on the Japanese who saw their value. Cannons were first used in warfare in Japan in about 1558 and within two decades the firepower of musketeer copras had become the decisive factor in battles in the field. The richer daimyo (a feudal lord, a hereditary samurai warrior in feudal Japan) who could afford the new weapons became more dominant over his weaker and less modernised rivals and thus moved swiftly toward a consolidation of political power.

Since the days of Hideyoshi (1536–1598), the Japanese shogun (the generalissimo and military commander, exercising absolute rule over Japan under the nominal leadership of the Emperor), Japan has been practising the principle of "learn from the West and forget the East" and implementing the policy of "revere the Emperor, expel the barbarians".

Since the Tokugawa era, the Japanese trend of thought underwent gradual change, deriving principally from Japan's success in modernisation and victories over Russia and China. The two wars had proved beyond a shadow of doubt that Japan had indeed developed into a "rich country and strong military power" and they started a course of foreign conquest and empire. Japan conquered Taiwan and Korea and ruled them as colonies.

Japan's perspective of China has evolved from a sense of inferiority to that of superiority during the last hundred years.

Sino-Japanese relations have gone through various stages of change since the days of Xu Fu. In the beginning, Japanese regarded the Chinese as their mentors. They derived their inspiration and cultures from China. There is practically very little in Japan's culture that was not copied from China. After Japan caught up with China in modernisation, they began to look down on the Chinese and started to compete with Western powers to control Asia, as they believe they were the leader and master in Asia. They began to feel that they were superior to all Asians as well as Europeans.

Throughout a millenium of contact down to the Meiji period, the Japanese looked to China as the motherland of their culture. The contrast with China in size, age and prestige also gave the Japanese collectively a certain sense of inferiority. Ever since the sixth century, Japanese leaders and people often praised Japanese national traits in an effort to compensate for China's indisputable superiority. Yet, this feeling of inferiority remained until the Meiji Restoration of 1868. After that event, a superiority complex was rapidly born from Japan's amazing success in its modernisation.

By the end of the nineteenth century, Japan's transformation was almost accomplished and its new institutional structure developed. The modernised Japanese maintained their independence and looked toward East Asia, where they could take an active role comparable to one that the West had taken in the underdeveloped world. By contrast, China was slow in accommodating itself to modern civilisation. As a result, it was humiliated at the hands of Western powers. One Western country after another bombarded China and demanded territorial control of her ports. Japan began to look down on China and felt that she had a duty to lead Asia against the West. So Japan invaded China and went on to invade Southeast Asia, ultimately taking on the United States by bombing Pearl Harbour. They became so arrogant that they took on the world.

With Japan's defeat in World War II, many Japanese feel a sense of guilt about past Japanese atrocities in China. Although defeated, the Japanese still maintain a sense of superiority because they believe that it was not China that had shattered Japanese forces.

After the Communist Party took over and with the establishment of the People's Republic of China, China became the only non-Western country with nuclear weapons and in 1971 became a permanent member of the United Nations Security Council. China is called a "superpower" more often than Japan. China and Japan now stand on an equal political footing. What will be the impact on the Japanese sense of superiority resulting from this new pattern?

I personally feel that the feeling of superiority of the Japanese vis-à-vis China will probably continue now that she has caught up in economic advancement and become a world economic giant, becoming the only Asian country represented in the world's seven economic powers.

Japan has also rearmed herself with a defence budget easily the largest in the world after those of the US and the former Soviet Union. Her military mission made its presence at Kompong Som in Cambodia as "peace-keeping forces" under the UN Peacekeeping Co-Operation Law.

Japan's fear of China since the Mongolian invasion and the Chinese hatred of the Japanese resulting from the Nanking massacre during World War II have created a complex feeling on both sides, which makes goodwill difficult to nurture. The strong hatred still harboured by some in the aftermath of a hundred years of conflict makes relations difficult to heal by any single effort.

A number of Japanese tourists and Japanese stationed in China had adopted an arrogant attitude towards local Chinese. These young Japanese, unconscious of the atrocities their ancestors had committed in China, found the Chinese rather backward and began to show signs of superiority and arrogance. There have been cases in which Japanese students were detained by the Public Security Bureau for two nights after beating up taxi drivers. The Japanese became rude and disrespectful to the Chinese. Japanese history books have not taught them what the Japanese did in China during the war.

The Japanese Emperor Akihito and the Empress visited China in 1993 and expressed the hope that the two countries will start fresh cordial relations for future mutual benefit. Emperor Akihito was the first Japanese Emperor to visit China.

Can this be the beginning of new era in the bittersweet relations between Japan and China? Only time will tell.

CHAPTER 2

Emperor Hirohito

It was one early morning in the small village of Butterworth, Malaysia, 49 years ago, that I first came to know about Emperor Hirohito, "God" to most Japanese. After coming out of the Bukit Brapit jungle, I went for a crash course in the Japanese language for three months and became a Japanese language teacher. I had gone into the jungle to avoid Japanese arrest because I had participated in anti-Japanese activities. My contact with Emperor Hirohito was more of a spiritual one. Every morning, students and teachers had to bow to the East, towards the direction of the Emperor's throne. They bowed 90 degrees and afterwards sang the Kimigayo — the Japanese National Anthem. The ceremony of bowing to the Emperor was called "Kyujoyohai". While I was bowing, I did not in my wildest dreams believe that I would one day see the Emperor face to face as Singapore's Ambassador to Japan, at the Tokyo Imperial Palace.

For several decades, Emperor Hirohito was "God" to all Japanese. No Japanese was allowed to raise his head to see the Emperor for he was "God". Japanese children were warned that they would be blinded if they dared look at the Emperor's face. He was the 124th direct descendant of Japan's first Emperor, Jimmu, who was believed to be descended from the supreme heavenly divinity, the Sun Goddess Amaterasu-Omikami.

Like most peoples, the first men of Yamato explained the origins of time and the world in terms of their own surroundings and their own fancy. The first Emperor was Jimmu, a legendary figure who was supposedly crowned in 660 BC. He was the great-grandson of the Sun Goddess Amaterasu, who had placed Japan under her protection. Japan's early history was written in Kojiki and Nihongi, the two great seventh-century chronicles written in classic Chinese. They were based on the crude belief that Japan was a God-favoured country and the Japanese were a superior race in the context of Asia.

According to the Nihongi, shortly after heaven and earth were separated out of chaos, the god Izanagi and the goddess Izanami stood on the bridge of heaven and peered below them. They thrusted down the jewelled spear of heaven and with it found the ocean. The brine which dripped from the point of the spear became solid and grew into an island. They came down to the island and started to produce offspring. Their very first children were the eight islands which made up Japan — called the Great Eight Island Country. Izanagi and Izanami continued to produce the mountains, rivers, trees, rocks and later animals. Then, they produced a human being who was Lord of the Universe, called Amaterasu-Omikami. She fought many battles with evil spirits and cleared the way for her descendants to inherit the "Great Eight Island Country" Japan. She sent her grandson down from the Plain of Heaven and gave him the three tokens of his divine rule — a divine sword, jewels from the mountain steps of heaven and the mirror into which she herself had gazed. Going down, he alighted on a mountain, and began his rule over the country of Japan. There has since been an uninterrpted line of Japanese Emperors in Japanese history, traditional descendants from one of his sons. Emperor Hirohito was the 124th descendant.

There is something very significant in the Japanese character, perhaps you may call it the "the Japanese wisdom". In the history of Japan, there have been numerous political and military struggles for power. However, whichever clan came into power, the Emperor was never harmed. They used him as a symbol of power possessing no real authority and he was always protected by the rulers who used him for symbolic functions. He could not be deposed of by any political authority, but neither could he step down from the royal position. That explains why there has been a straight line of descendents from the first Emperor. The fact that the Emperor should have become a symbol while real power was progressively transferred down to lower levels is of enduring interest, since the pattern of diffused responsibility — decisions made without anyone being identifiable as the decision-maker — persists in Japan to this day.

The peculiarly Japanese conception of the prestige of the Imperial institution has close relations to the traditionally fundamental concept of harmony. The atmosphere of "harmony" which prevails between the monarch and his subjects has enabled the Emperor institution to endure as an institution which has been characteristic of the political history of Japan. In both Western and Eastern countries, dynasties changed hands and Emperors were disposed of — some were killed, while others went into hiding. In China, for instance, one dynasty overthrew another, changing the Emperors,

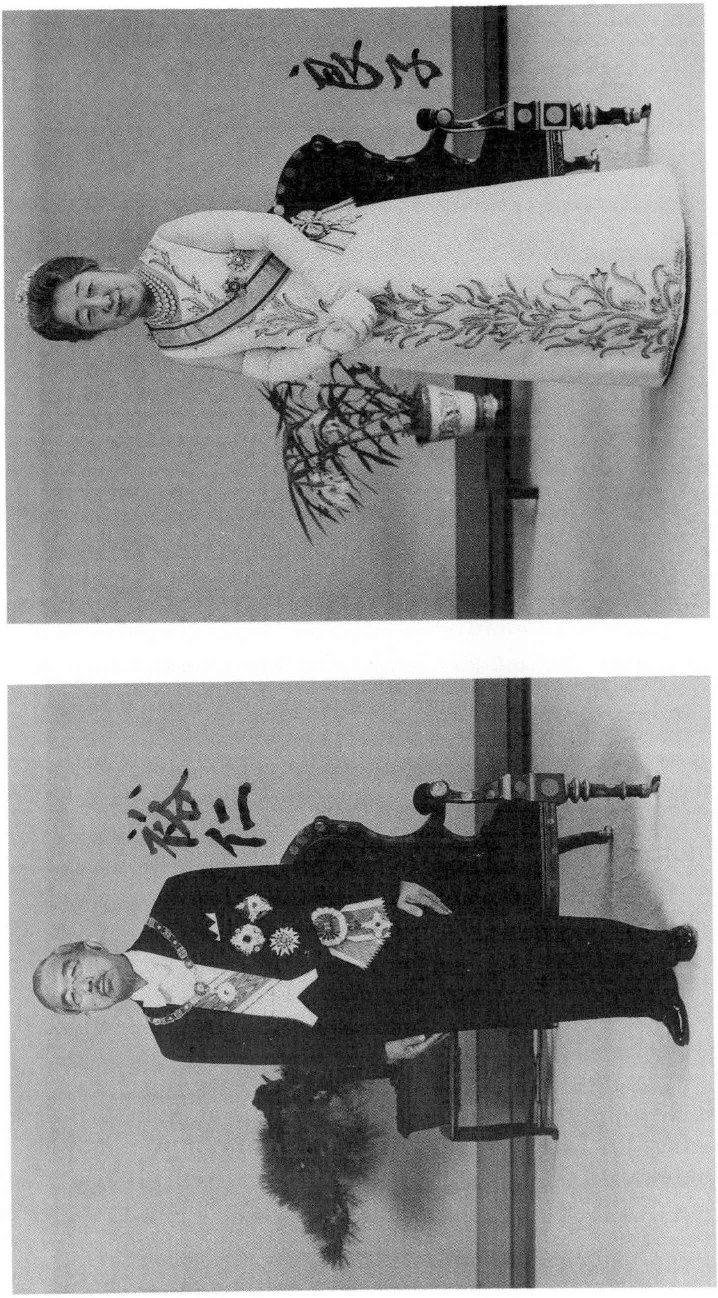

An autographed copy of a portrait of Emperor Hirohito and the Empress, sent to me before I left Japan.

and in many cases even killing them off. But in Japan, there has been only one ruling dynasty or "royal family", which has no specific family name, thus evidencing the remote antiquity of its relationship. This dynasty has survived for more than 2,000 years.

One reason may have been the existence of Japan as a nation that had hardly ever been seriously threatened by wars with foreign powers. Thus, there were really very few occasions calling for immediate decisions. Japanese internal wars generally involved struggles between sub-systems as to who would hold the actual power, and did not affect national policy as a whole. The Imperial Court, apart from realigning itself occasionally, remained unaffected.

It was only after the Meiji Restoration in 1868 that Japan's policy toward foreign powers had to be formulated. The Meiji Constitution of 1889 designated the Emperor as the possessor of absolute authority. The Emperor Meiji assumed political authority never before held by a Japanese Emperor except for a short-lived attempt at restoration of direct imperial rule in the 14th century. By the beginning of the Showa era in 1926, the Emperor had begun to assume an unusual role as the possessor of autocratic power in the modern sense. The nature of the system, however, compelled him to entrust this power to administrative officials. When Hirohito took over, the warlords who were the military leaders of the country, such as General Tojo, took over control and in the name of the Emperor conquered China and Southeast Asia, under the disguise of the "Asia Co-Prosperity Sphere".

When Japan occupied part of China and Southeast Asia, Emperor Hirohito was treated as "Tenno Heika", the God, and I was bowing as a subject of Japan's Imperial conquest. The warlords wanted not only Japanese citizens to regard him as "God", but also all subjects of Japan-conquered territories. All subjects of Japanese domination had to bow to Emperor Hirohito every morning.

In July 1984, when I presented my credentials to Emperor Hirohito at the Imperial Palace, I met him face to face, not as a subject but as Singapore's Ambassador to Japan. I was representing the independent state of Singapore as a "distinguished representative" to present a credential signed by the President of Singapore.

At about 2.45 pm, the protocol officer Nakajima came to my residence in Roppongi and briefed me about the procedure of presentation. He had been a diplomat in Amoy during the Japanese Occupation and after the war had been a diplomat in Europe and America. He was by nature cautious and methodical, and made me rehearse before the actual event. He took me to the Palace Hotel just opposite the Imperial Palace. I saw two old-fashioned British-styled horse carriages, mounted at the front by four blue-uniformed horsemen and four at the back. I was in a tailcoat, specially tailored for the occasion. Accompanied by Nakajima, I climbed into the carriage, followed by three of my staff who took the other carriage. The drivers of the carriages wore British top hats. As the horses clip-clopped towards the Palace, traffic halted for us to pass. The carriage passed the Imperial Gardens where summer flowers were blooming. As we entered the gates, a large gathering of visiting tourists stood by and waved to us. "Who could this Ambassador be?" I heard one of them asking, "Is he the Chinese Ambassador? He looks like a Chinese."

There was tranquility in the Palace compound and I felt a sense of serenity. I admired the well-trimmed pine trees which were very beautiful. The clip-clop of the horse shoes reminded me of my trip to Brioni when I presented my credentials to President Tito.

The Palace occupied a large green space in the centre of Tokyo. On a map, it looks like the hole in a doughnut. The grounds, 284 acres in all, have no tube lines running under them and until recently, no adjacent buildings could be built high enough to peer over. Amid the oppressive density and hurly-burly of the metropolis, the Palace is protected by moats, walls and Japan's finest electronic surveilance equipment. Inside, there exists a surprising profusion of flora, fauna and landscape styles, ranging from the classical Japanese garden to large patches of wilderness. The Emperor, being a natural scientist, favoured the latter.

Home of the Tokugawa shogun for nearly 280 years, the site passed to the Imperial Household with the Meiji Restoration at 1868. It was destroyed in World War II, but was rebuilt and completed in 1968. I saw no trace of any damage. On entering the Palace, I noticed a huge painting of the sea with three huge rocks. It was a Japanese-styled painting by Higashiyama, the famous Japanese painter who spent three years on the painting. I was quite impressed with the painting of the blue sea, greenest waves and grey rocks. I later became acquainted with Higashiyama, who was then 73 years old, and became his friend. I was introduced to Higashiyama when I had my first painting exhibition organised by Mainichi No E, a prominent Japanese painting organisation company, the proprietor of which was a friend of Higashiyama. I invited him to view my paintings at the Singapore Embassy one evening and he decided to write a forward for my painting album.

When I reached the outer chamber, the then Foreign Minister Shintaro Abe (who has since passed away) was waiting for me. He was also in a tailcoat. At all functions connected with Emperor Hirohito, all present had to wear tailcoats. I sat next to Abe and chatted with him in Japanese, a language which I managed to polish up a little before my departure to Japan. He told me of his successful trip to Korea and spoke about the security problem confronting Chon Do-Hwan on his coming visit to Japan. He said there were 800,000 Koreans in Japan and their loyalty was divided between pro-Kim I Sung and pro-Choon Do-Hwan. It made security arrangements difficult.

Before I entered the inner chamber, Abe warned me that the presentation ceremony would be short, for the Emperor was rather weak physically. At the appointed hour, a protocol officer came to inform us that the time had come. I proceeded to the Imperial Hall and saw a short figure with thick glasses wearing a grey suit, his habitual dress. When I came nearer, I tried to have a clearer look at him but I could hardly see his eyes. They were too small and were covered by thick spectacles. He was old and weak, and fumbled for words when it was his turn to speak. For a moment there was a sudden pause and I thought he had forgotten what he was supposed to say. Apparently, he was trying to remember what he had been told to say. When it came to my turn to speak, I told the Emperor that I had been appointed as Singapore's Ambassador to Japan and had brought with me the letter of credence. The Emperor said, "Welcome to Japan. I am glad that you have been chosen to better relations between Japan and Singapore." He then asked about the health of our President. He added, "I was told that you had visited Japan before with Prime Minister Lee Kuan Yew. What is your impression of Japan?"

I told the Emperor that I was impressed with Japan because it was a progressive and prosperous country where wealth was fairly distributed. He seemed happy with my remarks. He then warned me of the Japanese weather and said that I should take good care of my health during my stay in Japan.

After a short conversation, I introduced my embassy staff to the Emperor. Abe then came to warn me that we had to leave. I took leave of the Emperor by turning around and walking off. The whole ceremony was short and simplc. It was not as elaborate as the ceremony dictated by Ethiopian Emperor Haile Selasie when I presented credentials to him in 1969. On that occasion, I had to retreat three steps facing him and turned my back only after the third bow. The only similarity was the insistance of a cocktail suit being worn. There were no unchained lions inside the inner chamber to frighten me and no little chiwawa to pee on my shoes.

The Japanese Emperor was definitely luckier than the Ethiopian Emperor. Hirohito saw the country triumphantly rule Asia and also witnessed the miserable fall of the Empire. He saw the country rise again from the ashes of defeat and witnessed it overcoming all difficulties to become the world's richest nation. He died peacefully with great honour, whilst Emperor Haile Selasie died a miserable death in a small apartment where he was detained after the Communist rebels overthrew him. They were both short and stately. I found Hirohito easier to talk to. Emperor Hirohito was, however, a controversial figure in international circles and there was strong criticism about his involvement in the initiation of the Second World War and for the atrocities in the Nanking massacre.

The presentation of credentials was too brief a meeting. There was not enough time for me to talk to the Emperor. Then, a year later, I managed to talk more freely to Emperor Hirohito in a more congenial atmosphere, at a luncheon party specially arranged for me at the Imperial Palace. It is a custom in Japan for every Ambassador and his wife to lunch once with the Emperor. That was an Imperial protocol in order that the Emperor could have the opportunity to see every Ambassador during his term of office in Tokyo. This was a rare opportunity for me to meet the Emperor at close quarters.

The lunch was attended by Prince Hitachi, the second son of the Emperor, Princess Hitachi, the Gaimusho Vice-Minister and a number of Imperial protocol officers. All of us wore morning coats. The lunch was rather formal. No speeches were made but the Emperor, old and frail, was in a mood to talk. I talked to him for ten minutes with an interpreter.

As usual, the Emperor always asked about the weather to strike off the conversation. I took the opportunity to ask the Emperor which period of his 60 years of reign he liked best. He pondered for a while and said, "It was in 1921 when I visited Singapore on my way to Europe. I went to your beautiful Botanic Gardens, where rubber trees were grown." I said, "Oh, I was not even born yet." The Emperor laughed loudly and asked, "How are the rubber trees in Singapore?" Apparently he was under the impression that Singapore was a country with rubber trees. I was surprised with the question he had asked and told him that rubber trees were in fact grown more in Malaysia. He said he saw some rubber trees in the Singapore Gardens and I explained to him how rubber trees came to be planted in Singapore.

Emperor Hirohito visited Europe while he was still Crown Prince. It was a six month extensive tour, the first time in Japanese history that the heir apparent had made an overseas journey. It symbolised Japan's drive towards Westernisation at home and a peaceful rapport with foreigners. On March 21 1921, Hirohito and his entourage boarded the old battleship "Katori" in Yokohama harbour. They sailed out to Europe with stops at Hong Kong,

Singapore, Colombo, and Port Said. He was 20, a handsome thin-faced man who took his responsibilities seriously. Although not yet officially regent, he had begun to take the place of his father Emperor Taisho at state functions. Emperor Taisho, whose personal name was Yoshihito, was not of sound mind. As his brain weakened, he became progressively more embarrassing to his court officials. The last straw was when, at a formal convocation of the Imperial Diet, he rolled up the manuscript of the message which was meant for him to read and used it as a telescope to peer through at the distinguished audience.

Crown Prince Hirohito's behaviour during the European tour rather surprised the subjects who accompanied him. He did not behave like a Prince. When two stokers met accidental deaths, he visited the engine room wearing the sailors' rough working cloths and endured the heat of the engine room. Covered with oil and perspiration, he clambered up and down the hot iron ladders. He made enquiries concerning the whereabouts of the spot where the stokers had been scalded to death. Between formal calls and official dinners, Hirohito went to the London theatre and spent a holiday fishing in the Scottish Highlands.

He visited Eton, played golf in public, talked with Lord Baden-Powell and sat for a portrait by Augustus John. In Amsterdam, he went to see "The Night Watch" at the Rijksmuseum and in Rome he had an audience with Pope Benedict XV, and had an informal lunch with President Thomas Masaryk of Czechoslovakia. He celebrated the 100th anniversary of Napoleon's death in Paris and toured the battlefield of Verdun with Marshal Philippe Petain. In Paris, Hirohito went shopping on his own, quite an extroadinary act for a prince in those days.

Crown Prince Hirohito made a good impression. He was sincere. He spent much of his time studying the history and politics of the countries he visited.

Indeed, 1921 marked the most unforgettable days for Emperor Hirohito. According to the official diary of the trip, written in English by Count Yoshinori Futara and Setrsuzo Sawada, the Crown Prince made good use of every minute of his tour. For instance, in Rome, one of his attendants found him writing some letters to Japan at the height of a hot summer afternoon. He urged Hirohito to follow local custom by taking a siesta. According to the diary, Hirohito replied, "Oh, that's all right. I only mean to do as much as I can. As I have no time of my own, I can't take a rest. Really, I have no time. Why you know that I haven't time, don't you?"

The Crown Prince met King George V and the then British Premier, the wily Lloyd George. He played golf with the future Edward VIII, who became his ideal of the modern prince. It must have been an exhilirating experience for Hirohito, as from 1632 to 1865 no reigning Emperor had ever ventured outside the Palace in Kyoto.

Inbetween our conversation during the lunch, I told the Emperor that he must be very proud of his people, who have recovered from the ruins of war and have made Japan into an economic giant within the short space of 40 years. He smiled and said, "Yes, I am proud of my people." The Emperor then asked what I thought was the world's economic situation. I said the best thing was for the richer nations to help poorer nations and if they could do so there would be lesser chance of war. He said, "You are right. This is the way it should be. The rich must always help the poor."

The protocol officer then murmured to me that they had to rush through the lunch and finish it early because the Emperor usually took a nap in the afternoon.

The third time I met the Emperor at close quarters was during Singaporean Prime Minister Lee Kuan Yew's visit to Japan in June 1986. Premier Lee brought with him a calligraphy of the word "Longevity" written by my old friend Xiong Nien, a monk who was one of the leading calligraphists in Singapore. Premier Lee had visited Japan officially in 1979 and he had the pleasure of seeing the Emperor after seven years of absence. Lee said in the banquet that "during these seven years Japan made tremendous progress in all fields.

"You have overcome the oil crisis and have developed into the leading nation of the world, economically much admired and respected by the international community."

Lee added, "Your Imperial Highness must be very proud to see Japan emerge from a devastated and poverty striken country after the war, 40 years ago, into an economic giant with the highest GNP in Asia. I agree with the feelings you expressed during the anniversary celebration of your 60th year of your reign, when you said, "I feel overwhelmed with emotion when I consider that our nation has achieved an honourable status in the international community as a peace loving country after overcoming many hardships after the war through the efforts of my people." "

Lee said he agreed with the Japanese Prime Minister Nakasone when he said that although the Emperor was only a symbol of Japan, his position as an important pillar at the centre of national unity remained unchanged, and the bond between the Emperor and his people based on love and trust was becoming more solid through times of trouble.

During my four year stay in Japan, I had many occasions to meet the Emperor. On New Years Day and on his birthday, the Emperor would throw a party at the Imperial grounds for the diplomatic corps. There would be delicious Japanese food, Japanese music and dancing. All those attending would be wearing morning coats. I saw many oldish gentlemen wearing awards bestowed by the Emperor. When they met the Emperor when he went round greeting people, I noticed the older generation were still bowing to him in the same way as they did before the war. The Emperor would stop for a while to talk to his guests.

That was when I first arrived in 1984. When I left Tokyo in 1988 he was not in a position to walk too much and sat in a chair near the rostrum. The guests would bow to him from afar.

The Emperor performs duties stipulated in the Constitution. He appoints the Prime Minister as designated by the Diet (Parliament). He also appoints the Chief Justice of the Supreme Court as designated by the Cabinet, promulgates Constitutional amendments, laws, Cabinet orders and treaties. He sits in during convocation of the Diet, has the right to dissolve the House of Representatives, proclaims general elections, attests to appointments and dismissals of Ministers of State and other officials, and receives credentials from foreign Ambassadors. The Emperor also presents awards and honours to its citizens and performs ceremonial functions associated with Japanese customs and traditions.

Apart from the normal official duties, the Imperial Palace also helps to preserve a number of ancient customs and games unique to Japan. These include kamo-ryo — duck netting with scoop nets at the Imperial Preserves in Saitama and Chiba Prefectures. Almost every year, I attended this interesting duck netting game. We took a train to a station in Saitama and were brought by buses to a preserved land planted with pine trees. There were many trenches filled with water. We were divided into different groups, each holding a net with a long pole. We were led by a Japanese captain to a trench and waited on both sides. There was a little house with a small door which held back the duck from inside the house. Everyone was supposed to be quiet. Then, suddenly, the door opened and a fleet of ducks moved out from the door. When they began to fly away, we aimed at one of them and used our net to catch them. At the end of the game, there was a count to see who was the champion. I was not too good at the game but my wife was quite good at it. But we never won a prize.

After the game, we had lunch at the estate and some delicious ducks were served in a barbecue on a piece of stone, which tasted nice with sake. But they were not the ducks we caught. We had earlier enjoyed another game of letting off the ducks we caught.

The Imperial Household also organised visits for diplomats to enjoy viewing how trained cormorants caught fishes in the river off Gifu. This took place every summer around July. My family and I went there almost every year. We stayed overnight at a Gifu hotel and went on the river in little boats. This game is called "ugai" and was another game borrowed from China. The cormorants were wonderful birds. The fishermen tied up their throats so that they were unable to swallow. They were then thrown into the river to catch a kind of fish called "ayu". They were quite good at it and started swallowing fish only to have them thrown out of their throats when the fishermen brought them back to the boats. It must have been quite a frustration for the cormorants.

At the end of the game, there were fireworks which lighted the dark corners of the mountain. We could see a stretch of darkness and the firewords of different colours and shapes lighted up the sky, and we could catch a glimpse of the castle which was situated on top of the mountain. The fire torches used by the cormorant boats lighted up the river surrounding them. The diplomats who accompanied us had a good view of the river scene which had many comorant boats fishermen catching the "ayus". It was a beautiful sight.

Both the duck netting and cormorant fishing were ancient Japanese games carefully preserved by the Imperial family. We were also shown an ancient form of Japanese polo played at the Imperial Palace Riding Ground where the riders unfurl long streamers of cloth. The exercise was called "horoiki". We also visited the Imperial Stock Farm in Tochigi Prefecture.

All these activities were organised to give Ambassadors from abroad a glimpse of old Japanese customs and entertainments. We were invited in turns to attend such light-hearted excursions — all paid by the Imperial budget. These are some of the perks Ambassadors get with their assignments in Japan.

Japan does have a budget for the Imperial family. There were twenty-one persons in the Imperial family when I was in Tokyo. The Emperor's family, his son's family and his brothers' families and their children. Before the war, there were more people in the Imperial family, but after the war, the number was reduced considerably. The leaders needed a national head to unite the nation and used the Emperor as an effective means. The Imperial family are "servants" of the nation. They are given an allowance from the nation to live comfortably and no tax is imposed on any expenditures. The Imperial family normally take their vegetables, meat, milk and fruits from the Imperial farms and gardens. Once a year, I received a basket of apples from Princess Hitachi with my name carved on them. My relations with Princess Hitachi were a little extraordinary because on one occasion she honoured Singapore by consenting to be the guest of honour at an orchid show organised by the Singapore Government. My wife and I called on Princess Hitachi, together with Chandra Dash (a Singaporean Parliamentarian), and presented her with plenty of orchids as well as a golden orchid specially prepared for her. She was impressed by our hospitality. The basket of apples was a token of reciprocal hospitality.

The Japanese will always return hospitality to whomever gives it to them. It is a Japanese custom.

In 1986, on the Emperor's birthday, I arranged for a scroll of calligraphy written by me to him, describing his glorious days as Emperor. In return, he sent me an authographed copy of his photograph as well as that of the Empress.

Emperor Hirohito might have consolidated his power, like his grandfather, because by the Meiji Constitution he was already Commander-in-Chief of the Armed Forces. But, he was a studious man who would rather be a scientist than a monarch. His happiest days were Monday and Saturday when he would retire to his modest laboratory and study marine biology. Neither did he have the slightest wish to be a despot. From his trip to Europe as Crown Prince, he had already developed a taste for whisky, western music and golf, along with an abiding respect for the English version of constitutional monarchy.

Hirohito was a pious man who believed in monogamy. After Empress Nagako had given birth to four daughters he refused to take a concubine so that he could sire a male heir. Within a few years, he was rewarded with two sons by Nagako.

He did not care very much for his clothes and manners. In his leisure, he used to slouch around the Palace in frayed, baggy trousers and a crooked tie, dreamily peering through glasses as thick as portholes and occasionally his jacket would be fastened with the wrong button. He disliked buying new clothes on the excuse that he could not afford them. He was so frugal that he even refrained from buying the books which he really wanted and would wear down every pencil to the stub. He was completely devoid of vanity but had the qualifications of a great man. He wanted the best for the nation.

To every Japanese, Hirohito was "God". But they regarded him more as a father and oyabun. No matter how lowly a Japanese may be, he would have a feeling of kinship to the Emperor, who was the father for all of them. When Emperor Meiji lay on his deathbed, all Japanese prayed for his recovery and many remained in the Palace plaza day and night; the entire nation grieved his death as a single family. For Japan was one great family, a modernised clan which had evolved from a number of warring tribes.

Emperor Hirohito did not smoke. His face appeared on no stamps or currency. In no Japanese living room was his photograph propped up on the sideboard.

The Emperor was quite busy every day from morning to evening and sometimes did overtime work. The most important function of the Emperor is to scrutinise documents before signing them or affixing his seal. Counting just those approved by the Cabinet, there are some 1,200 documents annually. Beginning with New Year's greetings ceremonies on January 1st, the Emperor performs a variety of ceremonial acts of state throughout the year, including the appointment of the Prime Minister and the Chief Justice of the Supreme Court. He also confers orders and decorations and the acceptance of credentials presented by foreign Ambassadors. The Emperor also hosts numerous banquets and receptions, grants audiences and takes part in other ceremonies and programmes.

Besides his duties, he conducted research on the classification of marine life species at his biological laboratory located within the Palace grounds, and he published a number of books on his findings. Since he was busy, he had not enough time to pursue his hobby of marine biology, originally recommended to him as a less dangerous course of study than history. He liked plants but not wild plants, which he disliked as they were of foreign origin. Twice a year, on New Year's Day and his official birthday, he appeared on the balcony of the Palace to accept the banzai of the assembled crowds. He was fond of sumo wrestling and would be seen at sumo tournaments, especially when they fought it out to snatch the "Emperor's Cup".

He rarely spoke in public except from a prepared text, which he read in a halting monotone. Perhaps the only remarks he made on his own were when we talked about his past in our specially arranged lunch. The Japanese, who are suspicious of individualism in any context, prefer their Emperors not to do, but to be.

Hirohito — Hawk or Dove?

During my stay in Japan, Emperor Hirohito gave diplomats the impression that he was a gentle, soft spoken, peace loving, amiable and likable symbol of the Japanese nation. He behaved how Japanese should behave. How could one believe that the same gentle, soft spoken man was responsible for the brutality and inhuman acts of World War II, when Japan invaded China and southeast Asia? How could one believe that he was responsible for the Nanking massacre, when 300,000 captives and 10,000 innocent civilians were slaughtered? It is also difficult to believe that he was responsible for signing the declaration of war and the attack on Pearl Harbour.

Historians will argue over the exact role the Emperor played in Japan's slide to disaster. It was said that the Japanese Emperor had declared war on the United States "unwillingly" and that he was compelled to do so by the warlords. It was said that he would have been assassinated if he had tried to prevent the war. Apart from the challenge to his constitutional role, for the Emperor to have spoken out against the policy of military aggression would have been to defy the national consensus. After the 1936 coup attempt, the movement towards war was popular in nearly all sections of Japanese society. Japan's resounding victories had brought her useful overseas possessions and had considerably enhanced her prestige. Those easy successes had the unfortunate effect of spawning the myth of invincibility. But, according the research done by David Bergamini, who published a book entitled *Japan's Imperial Conspiracy*, all these assertions seem farfetched, for it was generally admitted that privates and generals were all ready to die for the Emperor and that the only Japanese irreverent enough to assassinate him would have been the few Westernised bankers and diplomats who opposed the war.

According to David Bergamini, Emperor Hirohito had stamped the orders sending troops into North China in 1937. It was later said that he did so unwillingly, yet he went on two months later to stamp orders for the dispatch of troops to central and south China as well. He opened an Imperial Headquarters in his Palace so that he could personally supervise the fighting. He became "so immersed in war planning that the Prime Minster at the time complained of his preoccupation". Finally his own uncle assumed command of the attack in Nanking, the Chinese capital, and moved into a hotel in Nanking to look on while the Japanese troops murdered over 100,000 defenceless civilian prisoners. It was the first act of genocide in World War II, but when the uncle returned to Tokyo, Hirohito went out of his way to confer decorations and honours upon him.

Bergamini said in footnotes to his readers, "I reviewed and reconsidered all the notes I had taken in my reading of source documents, and I became convinced that the modern history of Japan, as presented since World War II, was a skilfully contrived illusion fabricated late in the war, partly by counter-intelligence specialists in the General Staff and partly by high-ranking Palace courtiers."

Was it a myth that Emperor Hirohito was a "cultured biologist" who left the management of his realm to generals and admirals and devoted all his energy to pottering about with fungi and marine organisms, as portrayed by official versions? Or in reality was he a person described by David Bergamini as "a formidable war leader, a tireless, dedicated, meticulous, clever and patient man who inherited from his great-grandfather a mission which was to rid Asia of white men. Since his people were reluctant and backward, he had skilfully manipulated them for 20 years for the task"?

According to the memoranda by the Army Chief of Staff, Sugiyama Hajime who committed suicide in 1945 at the time of Japan's surrender, it was revealed that Hirohito was asking detailed questions about military and economic planning in the months before Pearl Harbour. The memoranda contradicted statements which General Douglas MacArthur said that Hirohito had made to him after the war, professing ignorance of all military and economic matters in 1941. The Sugiyama memoranda revealed that Hirohito had participated in the Pearl Harbour planning a full six months before any of his official military advisors were informed of it.

Sugiyama's papers were published in two handsome volumes, but not one Japanese newspaper carried a review of the set, or commented on it in any way. The silence which greeted Sugiyama's memoranda convinced David Bergamini that even today the Japanese remain extraordinarily discreet in matters touching the Emperor. Only 25 years ago, millions of Japanese had died with a prayer on their lips after the utter of "Banzai" and "May the Emperor live ten thousand years". They believe that the Emperor is "sacred and inviolable" and that he cannot be removed from the throne for any reason, and he is not to be held responsible for over-stepping the limitations of law in the exercise of his sovereignty.

David Bergamani's book *Japan's Imperial Conspiracy* was not easily available, even in the English language bookshops in Tokyo. I have not found a Japanese translation of the book. The Japanese are generally loyal to their Emperor and will not allow the image of the Emperor to be tarnished.

Other commentators and historians, however, pointed out that Hirohito had agreed to the war with great reluctance. He had little power to check the drive of the militarists at its zenith. Foreign critics were only partially correct. No historian can ignore the military elements in the Japanese tradition. The Japanese tragedy was that they were heirs to a society which had its morality and ways of thinking critically influenced by six centuries of civil war, then artificially frozen in their deformed state by three centuries of isolation. The Japanese were so indoctrinated during the three hundred years with the samurai spirit of serving the Lord that the spirit became the cornerstone of the Japanese society. It was essentially a military virtue. After the Meiji Restoration, the founders of Japan's modern army revived Bushido in another form. The Emperor was substituted for the clan chief as the focus of the soldiers' loyalty. Bushido, buttressed by the revived Shinto religion, became a kind of religious patriotism.The militarists have exploited the loyalty of the web society to lead Japan, the brave "island country", against the treachery and conniving of a hostile foreign world. The way to Pearl Harbour was charted.

The Emperor had in fact little sympathy with either the China Incident or the drift towards war with the United States. He had neither the force of character nor the training to halt the forward march of the warlike army. The old Meiji statesmen who had instructed Hirohito in the work of kingship had taught him all too well the duties — and the restraints — of a constitutional monarch. He was not supposed to interfere directly in government policies, as his grandfather had often done. He was to preside but not to act. The moderates around him, including his cautious distant relative Premier Fuminaro Konoye, were equally ill-equipped for a showdown with the Army. None of them had any alternative for Japan than the aggresive programme offered by the Army.

One incident demonstrated the Emperor's predicament in the early days of Japan's aggression against China. At an Imperial briefing session on September 5 1941, Field Marshal General Suguyama assured Hirohito that Japan could complete the capture of the "southern areas" within three months, whether or not the Americans intervened. Hirohito answered direct and frankly to him, "That's exactly what you generals told me when you started the China incident. You said it would be straightened out within three months. However, it has already taken four years. Are you now calculating more or less the same way?"

On another occasion there was a conflict of opinion between the military and civilian leaders over whether to go to war with the United States or to continue peaceful negotiations. The Emperor sided with the civilians. He pulled a piece of paper out of his pocket and read to the conference an old poem of his grandfather's:

"Though I consider the surrounding seas as my brothers, why is it that the waves should rise so high?"

The Emperor said, "I have always read and appreciated this poem and kept in my heart the Emperor Meiji's spirit of peace. It has been my wish to perpetuate this spirit."

Emperor Hirohito had often voiced his sentiments against war. But he had used the language of a gentleman to a bunch of military warlords who were not on the same wavelength as him. His language did not carry weight although he was their Emperor. He was not dealing with gentlemen, but with Hidejo Tojo who was not a gentleman.

The fact that Tojo and his militarist followers started the war is a classic example of men who were imprisoned by their own propaganda. They were able to so successfully evoke the armoured ghost of Japanese dualism and the "samurai spirit" because they firmly believed in that spirit themselves.

Tojo's army swept down on its enemies with a religious fanaticism that the West itself had not experienced since the Seventh Crusade. The spirit shown by the Japanese Army of 1941 was no different to the Hideyoshi's clan samurai or the Forty Seven Ronin.

Although the Emperor was too soft and weak to challenge the wishes of the military warlords, there were several occasions when he had to put his foot down and told off the military leaders. For example, in 1928 when Marshal Chang Tso-lin, the Chinese warlord in Manchuria, was assassinated by the Ishihara-Itagaki group, the Emperor was furious with the military leaders and reprimanded them.

During the military mutiny of 26 February 1932, a rightwing group of Army officials staged an assassination plot against those who were against Japan's expansion to annex Manchuria. The rebels' targets were Prime Minister Okada, the Finance Minister, the Lord Keeper of the Privy Council, Count Nobuaki Makino, former Privy Seal and counsellor to the Emperor, and eighty-seven-year old Prince Kimmochi Saionji, the Emperor's closest adviser, the nation's most honoured elder statesman, the last genro. The genro were important statesmen who had helped Emperor Meiji draw up the Imperial Constitution in 1889 and afterwards became advisers to the Emperor. The rebels also planned to seize the War Minister's official residence and force high-ranking officers to support them.

The rebels thought they had killed Prime Minister Okada, but he escaped death and was smuggled back to the Palace. The rebellion failed because the Emperor had issued a decree demanding that the rebels withdraw and return to the barracks. Anyone who dared to defy the Emperor's decree would be regarded as a traitor. The NHK broadcast the Emperor's message, which said, "You must not revolt against His Majesty and inflict upon yourself eternal disgrace as traitors."

The Emperor won the day. The rebellion fizzled out and the general in charge of suppressing the rebellion asked the rebels to commit harakiri. All of them except one decided to submit to court martial. The stubborn rebel wrote a final statement exposing corruption in high circles and lamented that he could not bear to see hundreds of Japanese soldiers shed their blood in Shanghai and Manchuria while politicians, businessmen and government officials were enjoying life in Japan through corruption. After signing the statement, he committed harakiri.

The rebellion cost the lives of seven people. Although it failed, it made an impact on Japan's decision to expand towards the Chinese mainland.

During a crisis, Hirohito was willing to defy the military authorities. On June 18 1945, despite strong insistance of the military leaders to carry on the war till the end, the Emperor decided to call off the war. On July 27, he advised the acceptance of the Postdam Declaration of unconditional surrender. The Emperor knew that Japan would not win and told the Cabinet: "We have a battle on the homeland? If all the citizens should die, we would hardly be able to perpetuate the nation. I think we must decide at this time to terminate the war, although it is an unbearable thing. Were we to terminate the war in this way, it would mean losing the Army, which we have had since the time of the Emperor Meiji. However, when I think upon all the men who have died, and the families of the dead, I feel as if my heart were broken... . In order to open the way to future peace, we must bear what is unbearable. It is needless to worry about the royal family or myself."

The warlords had argued that the acceptance of the Potsdam Declaration would mean the end of "Kokutai" (having the Emperor as the Head of the state and a system that binds the Japanese as a people). However, the Emperor could not endure the suffering of his people after the atom bombs were dropped at Hiroshima and Nagasaki.

The Emperor broadcast on 15 August 1945 declaring that Japan would surrender and would accept the Potsdam Declaration. It was the first occasion that the Japanese people had heard their Emperor speak. An entire nation listened attentively, awed by the high-pitched, almost unreal voice. The strange Imperial language, coupled with poor reception, allowed few of his subjects to understand exactly what he had in mind.

"Cultivate the ways of rectitude; foster nobility of spirit; and work with resolution so as ye may enhance the innate glory of the Imperial state and keep pace with the progress of the world...," the Emperor said.

Many were unable to comprehend the quavering, static staccato voice that came over the radio and announced that a "the war situation has developed not necessarily to our advantage". The people who assembled in village squares and factories all over the country knelt for the speech and heard it in silence. After the broadcast, millions wept. Some wandered around for hours in a daze — not so much because the war was lost, but because the Emperor had spoken to them. Underlying the humiliation of sorrow was an undeniable sense of relief. The terrible burden of the years of war, death and destruction was at last over.

The voice of the Emperor reached troops thousands of miles from the homeland, as far away as Harbin, Manchuria, Indonesia and the Philippines. All of them were taken by surprise.

Before the broadcast, a group of fanatical diehards had ransacked the Imperial guest house in search of the surrender recording, which they planned to destroy, to prevent the Emperor from broadcasting. They failed because a Palace official, anticipating such actions, had smuggled the tape out of the Palace.

The decision to broadcast Japan's surrender was one of the most significant roles the Emperor had played in Japanese politics. He made the decision against the will of the warlords who wanted to carry on with the war.

The American Occupation

After the war, Hirohito narrowly escaped being tried as a war criminal, which might well have meant execution or life imprisonment. About 70 percent of Americans felt that the Emperor should be punished as a war criminal. The United States was having a hard time deciding on the fate of the Emperor. It was left to the decision of General MacArthur, the Supreme Commander-in-Chief of Allied Occupations in Japan, to decide his future.

Some of the American press branded Hirohito as a warmonger. There were demonstrations outside MacArthur's headquarters advocating his removal. There were similar demands by the Russian and Australian press to bring Hirohito to trial. But MacArthur ignored all these demands. To bring the Emperor to trial would provoke guerrilla warfare throughout the nation and perpetuate a military government. At one time, Emperor Hirohito was contemplating abdication.

MacArthur was more than determined to treat the Emperor with respect — against the advice of his own staff, who wanted him summoned peremptorily to Allied headquarters as a show of power. MacArthur thought it over and felt that if he were to do that, it would outrage the feelings of the Japanese people and make the Emperor a martyr in their eyes. Instead of ordering the Emperor to see him, he chose the Eastern way of patience and waited for the Emperor to make the move.

Emperor Hirohito in full Imperial dress just before inauguration as Japan's Emperor.

Emperor Hirohito meeting General MacArthur at Alliance H.Q. on September 27 1945 for the first time after the Japanese surrender.

Two weeks went by without any response from the Emperor. Then, suddenly, news came that Tojo had attempted suicide and the Emperor himself requested an interview with MacArthur.

Wearing cutaway striped trousers, button shoes and top hat, Hirohito was driven to the American embassy with Grand Chamberlain Fujita. He stepped out of the ancient limousine and nervously allowed himself to be escorted up the spacious staircase to the second floor where MacArthur's office was situated. MacArthur was in an open-necked shirt. They shook hands and a photograph was taken, the publication of which the Japanese authorities tried to suppress. It showed MacArthur arms akimbo, towering over the diminutive and formally dressed Emperor. It was brutally clear who the boss was. The Japanese were always attuned to symbols and understood the significance of the newspaper photograph of the Emperor's first meeting with General MacArthur.

It being the first time he had met the Japanese King, MacArthur found it rather difficult to deal with a stranger who was once so powerful. He invited the Emperor to sit by an open fire and started to talk.

The Emperor's meeting with MacArthur marked the turning point in deciding Japan's future. His advisers had told him not to admit his guilt in the war. MacArthur had expected him to ask for forgiveness and for pardon. Instead, the Emperor had gone there to accept all responsibility for the brutal war and expressed his willingness to be punished. This took MacArthur by surprise and certainly gained his respect, which was revealed in his memoirs. The Emperor met MacArthur eleven times during the latter's six years stay in Japan. There were no written documents as the talks were held in top secret. MacArthur's memoirs stand as the only record of his encounters with Hirohito.

MacArthur was apparently impressed by the Emperor's frankness and courage. On 25 January 1946, he sent a report to Washington saying there was no evidence to show that the Emperor would have to be a war criminal. MacArthur felt that if the Emperor became a war criminal, Japan would be thrown into chaos and the country would be in a terrible confusion, as he was the only symbol who could unite the Japanese. If MacArthur had made the alternate decision to make the Emperor a war criminal and if he had been sentenced to death, Japan's future would not have been as rosy as it is today. The Japanese would not have known what to do without an Emperor.

MacArthur never paid a return visit to the Emperor after the latter visited him on 27 September 1945. This disclosure was made in a Japanese newspaper in December 1986, while I was Ambassador in Japan. The declassified US

Emperor Hirohito, whom the ordinary Japanese could not see eye to eye, came down from his throne to visit the people after the surrender to encourage them to work hard.

official documents showed that he was advised by Atcheson that he should never make a return call to the Emperor. He said it would be inappropriate for MacArthur to return the call since Japan was a defeated nation.

The document said: "It would be inadvisable for you to return Hirohito a call. Not only would such a gesture be likely to cause widespread adverse comment in the American press but it would, I believe, offend the sensibilities of the American people in general... loss of the war necessarily involves loss of face by the Emperor but is not necessarily undesirable from our point of view, and that to a reasonable extent, the contrary is true."

According to the document, an "official adviser of Marquis Kido has suggested to the US Secretary of State that the Americans should make a gesture toward the Emperor in return to his recent call on MacArthur".

On New Year's Day 1946, the Emperor declared that he was a "human being" and "not a god". He started his visiting campaign to a cross-section of the people — factories, coal mines, farmers, workers — donning a baggy suit. He shook hands with his people and was heartily welcomed by them. It was not a role to which he was suited by nature, yet he did it so well that he became a popular "hero". The people found a new inspiration to work hard to reconstruct Japan. He became the most visible link with native Japanese tradition.

Through his inspiration and encouragement, changes came about in the Japanese society: post-war chaos and inflation were followed by painful recovery, then a breakthrough in economic growth, industrial success and then unparalled prosperity. For the pre-war generations, the existence of the Emperor became one of the few signs that they were still living in the same country, and not occupied by a foreign power. Everything was in the right place. MacArthur had made the right decision. Without the Emperor, Japan would have been different.

On 11 April 1951, sudden news of the dismissal of MacArthur surprised the Emperor and the people of Japan. President Truman of the United States could not put up with MacArthur's dogmatic decision on the Korean War and fired him. The Imperial Household Agency asked MacArthur to come to the Imperial Palace, but he refused to do so. The last meeting between MacArthur and the Emperor took place on the day before he left the country. At the Haneda airport when MacArthur flew off on 16 April 1951, thousands of Japanese gathered to bid him farewell. They shouted "banzai, banzai" many times to show their appreciation for the things he had done for Japan.

When MacArthur died in April 1964, the Emperor was asked what he thought was the most impressive thing he had experienced during his 20 post-war years. He replied, "The most impressive thing was the meeting with General MacArthur right after the war."

Now that MacArthur had passed into history, events left Hirohito still warmly enshrined in the hearts of his people. The majority of the Japanese still feel the Imperial taboo and speak of their ruler with great diffidence. Politicians who were against him seldom dared to attack him personally except through veiled, technically inoffensive hints.

But the Japan Socialist Party and the Japan Communist Party still boycotted all functions held by the Emperor. They are against hoisting the "hinomaru" (the National flag) in schools, and in many schools, students refused to sing "Kimigayo" (the National Anthem).

The Emperor's image was particularly poor in Okinawa, where World War II claimed 200,000 Okinawans. The Emperor was scheduled to attend the National Athletic Meet in 1986, held in Okinawa, but had to cancel the trip due to ill-health. The Okinawans were preparing to stage demonstrations during his visit. Later, in October 1987, when the then Crown Prince and Crown Princess visited Okinawa on the Emperor's behalf, a man hauled down the Hinomaru flag and burnt it. Before giving himself up, this man held a press conference and condemned the Hinomaru and Kimigayo as "bloody history and sins". He said that the hoisting of the Hinomaru and singing of Kimnigayo had led to a mass suicide at Chibichirigama, Yomitan in 1945, after the United States armed forces landed in the main island of Okinawa.

Okinawa was the scene of the final and bloodiest World War II battle in the Pacific. About 100,000 civilians of Okinawa, 100,000 Japanese soldiers and 13,000 US troops were killed in the fighting. Okinawa was the only place in Japan where World War II battles were fought on Japanese soil. It was under US occupation for 27 years. Residents of Okinawa were still bitter over the fighting there, saying the Emperor was responsible for the war.

Divinity is like virginity — gone once, gone for ever. But, in Japan there is a strong desire by the right-wing politicians and businessmen, as well as scholars, to revive the role of the Emperor. One of them was Prime Minister Nakasone, who was influential when I was Ambassador in Japan. The desire grew from the obvious deterioration of the samurai spirit in Japan. The young nowadays are very much influenced by the permissiveness of Western culture. They are getting soft and like enjoyment and entertainment more than work.

I heard the Emperor speaking for the last time when Prime Minister Nakasone and others organised a massive celebration for the 60th anniversary of Emperor Hirohito's reign. It was held at the Ryogoku Kokugaikan (the sumo arena) and the diplomatic corp was invited to attend. There were 6,000 leaders from all walks of life including Government Ministers and Dietmen, with the exception of the Japan Socialist Party and the Japan Communist Party which as usual boycotted the function. After the attendants sang Kimigayo to the accompaniment of the Tokyo Metropolitan Police Band, Nakasone gave a congratulatory speech followed by the leaders of both Houses of Diet and the Chief Justice of the Supreme Court.

The Emperor clapped his hands enthusiastically like a child when the Tokyo Broadcasting Children Choir Group sang five songs which were all composed in the year 1901, when the Emperor was born, or in the year 1926 when he ascended to the throne. He seemed to like those songs.

The last speech I heard the Emperor make was when he said that his heart ached when he thought about his people having to sacrifice so much during World War II, adding that he could not help realising the importance of peace.

The Emperor said, "I feel overwhelmed with emotion when I consider that our nation has achieved an honourable status in the international community as a peace loving country after overcoming many hardships after the war through our own efforts." The Emperor said he believed that although Japan faced many problems, it would be able to carve out for itself a rich future if the people would use the lessons they had learned from the past.

After the Emperor's speech, Nakasone stepped down from the stage into a lower platform and shouted "Tenno Heika Banzai" three times, accompanied by all those present. After the ceremony, about 5,000 people from leftist extremist groups staged rallies against the ceremony in five parts of Tokyo. Leaders who spoke denounced the ceremony, saying that it was unforgivable that Nakasone had turned the country into a warlike nation with the Emperor sitting on top of the nation. There were disruptions all over the country, and signal and communication lines were set alight. The Bullet train running along the Tokaido Shinkansen Line was badly damaged and in Osaka the communication service was paralysed.

Emperor Hirohito passed away in 1989, after I left Japan. I scanned through all the newspapers to see whether anyone had committed harakiri as a result of his death. When Emperor Meiji died, the hero of the victory over the Russians at Port Arthur General Nogi, who had accompanied Meiji for a long time, committed harakiri together with his wife. In a suicide note, he said he was ashamed of losing the imperial standard in battle nearly 40 years before. Many other Japanese also committed harakiri. In the case of Emperor Hirohito, although thousands of Japanese flocked to pray outside the Palace for his recovery, none committed harakiri. This reflected the changing era and changing mood of the people.

During the mourning period, there was a complete ban on coverage of entertainment. There was no light music, nor happy drama or sketches, only solemn mourning music and stories of the Emperor's past. Even bars and nightclubs were prohibited from indulging in amusement activities. There was a hue and cry by the younger generation. Video-tape businesses did a roaring trade.

Nowadays, harakiri is not regarded as an act of bravery. In Japan the samurai spirit is gone. The right-wing leaders try to revive the spirit and they try to change the role of the Emperor as the head of state. I do not think the right-wing leaders can turn the clock back to make the Emperor a "God King" as he was before the war. They can at least revive the respect for the right-wing extremists are worried about the present crop of political leaders and other business and community leaders who have lost their samurai spirit. In the past, when a leader committed a blunder, he committed "harakiri"

Emperor Hirohito's funeral procession on February 24 1989 in Tokyo.

(suicide by slashing one's abdomen). Today, when corrupt politicians are blantantly exposed and in disgrace, they just bow out and say "sorry". They never commit harakiri. When the Japan Airlines planes crashed into the hills, the president of JAL just bowed out with apologies. Only very few people, like the driver of Tanaka, choose to commit suicide than to betray their master. Present lifestyles and Japanese responses to situations represent a change in the Japanese society. What will happen to Japan without the samurai spirit? Nobody knows.

I asked Japanese experts why not a single Japanese committed harakiri after Emperor Hirohito's death. One expert told me that after the Second World War, Hirohito had stressed the importance of keeping oneself alive to reconstruct the country. He had emphasised the importance of preserving life. Was that the reason why his subjects had not committed harakiri? Or was it the changing trend and mood of the new era?

The results can only be borne out by history.

CHAPTER 3

Sumo Wrestlers

Did sumo originate in Japan? Most Japanese would say, "Yes, of course." How could it be otherwise? I asked many sumo experts and they gave the same answer. I conducted research into the matter whenever I went to China. I found traces of stone walls in unearthed graves of the Qin and Han dynasties, depicting topless wrestlers similar to the Japanese sumo. The wrestlers wore only a covering over their loins. I read historical books and discovered that sumo, which is called "Hsiang Boh" (相樸) in Chinese, was mentioned as a royal sport and then became popular among the populace from Qin dynasty times. In the dynasties that followed, sumo was practised all over China until the late Ching, when China was too preoccupied with its struggle against Western invasion and domination.

How did sumo travel to Japan? Nobody has made any serious study into this matter. It could have been introduced by Xu Fu, when he settled in Japan with 3,000 boys and girls. In those days there was already sumo wrestling. It could have been during the Han dynasty when scholars from China visited Japan. Or it could have been introduced during the period of the Three Kingdoms, particularly the Wu or Go Kingdom, when a large number of Chinese troops crossed over into Japan to help Japanese kingdoms settle their internal disputes.

Recent archaeological discoveries in the Anhui Province found 140 lacquer wares, potteries, China wares and women's lacquer clogs in the grave of Choo Ran, the famous general of the Wu dynasty. Choo Ran was the military righthand man of Sun Chien, the King of Wu. The interesting thing was that the clogs were rounded and had two supports resembling the clogs worn by women in the Heian and Kamakura periods as depicted in old paintings. They also found in the grave low dining tables similar to the tables used by present-day Japanese.

The Japanese call their kimono dress "Gofuku", meaning dress of the "Go" or "Wu" dynasty, revealing that even Japanese dresses were introduced into Japan during the Wu period.

Sumo could also have been introduced to Japan during the Tang dynasty when many Japanese monks went to China to study Buddhism. They brought back the Kanji and Buddhism, and could also have brought back sumo.

The Japanese are not concerned where sumo came from. They believe that sumo originated in Japan. According to Japanese legend, the very origin of the Japanese race depended on the outcome of a sumo match. The supremacy of the Japanese people on the islands of Japan was supposedly established when the God Takemikazuchi won a sumo bout with the leader of a rival tribe. Apart from legend, Japanese believe that sumo is an ancient sport dating back some 1,500 years. Incidentally, it also coincided with the Three Kingdoms period in China.

According to Nihongi (Chronicles of Japan), a record which was completed in AD 720 describing the early history of Japan from the period of the gods through to the reign of Empress Jito which ended in AD 679, sumo started in 23 BC in the 7th year of the 7th month during the reign of Emperor Sumin. According to Nihongi, certain courtiers informed the Emperor of a man named Kuyehaya, from the village of Taima, who could break horns and straighten out hooks. The Emperor asked for a person who could challenge this "champion of the Empire". One man named Sumi-no-Sukune came along and volunteered himself. The bout took place and Sumi-no-Sukune raised his right foot and kicked Kuyehara to death. It was the first sumo contest and the first recorded match in Japan's history.

Legend plays an important role in Japanese history. Even today, every 7th July, a sumo festival is held in the place where the classic struggle was supposed to have taken place, to commemorate the occasion.

In the Heian period there were many miraculous stories concerning sumo which made interesting reading. One of them tells of a dispute between two sons of Emperor Montoku (AD 850–858) over succession. They decided to settle the dispute by a sumo bout. The elder son Koretaka chose a giant named Ki-no-Natora to fight his rival. Ki-no-Natora had the strength of 60 men and was tall and muscular. The second son Korehito chose a tiny man named Ootomo-no-Yoshio who was thin and most unimpressive. When the bout started, the giant threw the tiny man into the air. Yoshio straightened his body and fell down within the ring. But, Yoshio was a close friend of the Chief priest who had spiritual powers. Hearing of Yoshio's danger, the Chief priest began to mumble some mantras. Suddenly, a huge water buffalo, bearer of dignity and virtue, appeared and began to let out a great bellow which carried all the way to the Palace where the bout took place. This wind took away all the strength of the giant. Yoshio seized the opportunity and threw the giant to the ground, thus securing the throne for Korehito.

Military dictatorship was established in the Kamakura period in 1192 and a long period of intense warfare ensued. Sumo was quite naturally regarded chiefly for its military usefulness and as a means of increasing the efficiency of the warrior. In about the middle of the Muromachi period (AD 1336–1573) sumo bouts took place in temples and shrine compounds all over the land, continuing the sumo tradition. They were primarily for entertainment. The shrine would benefit from the spectators' donations. In return, temples would share the proceeds with the wrestlers who drew the crowds. This generally gave rise to semi-professional groups of wrestlers who toured the countryside plying their trade at religious festivals before warriors and commoners.

During the Tokugawa period, sumo became fully professionalised in the expanding urban centres and took on the form we know today. With the advent of professional groups of wrestlers, performances as part of religious festivals were discontinued. Money was raised for private profit and less for religious purposes.

During the Edo period, sumo bouts were often scenes of bitter quarelling and fighting among the samurai, prompting the Tokugawa government to issue decrees of prohibition of sumo performances. Despite the ban, sumo's popularity remained undiminished and promoters often staged matches on street corners and in temple compounds without permission. But such precarious employment was hardly enough to fill the wrestlers rice bowls.

To save the situation, professional sumo groups started to work out a series of rules and regulations to govern the sport and selected supervisors to enforce them. This would prevent disputes and unnecessary fights among sumo wrestlers. Winning techniques were carefully defined and matches were confined to a limited area — the ring "dohyo" as they are known today.

These efforts finally led to official sanction. As early as 1684, in Edo (present Tokyo), sumo wrestling started again with official blessing. At the outset during the Tokugawa period, the best wrestlers were employed by Japan's great feudal lords, given samurai status and treated like retainers. Rich merchants also contributed to the sport's prosperity by giving money to their favourite wrestlers.

When the Black Ships of Commodore Matthew Perry landed in Japan in 1853, signaling the end of Japan's closed door policy of the Tokugawa regime, giant sumos were mobilised to show the unwelcome Western intruders the size and strength of the Japanese nation, just as the Ching dynasty had used the "invisible" boxers against the Western intruders. Giant wrestlers went to the port of Yokohama to intimidate persistent strangers by lifting and carrying heavy rice bales, staging bouts and throwing with ease those sailors foolish enough to accept their challenge. The wrestlers' efforts, however, did not deter Perry's determination to make Japan open its doors to the West.

The years of the Meiji Restoration of 1867 were the worst days for sumo wrestlers. The early Meiji rulers had a sudden craze for things Western and they copied practically everything Western. They craved for Western culture and despised anything Eastern, particularly culture and civilisation from China. Caught up in a revolutionary wave of copying the West, sumo was denounced as an anachronistic leftover from Japan's feudal days. Newspapers took up the cry, arguing that the "uncivilised" sport should be banned and the near nakedness of the wrestlers was ugly and shameful.

One high ranking wrestler, Takasago, emerged to save the situation. He went to Tokyo and staged a demonstration exhibition in Akihabara to challenge the ban. The police at first disallowed the exhibition. But the ordinary populace supported the demonstration and nearly clashed with the police. Even influential Japanese supported the sumo exhibition and gave money to encourage it. Takasago's determination and the people's support turned the tide. In those days, many Japanese were getting fed up with the wholesale mimicking of Western behaviour and thought that sumo, a Japanese tradition, should be allowed in Japan.

Takasago later became the Head of the Sumo Kaisho, an organisation which was formed to encourage sumo wrestling. This organisation later changed its name to Tokyo Ozumo Kyhokai (Tokyo Sumo Association) in 1889, which was the forerunner of the modern Nihon Sumo Kyokai (Japan Sumo Association) which controls the sport today. Under the guidance of the association, wrestlers performed for the organisation and shared the proceeds with its administrators.

The headlong rush to Westernise produced an inevitable counter-reaction. The ban on sumo sparked off a campaign by tradition-minded Japanese to protect their traditional culture and characteristics. Many Japanese felt that the people of Japan could learn Western modernisation but not Western cultural behaviour. They coined the slogan "Modernisation but not Westernisation".

A key turning point for sumo came in 1884 when Emperor Meiji, a practitioner of sumo himself, had an exhibition held in his presence to

A view of Japan's Kokugaikan in Kurame.

Sumo wrestling at Kokugaikan.

emphasise his support. Those Japanese who were against Westernised behaviours had used Emperor Meiji — then regarded as the God for most Japanese — to sink home their slogan of "Modernisation but not Westernisation". After Emperor Meiji's association with sumo, the sport gained a new sense of national confidence and patriotism. This was further solidified by Japan's victories in the war against Russia and China.

The sport's complete recovery was symbolised by the successful completion in June 1909 of a permanent home for sumo tournaments, the Kokugaikan (Hall of the National Sport) in the Ryogoku section of Tokyo. The present home of sumo, called Kokugokan, is a post-war structure located in Kuramae, just across the river from the home of the original Kyogoku building. It is the site of the three tournaments held in Tokyo every year in January, May and September. Three additional tournaments are held annually outside Tokyo in Osaka (March), Nagoya (July) and Fukuoka (November). In April 1925, the Tokyo Sumo Association created the Emperor's Cup to be presented to the winner of each tournament.

Sumo became even more popular during World War II when Japanese soldiers invaded China. With the escalation of the war with China in the late 1930s and the outbreak of the Pacific War in December 1941, the phrase "the undefeated Imperial Army" was the common slogan. Sumo wrestlers crossed the ocean to perform for the Imperial Army in occupied areas of China and Manchuria. During the war, sumo was included as a required subject in the physical education programmes of the elementary schools.

During the war, when the building of the Sumo Association was requisitioned by the military forces in 1944, the summer and winter tournaments were held on the baseball ground at the Koraku-en park. By 1945, the air raids over Tokyo became so severe that the January tournament was called off and in March, when the stadium and most of the stables were heavily damaged by fire, a number of wrestlers perished in the association building. Then, in August 1945, Japan surrendered to the Allied Forces.

In November 1945, the Sumo Association received permission from the Occupying authorities to hold a ten-day sumo tournament in the damaged Kokugaikan. Sumo wrestlers who took part in the tournaments were not as huge as before because of the scarcity of food. In 1947, the association obtained permission to use the sumo arena in the Meiji Shrine Outer Gardens for tournaments. Spectators entering the grounds were confronted by volunteers collecting signatures to demand the restoration of the Kokugaikan for the wrestlers but the movement never got off well. However, promoters of sumo raised funds to build the Kokugaikan, which was finally completed in 1954.

Sumo became more popular with the advent of television broadcasting, with four different channels then competing to display sumo tournaments. By the early 1960s the government station NHK emerged with a monopoly over sumo.

The new Hall of the National Sport (Kokugaikan), a great collisseum made of steel, is situated in Kuramae and occupies several acres of land. It has a typically Japanese style roof resembling an umbrella. The building is modern but the atmosphere is of the feudal era. There are sliding steps leading from the four directions of North, South, East and West to the main hall.

I was invited on many occasions to witness sumo wrestling. It was always the Emperor's Cup Tournament. My hosts were the owners of Kajima Corporation, the biggest construction company in Japan which had built the Singapore Embassy. I came to know the boss Kajima personally, as he invited all Asean Ambassadors to golf and then adjourned to his home in Roppongi for dinner. He was a charming gentleman, short and slim. He also invited Asean Ambassadors to the Kajima holiday resort in Karuizawa golf course and I stayed overnight in their hotel in 1985. There were also many multi-national companies who often invited ambassadors to view sumo wrestling. We were also the guests of Gaimusho (Ministry of Foreign Affairs) having a glimpse of Japanese culture.

As you enter the hall at the Kokugaikan, you see stone carvings on the walls showing the bouts between Sumi-no-Sukune and Kuyehara, the first sumo wrestling in Japan's history.

On my visit there, as I entered the main hall, I saw right in the middle of the four flight of steps a ring called "dohyo". It is a hard clay platform of 18 feet square and two feet high. In its centre is a circle of 20 small rice straw bales sunk into the clay to form a ring just under 15 feet in diameter. One bale is removed from each of the four cardinal compass directions and set slightly outside the circle. Beyond the fighting circles lies a square marked off by a further 32 bales.

Building a dohyo takes three days, requires seven truckloads of special clay and involves an elaborate ritual, supervised by a Shinto priest and ending with the ring ceremony, or dohyo matsuri, on the day before each tournament.

Directly above the dohyo is a wooden roof in the style of a Shinto shrine. This used to be supported by four wooden pillars, but an improvement was made later to do away with the pillars, and the hanging roof enabled visitors to have a better view of the bout. This wooden roof is now suspended from the ceiling with cables. The pillars have been replaced by silk tassles in the colours of four seasons — green for spring (to the East), red for summer (to the South), white for autumn (to the West) and black for winter (to the North). The four colours and directions were based on the I Ching and together with the inner ring represent the five elements and five virtues of Confucianism.

The slopes of the four corners are divided into small boxes holding four people sitting cross-legged in the Japanese style. The boxes are like little stalls. No chairs are provided and we sat on tatam (mats). As soon as we were seated, Kimono-clad waiters brought us sake, beer, boxes of chestnuts and Japanese cakes. Most of the spectators wore casual dress, some however came in kimono. All of them talked loudly and munched their food and drink in a picnic atmosphere.

The boxes are normally reserved by rich patrons and were always booked. It is almost impossible for the ordinary customer to get a seat. If one is available it would probably cost about US$500. Most multi-national Japanese companies are patrons of sumo and they book up the boxes to entertain their guests. The various ministries also have their fair share of the boxes.

There is a special box for the Emperor, who is a great fan of sumo. Emperor Hirohito often appeared during the Emperor's Cup Tournament as he enjoyed viewing sumo.

My first impression of the Kokugaikan and sumo viewing was an exciting one. I have never seen so much pageantry and ceremony in any kind of sport. Possibly nowhere else in the world do colourful festivals abound in every corner of the land as in Japan. In Japan, thousands of festivals are held in every town and village annually. Sumo is no exception. It is crammed with pageantry. This is only natural when one considers that sumo was originally closely linked with religion.

For a few hours of the 15-day long tournament, a long succession of lower ranking rikishi (sumo wrestlers are called rikishi) did battle with each other almost without pause under the eyes of teenage officials. Then later, the television lights came on for the real contenders.

The referee (gyoji) enters the dohyo. He wears a magnificently colourful kimono patterned after the style worn by the samurai of the Kamakura period, some 600 years ago. His black court hat of gauze resembles the traditional Shinto priest's hat. He stands at the centre of the dohyo and starts to call out the names of the contestants in his high-pitched voice. The names are poetical. The rikishi are divided into two teams, one group entering from the East and the other from the West. Traditionally, those on the East side are one rank above those from the West.

Then the wrestlers march in one by one. About 20 of them form a circle round the dohyo. They clap their hands in unison twice and go through an amusing little routine in which they saucily hitch up their aprons half an inch or so and walk around the dohyo. They stop and raise their arms, and after one round of the dohyo withdraw, descending from the opposite aisle.

This ring-entering ceremony dates back to the 17th century and like much else in sumo has Shinto overtones. Clapping is a ritual performed in front of all shrines to attract the Gods. Lifting of the apron is the ritualised version of a more robust gesture usually made to drive out devils. And they raise their arms to indicate, like the samurai, that they are not concealing weapons.

I watched a number of high ranking sumo bouts with great patience. A great deal of patience is required when watching sumo wrestlings. There is lot of motion but no action. Sometimes one has to wait for four minutes before an action takes place.

The most exciting match is usually the last bout. I saw the highest ranking and most popular sumo wrestler Chiyo-no-Fuji appear on the stage amidst thunderous applause. He was having a bout against the twenty-three year old Hawaiian Konishiki. Apart from the usual mawashi (loincloth), he wore a snow-white belt of thick hemp rope tied behind him in a sweeping bow. Only wrestlers of high rank can wear such belt. He was a yokozuna, the highest rank in sumo wrestling. He wore a hair-style like a fan, like the leaf of the sacred gingko tree. This hair-style is known as O-ichomage, in which a small circle is shaved on the crown and the hair pulled back.

Chiyo-no-Fuji looked handsome, about 32 years old. He had the size of a normal fighter, not overweight, but muscular. As he reached the dohyo, he put his hand to his heart, extended his right arm out to the east and raised his right leg as high as he could, and then slamed it down into the clay. This action is called "shiko", a gesture that both frightens evil spirits out of the ring and indicates to his opponent that he could trample him into the dust. The crowd loved the stamping exercise and the more he stamped the louder the applause. He repeated the stampings with his left and then right legs. His opponent, Konishiki, also did the same act.

Chiyonofuji and Konishiki spent about four minutes throwing salt (to purify the proceedings), stamping their feet into the ground, rinsing their mouths with water (ritual cleansing) and spitting with phenomenal accuracy into a pail, and then throwing more salt, sometimes licking their salted fingers. Finally they crouched down on their marks and glared at each other. The glaring is a psychological warfare strategy to frighten the opponent. Sometimes, it looks like the bout is about to begin, but the contestants suddenly decide to withdraw again. The shadow boxing goes on and on, only to bring the spectators into great suspension. The psychological moment has not arrived.

These pre-bout actions are called "shikiri naoshi", considered by Japanese fans as the most interesting part of sumo but to foreigners these are dull moments and they wear out one's patience. In the old days "shikiri naoshi" could drag on and on for hours without limitation. Nowadays it is confined to four minutes. Viewing the pre-bout sumo motion reminded me of my first experience viewing the Kabuki. Movements were so slow that foreign audiences could easily drowse into sleep.

The moment of excitement comes when the referee turns his broad-face fan towards the wrestlers to indicate that they must begin the fight. I saw the tremendous impact when the two giants clashed. Chiyonofuji turned his body and grabbed the mawashi of Konishiki. He did a "shitate-nage" on his opponent. The fight was over within a few seconds. With the belt grip, Chiyonofuji threw Konishiki off his balance and out of the dohyo. The warming-up took time but the bout was over in a few seconds. It is like blowing up a balloon. It takes some time to grow big, but a split second to burst.

When the victor was declared, both the rikishi bowed to the referee and Chiyonofuji squatted on his side of the dohyo to receive his reward. He received an envelope containing cash prizes donated by sponsors. Before he accepted the envelope, he raised his right hand, chopping with his open hand to the left, to the right and then to the centre, indicating giving thanks to heaven, earth and man. He then retired from the dohyo. He waited at the corner of the dohyo and offered a bale of water to the next wrestler of his team "to share his fortune".

At the end of the show, a senior rikishi comes out to perform the bow dance called "yumitori shiki". This bow dance originated from the Tensho era (AD 1575) when Oda Nobunaga presented a bow for the winner of the sumo tournament held. To commemorate this historical occasion, the winner of each tournament is given the privilege of performing the yumitori shiki after the final bout on the last day. A change was made in 1952 and the show is now performed by a hand-picked wrestler who has made the bow routine his speciality.

Chiyonofuji was a native of Hokkaido and a member of the Kokonoe stable. He showed fighting spirit which won him the nickname "the Wolf". His slight build combined with his frequent dislocated shoulder gave him an uneven record for some years. But, he added ten kilograms and with a weight training program developed great physical strength. His success in sumo depended more on skill than on weight. He was the first wrestler to win the Emperor's Cup in the new Ryogoku Kokugaikan, with a 15 to zero record that gave him his eleventh tournament.

Konishiki had a tremendous physique, tall and easily the most flashy and heavy among the wrestlers. He had dark skin and looked rather fierce, especially when he stared at his opponent. To most Japanese, Konishiki seems rather rough and crude with no refinement in his behaviour. He depends very much on his weight and the first impact on his opponent to determine his victory.

Those who decide on the victory of a sumo bout are the honourable judges who are rather inconspicuous. They sit around the ring, clad in the traditional ceremonial attire of the haori, a loose black robe flopping over the hakama, a thicker black shirt. The haori bears the family crest. In sumo history, there have not been any cases of favouritism.

In present-day sumo wrestling, a display of temper such as often seen in boxing and Western wrestling matches is not seen. Foul tactics are extremely rare. Seldom do the spectators boo or make cat-calls. A sumo wrestler is a good loser who never betrays dissatisfaction, whether in word or deed, with the referee's decision. He is courteous toward his opponent, however roughly he may be slapped or flung about.

Sumo wrestlers are treated with respect in Japanese society. They are regarded as descendants of samurai and are expected to behave as one. There are at present over 800 rikishis in professional sumo from the lowly trainee to the yokozuna at the top.

At every match, a "banzuke" showing the names and ranks of wrestlers written with beautiful calligraphy is hung on the wall or is printed in programmes distributed to spectators.

Sumo wrestlers are divided into five ranks. The lowest is the Makushita, who wear a dark cotton belt in the ring. One wears white cotton belts for training. Then, when he wins a fight in more than one tournament, he is promoted to Kumushi, then Sekiwake, then Oze and finally the highest rank Yokozuna.

Life in the stables revolves on tradition, nurtured over the centuries of absolute obedience to and respect for the superiors. Each wrestler must acknowledge the prerogatives of higher rank and act accordingly. Rank is a reflection of a wrestler's success and nothing else, and rank is the only important consideration. It dictates how a wrestler is dressed, what his wages will be and how he will be treated by other members of the sumo world.

The position of Yokozunais is unique. In the past three hundred years since the title was created, only 50 rikishi have been so honoured. The yokozuna alone of all the ranks can never be demoted even if he makes a poor show during a tournament. Instead of demotion, he is expected to retire if he continues to lose matches. Before a rikishi can be considered for promotion to Yokozuna, he must have won two consecutive tournaments while holding the rank of Ozeki. He must have proven himself capable of turning in consistent performances and in the critical eyes of the Sumo Kyokai is a man of character worthy to hold such an exalted position.

How is life as a sumo wrestler? To have a clearer understanding of this aspect of sumo wrestlers, I made arrangements to visit the stable of the then President of the Japan Sumo Association, Futagoyama Oyakata. Futagoyama was himself a champion sumo wrestler at one time.

There are 39 stables, called heya in Tokyo, and most are concentrated in the suburb of Ryogoku near the Kokugaikan stadium. Futagoyama was the mentor (or foster father) and nominal lord of his stable. When I visited his stable, I saw young sumo wrestlers practising sumo skills. It was a single storey building with a platform raised above the ground with the recruits practising sumo lessons below us. As there were no chairs, we sat crossed legged and witnessed how recruits were being trained. There were a few tall, huge wooden pillars meant for recruits to slam their hands on to harden them. The ground was covered with earth and mud. I saw them stamping their feet all the time. Then a series of bouts started, with bigger wrestlers pushing the smaller ones to learn the art of falling. I also saw some recruits scraping the backs of more senior wrestlers.

Futagoyama explained to me the life of young sumo wrestlers. He said that most new recruits joined straight from junior high school at the age of 15 or 16, usually as a result of recommendations from their local supporters group or amateur sumo clubs. Once accepted, they were offered nothing but the three necessities of life — food, clothing and shelter — in return for total loyalty and unquestioning obedience, with no day off. For instance, the sumo day begins at about 4.30 am when the dormitory is roused and set to work. The recruits would loosen up with exercises such as shiko-high stamps with each leg in turn, teppo slamming the open hands into the wooden pillar; and the painful matarari — a sort of sumo split in which the legs are held out sideways at right angles to the body, while the trainer forces the seated novice's chest down to touch the ground. Then comes moshiai, a noisy elimination contest in the ring, and a long series of bouts against the same opponent to test endurance.

Throughout all this, a coach and the stable master would watch and scold them with sharp words of instruction and an occasional slap with a bamboo stick or the handle of a broom. After two and three hours of hard work, the novices would stand around sweating and covered with dirt, ready to offer a towel or drink of water to the senior to whom each had been assigned as tsukebito or servant. They had to rub the backs of the seniors and do errands for them. They do not get to sleep during the day. While the elders lie about, they go shopping or run errands until it is time to prepare the evening dinner for the seniors.

Some recruits stick at this level throughout their sumo careers, going on to become cooks or, if they good enough, trainers in the same stable and retire at thirty. In many ways, they are the life blood of sumo, vital to the system, but they are at the service of the champions, the men who go on striving for perfection and win titles.

After the viewing, Futagoyama invited my family to a Chanko-nabe lunch and I went there with my wife and daughter. Chanko is whatever is available. It was a stew with no set recipe. It consisted of fresh vegetables, mixed with poultry, pork and fish with a flavouring of sugar and soya bean sauce. It also contained carrots, onions, cabbages, leeks, spinachs, beansprouts, tofu and fermented bean pastes in rice vinegar or sake. It was a huge pot, the contents meant for a large group. For small eaters like us, it was too plentiful. But wrestlers might think it was not enough. Sumo wrestlers are great eaters, which is why they are so huge. It seems that they are forced to eat so that they can become sumo wrestlers.

I enjoyed Chanko-nabe. It was the first time I had tasted the food meant for sumo wrestlers. The recruits had to serve us and only after we have finished the lunch could they start to eat. I saw them take bowls and bowls of soft rice. The kitchen was busy turning out the vast quantities necessary to feed 30 or 40 ravenous and rapidly growing young wrestlers.

Sumo is tough and very few rikishi remain active after 40. Most retire in their early 30s. Retirement is marked by an emotional ceremony called danpatsu-shiki which involves cutting off the rikishi's distinctive topknot. I witnessed Chiyonofuji's danpatsu-shiki ceremony. He sat in a chair on the dohyo while hundreds of patrons, friends and fans filed by and took turns to snip tiny pieces of hair from his head. The last inch or two was ceremonially removed by his own stable master with a long pair of brass scissors.

There were tears in the eyes of Chiyonofuji. It was a sad occasion when he had to give up his sumo career. The glories of victories over opponents and the thunderous applause of the crowd would forever be gone. Retirees can no longer participate in bouts. They have to give way because as younger and stronger sumo wrestlers appear in the arena, they find difficulty in triumphing over them.

The ceremony is followed by entertainment that serves to lighten the sombre mood of the main event. There are songs and dances, and much drinking. Everyone would be in a festive mood.

Sumo is fast becoming popular outside Japan. London's Royal Albert Hall, in November 1991, hosted a number of distinctive events. The British got their first taste of sumo a few years ago when matches from Japan were broadcast on television. At first a novelty, it quickly gained popularity. The British fans enjoy the sport on a less reverent level, attaching nicknames to their favourite wrestlers. For example, Hawaiian-born Konishiki, who weights about 262 kg, is known as "Dump Truck". Sumo wrestling went to the United States much earlier. Starting even before the Meiji Restoration, Japanese performers were great hits on the stage of variety halls in New York, London, Paris, and lesser cities. The first sumo wrestler performed in the White House for President Teddy Roosevelt when he arrived in Washington.

Konishiki or "Dump Truck", but known to Japanese as "Little Brocade", came from Hawaii ten years ago. Since then he has had 28 promotions and aimed at becoming the first foreigner to attain the ancient sport's highest rank of Grand Champion. He won 1992's first sumo tournament and was elevated to the rank of yokozuna. In the 300 years of recorded sumo history there have been only 50 yokozuna, none of them a foreigner. To earn this rank, a fighter must not only have performed consistently well, for example winning two tournaments in succession, but also convince the Sumo Association that his character is worthy for him to hold such an exalted position.

For Konishiki, it was a dream come true. He told the press, "For many years, I have had the dream of becoming a yokozuna. Every sumo wrestler wants to attain the highest rank. Wouldn't I be making history?"

Recently Konishiki applied for Japanese citizenship. He needed the citizenship because he wants to start his own stable when he retires from active wrestling. To open a stable, Japan's sumo rules insist that the owner of a stable is a Japanese citizen. In February 1994, he was granted citizenship, clearing the way for this ailing colossus sumo wrestler to retire and make a second career managing other fighters. A Justice Ministry spokeman said that the Hawaiian-born Salevaa Atisanoe, who was given the name of Konishiki, would now be known as Yasokichi Konishiki.

The strain of carrying his huge 262 kg weight had caused chronic knee problems for years, but his physical decline had been rapid since the middle of 1993. Commentators generally agreed that he only kept on fighting because

The Hawaiian-born giant sumo wrestler Konishiki squeezing the champion sumo wrestler Chiyonofuji out of the ring. It was the first time he beat Chiyonofuji.

he would have no chance of a post-retirement role in the sport without Japanese citizenship.

The Sumo Association is under the jurisdiction of he Ministry of Education, one of the most conservative bodies in the Japanese Government. When I was in Japan, the Ministry refused to change the content of distorted history which tried to cover up Japan's atrocities of the Nanking massacre. It must have taken a great deal of "nemasasi" (consultation) for the Association to reach an agreement to allow Konishiki to become a Japanese citizen.

Konishiki was realistic enough to realise that if he had remained a foreigner, his chances of survival would be remote. He overcame the dilemma by announcing his intention of applying for Japanese citizenship after he married fashion model Susmika Shsioda. He had adapted well to his new home. He lived the same life as the other sumo wrestlers and spoke excellent Japanese, cracking jokes and singing lovesongs on television variety shows. In other words, he behaved like a Japanese and was acceptable as a Japanese. He said last year, "If I apply for naturalisation, I would feel more at ease. I have been able to come this far due to the warm support of the Japanese people. Now I want to return their favour." His stable master is Jesse

Takamiyama, a fellow Hawaiian who became grand champion many years ago and who also became a Japanese citizen.

The Japanese have not been able to accept the fact that a foreigner can become a sumo champion and beat all Japanese in the game which they think was originated in Japan.

Sumo, like other professions in Japan, is facing the problem of survival as the younger generation become very sensitive, impatient and easily frustrated due to Western influence. When I was in Japan, I was concerned about the future of sumo because of the Futahaguro incident. Futahaguro, 24, was an up and coming wrestler who had climbed very fast. He was a good fighter, but was rather rash and abrupt. He created news when he injured his stable master's wife, after being reprimanded for his overbearing attitude toward his attendants. The incident was unprecedented in the history of the tradition-bound Japanese sport. Whatever reasons Futahagauro might have had for injuring Tatsunami's (his stable master) wife, Chieko, and his walking out of his stable, he could never justify his actions in the eyes of the Sumo Association, which was run by sumo leaders with old traditional concepts. It seems that he not only struck his stable master's wife, he also struck six of his attendants during a sumo barn storming tour. He was forced by the Sumo Association to take early retirement because they could not demote him, as he had attained the title of yokozuna. His father had to cut his hair in a ceremony of Danpatsu at the Imperial Hotel where some 300 guests, but no rikishi, were present.

Futahaguro belongs to the shinjinrui generation — the new breed said to be very sensitive, impatient and easily frustrated. These youngsters are selfish, likely to get angry when things do not go as they wish, and have what is sometimes called a "short circuit response". It has been said that Futahaguro was pampered by his stable master from the start. There was criticism of his quick promotion to yokozuna, particularly as he had never won an Emperor's Cup tournament.

The Futahaguro incident raises the question of how to deal with the younger sumo wrestlers whose dispositions differ from those of the older adherents. The traditional idea that the dominance of superiors outweighs reason and that lower rank wrestlers should be treated as little more than slaves can no longer hold. The Sumo Association may have to re-examine the stable and attendant system, where young wrestlers must cater to their higher ranking stablemates and act like slaves as in the olden days.

The sumo world cannot survive if it cuts itself off totally from changes in society. It is understandable that the Japanese want to keep the sumo tradition to remind themselves of the samurai tradition. It is necessary for the sumo promoters to keep the charm of the old traditions. But they must face reality and make the sport more attractive to the younger generation if they want sumo to survive.

CHAPTER 4

The Myth of Nihongo

When I first heard Japanese soldiers speaking Nihongo (the Japanese language), when they invaded Malaya and arrived in my hometown of Penang at the end of 1941, the language sounded very much like Fukienese (a southern China provincial dialect). There are many Japanese words which sound very much like Fukienese. For instance, the Nihongo word for "world" is "sekai", exactly the same as the Fukienese. Similarly, words such as "jinrui" (human kind), "Bukkyo" (Buddhism), "ki" (air), "ka" (home), "jinmin" (people), "kunjin" (military) and "anzen" (peaceful) have the same Fukienese pronunciation. Even the names of fruits such as "budo" (grapes) are almost identical to Fukienese. The numerical counting in Japanese such as "ichi" (one), "ni" (two), "san" (three), "si" (four), "go" (five), "roku" (six)... have almost the same sound in the Fukien language, which pronounces them as "it", "ji", "sa", "si", "go" and "lak". I could produce a few pages of Japanese words which are similar to Fukienese, but it would be superfluous.

How is it that the sound of the Japanese language is so similar to Fukienese? I began to ask the question 48 years ago when I first learnt the language. Can it be that there was a large scale migration of Fukienese to Japan in the early period of Japanese history? When I was sent to Japan as Ambassador in 1984, I began to take a keen interest in finding out the answer and started to do some research. I read up on the history of Japan and China, and tried to find out the reasons for the similarity between Japanese and Fukienese. It was a tedious affair but I think I have found some clues.

It was not the migration of Fukienese to Japan that resulted in these language links. There was no such movement in the history of Japan, nor the history of China. The similiarity has to do with the journey of Buddhism from China through Korea to Japan, and the "Go On" — the phonetic sound used in China during the Tang dynasty to translate Buddhism from Indian Sanskrit to Chinese.

Chinese languages were pronounced according to three major systems of phonetics — the Han On, the Tang On and Go On. Although Chinese characters were unified under Emperor Qin Xi Huang, people from different provinces read Chinese characters in different phonetic accents based on the three phonetic systems. Han On sounds quite different from Tang On, and so with Go On. During the Han and Tang dynasties, Go On was popularly spoken and in fact it was the official language of Mandarin circles in Xian.

When Buddhism spread from India to China, Chinese scholars wracked their brains trying to translate the teachings of Buddha, which were written in Sanskrit, into Chinese. The Chinese Buddhist sage Dang San Zhang spent many years in India and brought back large volumes of Buddhist scripts to Sian, storing them in a specially built pagoda. He also spent almost his whole life trying to translate the scripts. The translators were particularly concerned with Sanskrit "Mantras", which should never be wrongly translated, for the "Gods" would not understand the "Mantras" when they were chanted by the worshippers. The "Mantras" would not be effective if not properly pronounced. The scholars found Go On most suitable for translating Buddhism because it produced the desired phonetic sounds, similar to Sanskrit. For instance, in the Chinese language, only Go On has the word "Bud" to pronounce Buddha. Other phonetic systems do not have the "bu" sound.

What then has Fukienese to do with Go On? Following the Han dynasty, people of the Yieh tribe (the ancestors of Fukienese) migrated to Fukien because of the upheaval and purging of the tribe, which then tried to found its own kingdom. Migration peaked during the Tang dynasty when there was a widespread struggle for power in a serious upheaval which brought many thousands of Yieh people to Fukien. They brought with them the Go On language and culture. Being conservative, the Fukiens stuck to their Go On phonetic and the Fukienese language was therefore Go On oriented. When Buddhism spread from China to Japan through Korea, the Japanese picked up Go On phrases by reading Buddhism and chanting Buddhist sutras.

It is generally agreed that the Japanese people did not have their own writing system before the introduction of Chinese script. The Japanese language has an Altaic origin which belongs to the same family as Old Turkish, Mongolian, Korean and early records of the Manchu founders of the Qing dynasty in China. The syntactic similarity of Japanese to Korean is widely acknowledged, and its general resemblance in certain respects to the Altaic languages has been pointed out. There is a growing consensus among Japanese scholars that, syntactically, Japanese shows an Altaic affinity, but at some time in its prehistory it received an influence in vocabulary from the Malay–Polynesian languages to the south.

Before the Chinese script came to Japan, the Japanese had no written language. The construction of the Altaic language is very different from the Chinese language. But the superiority of the Chinese culture during the Tang dynasty captivated and overwhelmed the Japanese. They so admired Chinese culture that they wanted to import everything Chinese, including the Chinese language, despite the fact that the two languages were so different. In fact, the two major historical documents, the ancient Japanese chronicle Kojiki (Record of Ancient Matters) written in 712 and the Nihon Shoji (Chronicles of Japan) written in 720, were written in Kanji (Chinese script). Kojiki records the ten volumes of Senjimon (Ch'ientzu wen — the Thousand Character Classics). Both these historical documents were Go On oriented, although some of the words also had Han On and Tang On.

These documents were brought to Japan by a Korean scholar named Wani in the 16th year of Emperor Ojin's reign. In those days, Korean scholars were highly proficient in the Chinese classics and were influenced by Go On through Buddhism. The earliest known Buddhist temple, Hokoji, was erected at the end of the 6th century in the area of Yamato, where the Emperors took their residence before 710. The Japanese court must have been involved in studying various aspects of Buddhism, including reading Buddhist literature in Chinese, for a long time before they built the temple, which was the embodiment of their faith in Buddhism.

Having imported Kanji from China through Buddhism, the Japanese had the difficult task of spreading Buddhism because it was written in classical Chinese which was used by only a small number of people, namely the court nobles and priests. In order to spread Buddhism, the Japanese had to find a way to make the reading of Kanji easier, so that Buddhism could be introduced to more people.

It seems that around the beginning of the 9th century, priests who were studying Buddhist texts in Kanji began to use certain marks as an aid to reading Kanji. The marks were, in the beginning, created individually for personal use. The oldest copy of a Buddhist text which has these marks is dated 828. These marks are called okototen (after O, the object marker, and koto, the nominalisation marker). These were used to indicate the ways to read Kanji. Apparently, the priests who used okototen were translating Chinese into Japanese. In other words, they were giving the Japanese approximation of the Chinese pronunciation. They probably used Go On reading to deal with Chinese characters, as Buddhist priests today still recite Buddhist sutras in Go On.

These otokoten began on an individual basis but eventually became a regular feature in the teaching of Chinese and developed as a means to study Buddhism. When the priests studied Chinese under a lecturer, they had to write quickly and they developed their own personal, simplified letters. They started to write a part of a character in place of the entire character. The priests in the early Heian period might have taken some hints from these abbreviated characters and invented the Katakana.

Japanese scholars picked 50 Chinese characters and simplified the strokes according to their sounds to compose the Katakana, which became a useful alphabet to read Chinese and developed into a valuable alphabetical system for the Japanese language. By the end of the Heian period, Katakana was used to write Japanese sentences, along with Chinese characters.

The emergence of Katakana to write Japanese was extremely important in the history of writing in Japan, since it made the writing of Japanese grammatical elements possible and easier than depending on Kanji alone.

Another phenomenon in Nihongo which helped boost the Japanese language was the invention of Hiragana, which was another system of applying Chinese characters into a different type of Japanese alphabet. Hiragana was called onnade (woman's handwriting) or onnamoji (woman's letters) in the Heian period because women were excluded from the study of Chinese and started writing poems and letters in Hiragana. There is a legend which says that Hiragana was created by Kobo Daishi (also known as Kukai, 774–835). Kukai went to China to study Buddhism during the Tang dynasty and returned to Japan with a large collection of Buddhist scripts. He was a prominent calligrapher and many people in Japan believed that he contributed towards the invention of Hiragana after returning to Japan.

Katakana was never written for aesthetic purposes, but Hiragana was written to appeal to the aesthetic sense of the reader. While Katakana was a convenient reading aid and was developed in the austere society of priests, Hiragana was created in a more leisurely aristocratic environment, for writing poems and letters in beautiful handwriting.

Hiragana consists of the simplified strokes of another 48 Chinese characters and is pronounced according to their sounds. It is written in the flowery style — a creation of the Japanese mind. The emergence of Hiragana was perhaps a more significant phenomenon than that of Katakana in the history of the Japanese written language, since Hiragana came to be used for establishing the wabun (Chinese language) style of writing. By the beginning of the 10th century, after many centuries of studying Chinese characters and writings, the Japanese people found a way of writing that was completely free of Chinese domination. This is what I would call the Japanese genius.

The Chinese have been using Kanji for centuries and they have not yet found a suitable alphabet for reading Chinese characters. That makes the study of Chinese most difficult. Until today, readers of Chinese characters have to memorise every word without any spelling system. This is what makes Chinese the most difficult language in the world and it requires a lot of effort for even the average Chinese to learn the language. Consequently, illiteracy is still very high in China.

The durable and intrepidly outspoken Chinese political leader Deng Xiaoping astonished a visiting delegation of Japanese in June 1977 by commenting frankly about the Chinese script. The Japanese delegation began their meeting with Deng with a ceremonial apology for the damage and destruction that Japan inflicted upon Chinese life and property during World War II. Deng replied, in his characteristically sharp and frank fashion, that no apologies were necessary. China, he said, had itself done much more wrong to Japan during the years of their historical association than Japan had ever done to China. The visiting Japanese delegation was surprised by his statement and asked what he meant. Deng said, "In years gone by, we managed to inflict upon your nation two of the greatest burdens known to mankind — Confucianism and the Chinese writing system. Now, we in China have got rid of the first and are on our way to getting rid of the second. But it seems that you Japanese are to suffer the consequences of both the rest of your history. This is a crime that China can never be forgiven for."

To my mind, Deng was wrong in his statement. Today, China has not got rid of Confucianism, which is making a comeback with the blessing of the Chinese authorities. Deng was also wrong about the introduction of Chinese characters into Japan. Unlike China, the Japanese invented the Hiragana and Katakana out of Chinese characters to become their reading alphabets. Today, literacy is higher than 94.5 percent in Japan. Literacy in Japan has helped its modernisation, whereas China is still generations from becoming a modern industrialised society. It is not possible for China to get rid of Kanji without causing great harm to the country and people. Events have proved that it is impossible for China to romanise the Chinese language. The most China can do is to simplify the writing, which she is now doing.

Admittedly, the most formidable element in the Japanese writing system is obviously the Chinese characters. What makes the Chinese characters a formidable burden is the complex and cumbersome way they are being used. During the Meiji Restoration, Japan was caught up with the euphoria of the westernisation of everything Japanese. Some Japanese scholars felt that the written language too needed liberalisation from its dependence on classical Chinese. The only way to modernise was in affiliation with the

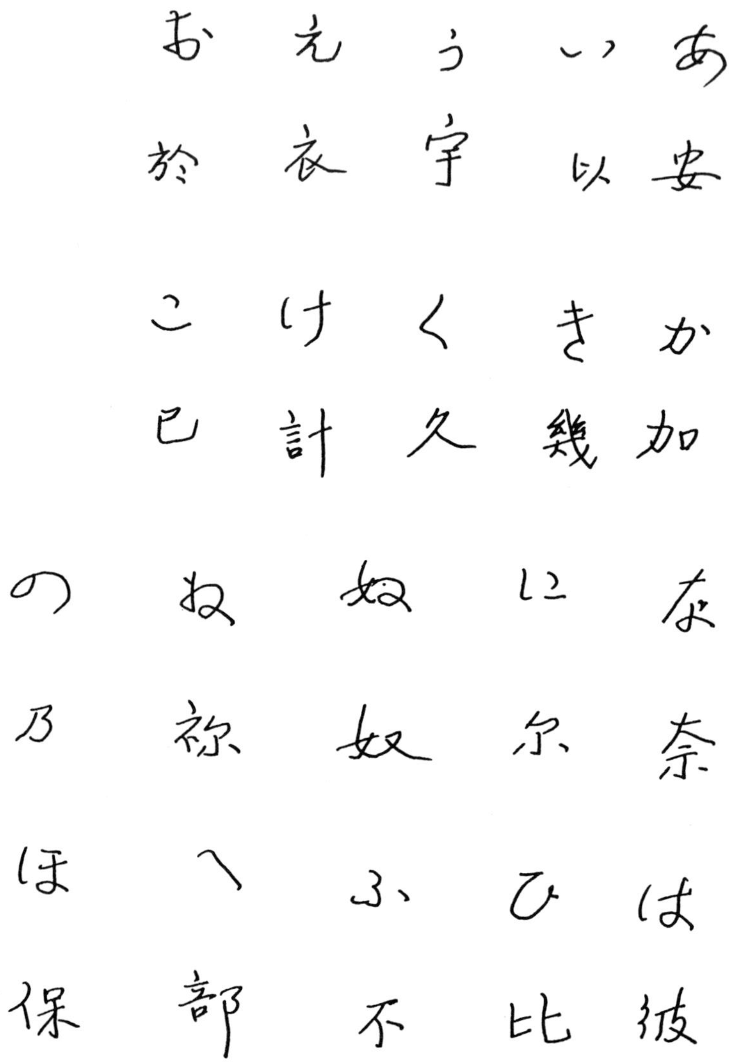

All Japanese alphabets are derived from Chinese characters. The pictures show how each hiragana was taken from a Chinese character.

そ	せ	す	し	さ
曽	世	寸	之	左
と	て	つ	ち	た
止	天	川	知	太
も	め	む	み	ま
毛	女	武	美	末
		よ	ゆ	や
		与	由	也

modern languages of the developed West. At the outset of the Meiji period (1868–1912) one scholar, Mori Arinori, contemplated giving up the Japanese language and adopting English as the national language of Japan. Mori was one of the most important intellectual leaders of the Meiji era. More than any other individual, he was responsible for the development of the entire Japanese national education system. He travelled widely in Eastern Europe and North America and was convinced that the Japanese language would never be able to serve as a viable medium of instruction in the new European-styled education system that he was in the process of devising for Meiji Japan. Within the next three decades, however, the Japanese solved most of their basic problems and Mori's idea died a natural death.

In 1866, a scholar Maejima Nisoka made his name by calling for the abolition of Chinese characters in favour of Katakana syllabary. Three years later, another scholar, Nambu Yoshikazu, suggested the use of romanisation instead of using Katakana and Hiragana. Associations were formed to implement the idea. However, due to lack of public support, his suggestion also did not come to anything. This was the first period of Japanese language reform when the basic issues were discussed.

The second period, which started in 1900 and ended in 1960, concentrated more on adjustments to the existing language and paid more attention to its efficiency and effectiveness. There was a proposal in 1923 that Kanji should be restricted to 1,962 words and by 1925 Japanese newspapers were already using the suggested words. The era was characterised by a struggle between the utilitarian reformists and the nationalists. The former approved of the reforms because they aimed at efficiency. With the colonial expansion of the Showa period, the difficulty of teaching Japanese to colonised people contributed to the arguments of the reformists, and it is interesting to note that both the army and navy supported the reformists. It was, however, the nationalists who won the battle.

The defeat of Japan in 1945 gave the reformists a golden opportunity to push through their long prepared reforms. They had the backing of the progressive forces within the country, which aimed at a real democratisation of the country's administrative system and language, and the Allied Occupation Forces. A series of exercises to "phoneticise" the historical Kana spelling and restrict the number of Kanji to 1,850 was initiated. By 1949, the number of Kanji characters was reduced to 881.

The third period of reform started in 1960 and still continues today. After long years of reform, it dawned on the Japanese that however difficult the language may be, it is not incompatible with the functioning of a modern society. It also became clear that within contemporary Japan a radical language reform of any kind is politically unfeasible. The Japanese have accepted the existing pattern of the Japanese language of mixing Kanji with Katakana and Hiragana. The only problem was how to reduce the over-dependence of Kanji. The Ministry of Education raised the number of Kanji taught in schools from 881 to 996 in 1968 and by 1981, the number had increased to 1,945 characters.

The Japanese vocabulary has been so deeply influenced by China-imported culture and knowledge that it has become impossible to do away with them. Each Chinese character gives an impression and meaning of a "thing" whereas an alphabetic combination of words do not convey anything except sound and letters. The influence of Chinese culture is so deeply intertwined in the Japanese culture that it is not easy to dig out its roots without harming the body.

There is no doubt, however, that since Meiji, Japan has been moving away from China's influence and beginning to worship the West. The influence of China had been diminishing ever since the court ceased sending its official embassies to the Chinese capital and the glory of the Tang dynasty came to an end in 907. After Tang, the Japanese gradually felt that they had nothing much to learn from China. With the Meiji Restoration, Japan shifted their attention to the West to learn Western technology. It used Katakana to take in Western phrases and scientific terms. They also used Western culture, civilisation and scientific knowledge to equip themselves with modern technologies and modernise the country. And when they grew stronger militarily, they began to compete with the West in the adventure of dominating the Asian continent. The Japanese are experts in coining phrases and the Japanese had a new slogan which said "Learn from the West and forget the East".

Through Katakana, the Japanese started borrowing Western languages, especially English. Borrowing the English word "rice" and turning it into the Japanese word "raisu" happened when the society decided to imitate Western eating habits, including using a fork and spoon. It is not easy for an Englishman to understand the word "raisu" when it is pronounced by a Japanese. Similarly, there are hundreds of Japanised English words which are not understood by an English-educated person when spoken by a Japanese. For instance, when a Japanese says "raito ranchi" he means light lunch, "suppu" means "soup" and "kurisumasu" means "Christmas".

An American scholar of the Japanese language recently started to count the number of words borrowed from English used in recent issue of the popular Japanese literary journal Bengei Shunju, a famous Japanese magazine whose article brought about the downfall of Prime Minister Tanaka.

"I gave up counting," he said, "after 7,000 occurences of borrowings from English, or an average of more than 15 per page."

A Myth Created

Although the Japanese language is a combination of Kanji, Hiragana and Katakana with a vast resource of English and Western vocabulary, the Japanese have learnt to be proud of their language, especially after they achieved an economic miracle after the war. Before and after the war, various attempts were made to modernise the language but the nationalists resisted each move. Japan's long period of national seclusion from the 17th to the mid-19th century and the absence of readily apparent genetic relations with neighbouring languages have resulted in a broadly accepted myth in Japan proclaiming the "uniqueness" of the Japanese language. Nowadays, Nihongo has become a myth to most Japanese. In modern Japan, the Nihongo is never allowed to be taken for granted, not by anyone, not for a single moment. It is constantly being made the subject of security, the target of self-examination and of soul-searching. The language not only serves the society as a vehicle for daily communication, but also manages to be a cult and myth. It has assumed the dimensions of a national myth of vast proportions. The myth equates the Japanese language with the Japanese race and culture.

After World War II, the Japanese found nothing of Japanese life to bind people together except for the language. The sustaining myth that was once erected on the foundation of Mahayana, Buddhism had begun to lose its credibility in Japan by the latter part of the 14th century. Using Buddhism to bind the people was no longer an effective force in Japanese life after the 100-year civil war that ravaged most of the settled parts of the country between 1467 and 1568. After 1568, when Oda Nobunaga, the victor, finally fought his way into the smouldering ruins of the city of Kyoto, very few who were not on the payroll of a temple or other religious foundations would take religious ideas seriously. Buddhism failed to create a united people.

The nationalist–fascist dictatorship that led Japan into its ill-advised military ventures on the Asian mainland, its attempted rape of China and its final demented challenge of the industrial powers of the West in the skies of Pearl Harbour was spectacularly effective but short-lived. The perverted myth of a "master race" and "superman" ideas, inspired by a selection of 19th century nationalistic fantasies borrowed from Western Europe, evaporated after the defeat in 1945. Those Japanese who were lucky enough to survive found their cities and villages overrun by hordes of tall, strong, well-fed, and generally genial foreign troops. How could any Japanese believe for a moment that he belonged to a race that was in any way superior to these great, smiling, robust pink-faced lads? The myth of the Emperor fell apart overnight when MacArthur proclaimed, "The prerogative of the Emperor to rule the state shall be subject to the Supreme Commander of the Allied Forces of Occupation."

The Japanese who were trying to create a myth out of race and the Emperor failed, and had nothing to hold onto except the Japanese language. This was the only thing they had which was "unique" and which supposedly was not shared by any other language on earth. What in all Japan had survived intact? Only the Japanese language. What was the common possession of very Japanese alive, while at the same time the only thing that the invading American did not have at their command and in abundant supply? The Japanese language. This was the single, possibly unifying, factor that the Japanese nationalistic scholars wanted to appropriate and turn into a myth.

The average Japanese believes in the myth of Nihongo, a language that can pull and bind all Japanese together and a language that is meant and reserved for the Japanese. Only the language can bind the people together. The myth of a superior race to keep the nation together is no longer valid after Japan's disastrous defeat in 1945.

In most cultures, a foreigner who attempts to learn the language of the society in question is believed by the society to be providing a significant indicator of the high esteem in which he or she holds both the society and the language. In the case of the Japanese, the reaction is reverse. Japanese society usually distrusts and dislikes any attempt by a foreigner to learn and use the Japanese language. This dislike grows stronger as the foreigner becomes more fluent. Fluency in Japanese by a foreigner is regarded as an attempt to acquire Japanese racial identity and to enter Japanese society.

A well-respected old-time Japanese Ambassador who served in Singapore in the early 1970s once disclosed a secret to me. I was talking to him in Japan when I first became Singapore's Ambassador. He said that the average Japanese normally does not like to see a foreigner speaking too fluent Japanese. He warned me not to speak Japanese fluently and said that it would be wiser to speak in English. When a foreigner becomes too fluent in Japanese, they get suspicious. After more than four years posting in Japan, I begin to realise that my friend was telling the truth.

Basil Hall Chamberlain (1850–1935), a pioneer student of the Japanese language and a trenchant observer of "things Japanese", put it in the following way: "Seeing that you speak Japanese, they (the Japanese) will wag their heads and smile condescendingly, and admit to each other that you are really quite intelligent — much as we might do in the presence of the learned pig or an ape of somewhat unusual attainments."

Foreign correspondents I met in Tokyo often mentioned the name of Cox, a journalist who was arrested by the Japanese secret police in 1939, along with a number of other British nationals rounded up at that time on suspicion of espionage. The affair appears to have been instigated by a pro-Nazi element active within the Japanese Foreign Ministry at that time. Their aim was to enrage Britain by mistreating British subjects by lodging absurd charges of spying, in the hope that Britain would declare war against Japan. The trouble with Cox was that he spoke Japanese perfectly well. He understood the questions when they interrogated him and answered in fluent Japanese. He made a mistake by displaying his linguistic abilities and he got into serious trouble. The Secret Police were so outraged that they threw him out of the window to his death.

Those were the inner feelings of the Japanese towards foreigners who tried to master their language. As the Japanese find it difficult to study English or other foreign languages, it is quite natural for them to feel that foreigners will never be able to master Japanese as they have. They would always tell foreigners that the Japanese language is difficult and that only the Japanese can master it. They also distrust foreigners who try to master the language. They are happy when they hear foreigners utter a smattering of Japanese and would comment that "Oh, you speak excellent Japanese." But when a foreigner speaks perfect Japanese with impeccable grammar, they become uneasy and suspicious.

It was just as well that the American Allied Occupation Forces were not instructed to learn Japanese. It was felt that after its surrender, Japan would simply be reduced to an agricultural community of no importance to the world at large and hence it would not be worth the time and trouble of a protracted military occupation. There was no need to train large numbers of Americans for a long occupation of Japan. But the prediction was wrong. Japan was not reduced to a simple agrarian economy. Soon, it was encouraged to reindustrialise so as to serve as a weapons-maker for the new American war in Korea and later Vietnam. The Allied Occupation of Japan was an all-English speaking, all-English writing enterprise. It was up to the Japanese to learn English if they wished to cope. It was never in the minds of the victors at that time to rule Japan with a Japanese speaking elite.

Within a short period of time, Japanese diligence, skill and determination, combined with material help advanced by the Occupation Forces, paid off.

The economy responded to ever-increasing export sales of Japanese goods throughout the world and particularly the United States. Slowly but surely, Japan entered a new period of growing prosperity, finally achieving outright affluence. Japan's GNP soon outstripped that of West Germany and the United States. It has become the world's No 1 economic giant. With this, the stage was finally set for the revival of the modern myth of Japan — the Nihongo. As Japan's industrial products swept the world and Japan began buying up the world, it was necessary for the Japanese to embark on a program of teaching their language to foreigners, imitating the model that the British, French and West German governments had set for them. The die has been cast. Since the Japanese find difficulty in learning foreign languages, why not let foreigners learn Japanese if they wish to trade with Japan? The aim is to make Japanese a world language and a language recognised by the United Nations.

To a certain extent, the Japanese have succeeded. All over the world, the Japanese language has become more important than the Chinese. In many European and American airlines, the Japanese language is announced to customers whereas the Chinese language is completely ignored. Perhaps there are more Japanese travellers going around the world compared to Chinese. With the emergence of Chinese prosperity and growing wealth today, and perhaps more Chinese travellers, the Chinese language may be better respected in the world arena.

A new problem emerges as to what kind of Japanese the foreigners should be taught. To the English, French and Germans, such a problem does not arise. The Englishman would like foreigners to learn the same kind of English as is taught to all Englishmen. The Englishman does not care whether the foreigners turn the King's English into pidgin English, Singlish or English with a heavy Indian accent. The French, who have always thought that French is the most beautiful language in the world, demand that all French should be spoken just as a Frenchman would speak it, in other words perfect French. The French normally look down on a person speaking broken French. Generally speaking, a Frenchman would even like to see French colonised subjects thinking and behaving like Frenchmen. In the case of Germans, they are not serious in wanting to convert foreigners into speaking perfect German.

In the case of Japanese, however, the problem does not appear to be that simple. Most non-Japanese would like to learn the same kind of Japanese that the Japanese have learnt, spoken or written. But the Japanese do not want that to be so. They would like the foreigners to learn Japanese the same way as the Japanese in Japan have been learning English.

The Japanese distinguishes between the kind of English he learns to pass the university entrance examinations and the kind of English he learns if he wishes to talk to foreigners and understand what they say. No amount of Eigo or Eigo Kyoiku, literally English or English education, will make it possible to speak a single word to be understood by a foreigner or comprehend a single word of English as spoken by anyone not similarly adept in the same arcane game. To learn English in the practical sense so that one can be understood, one has to study English as a language which the Japanese call Eikaiwa, literally meaning English conversation. The subject is not taught in Japanese universities and plays no part in university examination procedures. It must be purely privately learnt in special schools specifically for that purpose, the same kind of school at which one would study welding, carving, book binding and sewing.

The Japanese would like foreigners to learn Japanese in exactly the same way that they learn English. That was why they were not certain what type of Japanese to teach foreigners. After lengthy debate on this issue, the Foreign Ministry and the Ministry of Education both finally decided to set up and finance a private organisation comprising of independent scholars to be known as the Nihongo Kyoiku Gakkai (the Society for Japanese language education), headed by a professor of French language who had recently retired from the faculty of Tokyo University.

The Nihongo Kyoiku Gakkai hosted an international conference in Tokyo and Osaka in March 1978 and invited a small group of foreign educators from the United States, France and Australia, all of whom were professionally engaged in directing or supervising instruction in Japanese as a foreign language in their respective countries. The foreign professors were at first surprised with the Japanese concept of teaching English when they were told that the NKG was meant to implement a new Japanese policy of teaching the Japanese language to foreigners as "a special kind of Japanese language", the same way Japanese would learn English in Japan.

Stressing the importance of the Japanese language, Professor Suzuki, chairman of the NKG, said, "Everybody who is a human being is going to be better off by learning Japanese. Nihongo must be taught to the foreigners because the well-known post-war Japanese constitution outlaws war as an instrument of Japanese national policy, and so Japan does not have modern military weapons like rockets and atom bombs. What it does have is Nihongo, and we ought to use it our weapon; it is the only one we have. Teaching Nihongo to foreigners will not only make them better people and defend weaponless Japan, it will also contribute to the peace of the world.

"The greatest contribution of all would be if Nihongo could be made one of the official languages of the United Nations assembly in New York." Suzuki added that the reason why the UN does not now function effectively is because Japanese is still not one of its official languages. He sounds rather arrogant.

What Japan had failed to achieve through military conquest, it tries to do through the spread of Nihongo — the new weapon of Japanese adventure. Japan tried to conquer other nations in order to sell its goods before the war. Today, Japanese goods are sold throughout the world without having to fire one bullet. It has dawned on the Japanese that it is unnecessary to conquer a nation in order to sell goods. It is easier to spread Nihongo and let the world benefit by Japan's superior technological knowhow. Let the world learn Japanese instead of Japanese learning foreign languages.

I would like to quote what Suzuki said at the 1978 conference when he tried to make a stirring call at the altar of Nihongo. He said, "The nation of Japan is one in which religious ideology has always been quite shallow. We Japanese have been a docile race. We have not developed ideologies or principles that explicitly define things in definite terms. We have lacked a messianic urge, the ideological strength to spread our ideas aggressively to other countries. For us Japanese to now found a new religion, something that we could spread throughout the entire world, would be a task requiring enormous time, nor are the other usual possibilities for extending our influence abroad anymore feasible.

"What we must do, therefore, is to make a religion of Nihongo. We must think of the Japanese language as the Nihongo Creed, and spread this new religion of Nihongo throughout the nations of the earth."

A standing ovation followed when Suzuki finally concluded his lecture at the Aoyama Gakuin auditorium in Tokyo on the afternoon of March 18, 1978.

That was the myth of Nihongo and the dream of most Japanese. To the Japanese, Nihongo is a language of success, achievement, prosperity and a language which every Japanese should be proud of. But, what is Nihongo if one perceives it objectively? It consists of Kanji, Katakana, and Hiragana. Take away the Kanji, which is a product of Chinese civilisation, and take away Katakana, which contains thousands of English words and Western vocabulary, and Japanese is left only with Hiragana. I doubt that the Japanese language could survive if the Japanese wrote their language with Hiragana alone. It would not make sense to most Japanese. Can a Hiragana oriented Japanese be intelligible and comprehensible? This is what I mean by referring to Nihongo as a myth.

But, there is reason for the Japanese to be proud of their language. They had the wisdom and genius to borrow from the Chinese characters, simplify them and turn them into useful alphabets. The Chinese had five thousand years of civilisation and history, but were unable to invent any suitable alphabet to simplify the Chinese language. After inventing the Katakana, the Japanese were able to use it to absorb English and Western terms to enrich their vocabulary and thus the language.

The Japanese are masters in copying from other civilisations. The beauty of the Japanese culture and civilisation is that whatever they adopt from foreign culture, they adapt to suit local conditions and make them something of their own. They have the wisdom of treasuring and preserving old cultures and weaving them into their Japanese way of life. Many of such borrowed cultural treasures have long ago become extinct in their original homes, but the Japanese continue to treasure them as their own.

The Japanese have reasons to be proud of their own language. It is unique in a certain sense because it is a fusion of the East and West and practicable as far as they are concerned. The Japanese are a practical and pragmatic people. The language has undergone many changes but has gone through the test of time. All sorts of changes including banning the language have been suggested by leading Japanese intellectuals and educationalists. But Japanese common sense prevails and the language remains very much intact and continues to serve the community with some minor changes.

The Japanese have a practical mind to select what is good for their society. It must have taken a long process of "nemasasi" (consultation) of Japanese scholars from all levels before a decision was made. The collective view of the Japanese is that the Japanese language, though it has handicaps and is viewed at times with misgivings, serves the society effectively. So, the Japanese language has not only come to stay but is being propagated as a myth.

In the eyes of the world, Nihongo has arrived and the Japanese would like it transformed into a myth.

CHAPTER 5

The Utilitarian "Gods"

There is an anecdote describing the Japanese and it goes something like this. "A Japanese undergoes a Shinto ritual when he is born, marries in a Christian church and is buried according to a Buddhist ceremony. The reason for this mixture of religious activities is for practical reasons. He goes to a Shinto shrine because his parents want him to remember that he is a Japanese; he is wedded in a Christian church because it looks grand to be married in a church; and he has a Buddhist burial because the Shinto shrine does not perform the burial ceremony. In any case, he had covered all the options for the after life. He is safe."

Religious observance in Japan is indeed rich in a healthy interchange between different religious traditions. People who go to Buddhist temples are just as likely to visit Shinto shrines, whilst Christian churches, though small in number, are not without their congregations. However, many religious beliefs and practices exist outside the boundaries of organised religion, and it is difficult to define where religion begins and tradition and custom end.

My impression of the Japanese during more than four years stay in Japan as Singapore's Ambassador is that the Japanese generally take a utilitarian approach to religion. Nearly every Japanese believes in the existence of the soul. He believes that there is soul or "kami" in everything under the sun. He has a special liking for the "Sun God", which is based on the cult of the sun, which is among the deities of Japan. Significantly, too, that deity is female. He also worships the moon, the stars, mountains, rivers, trees, rocks and various kinds of animals, particularly the fox which is believed to be the god for prosperity.

The Japanese concept of kami may be described as a syncretic system of animism and pantheism. This system of belief has evolved and been refined over a period of 2,000 years, and it has received considerable influence from other cultural systems, primarily that of China. The interaction of man and kami, and of man and innumerable souls, is sometimes the occasion of diverse and dramatic events and that interaction is at the very core of Japanese culture.

In ancient Japan it was believed that trees and plants conversed with one another. Birds and beasts had spirits and could speak, just as human beings could. The same rules and order seen in the world of man were thought to exist in the animal kingdom, although these creatures were graded one step below man. It was often believed that the spirits of animals could, if worshipped, bring luck and fortune to human beings. Take a stroll along Ginza, Tokyo's busiest shopping street, and you will invariably find a procelain cat raising its forepaw beckoning to customers. The beckoning cat is called "maneki neko" in Japanese and is a symbol of good fortune, for the Japanese believe that cats have special powers. The display of maneki neko has become the most auspicious symbol of merchants, promising that his shop would attract numerous customers and make plentiful profit.

The Japanese utilitarian approach to religion makes them identify the various "gods" as targets of worship. At the age of 3, 5, 7 and 13, which are considered to be important turning points in a child's growth, arrangements are made to visit shrines which house the God of scholarship, so that children can pass their examinations easily. When I visited Kagoshima, the southern part of Japan, I visited one of the biggest Shinto shrines, the Tenmangu, which is the most popular shrine in Japan for scholarship. The Tenmangu takes in one-eighth of Japan's younger population and there are 1.2 million Tenmangus throughout Japan.

It was the fifth day of May, and on this day each year the whole shrine, and in fact the whole city of Kogoshima, is decorated with gigantic fish floats in the air like kites. Almost every home with one or more sons has a tall pole in the garden attached to the roof upon which are hoisted carp of brightly coloured paper or cloth. The carp exemplifies fortitude, courage and perseverance in overcoming obstacles. The hoisting of such carps was an expression of hope that each boy in the family would have good health, vigour and success in all his undertakings. That day I saw many boys in the streets, dressed in their best attire going about visiting the Tenmangu to pray to the God of scholarship.

"Who is this God of Scholarship?" one would ask. The day that the Japanese celebrate the God of Scholarship coincides with the Chinese "Tuan Wu" Festival when the Chinese eat dumplings and have dragon boat competitions to commemorate Qu Yen, the famous poet and scholar from Chinese history. Qu Yen committed suicide by jumping into the River because the Emperor, who was obsessed with wine and women and listening only to poisonous gossip, no more listened to his advice. Nobody knows whether there was any connection between the God of Scholarship and Qu Yen.

Japanese sometimes use the expression "Kurushii toki nokamidanomi" (seeking God only in time of tribulation) to indicate their sense of contigent "faith". Such faith is not equivalent in their minds to religion, however, since it is not a full-time avocation or way of life, but rather something one does only on isolated occasions of specific need. Most Japanese claim no religion for themselves. No specific day is set aside for rest or worship as in many Western countries. But when trouble arises, Japanese call upon their "gods".

In the late sixties, a major Japanese construction company was plagued with on-the-job accidents that resulted in a number of deaths. Stringent safety precautions were implemented, and every man on every site was constantly reminded of the need for safety first. Still, the accidents continued. Management was confounded. It seemed that every precaution had been taken, and yet accidents occurred. In desperation, the entire executive management corps made a pilgrimage to the Ise of Jinggu — the Grand Shrine of the Ise, the guardian of the Japanese archipelago — to appeal to the guardian and receive the cleansing "oharai" (shinto purification) of the high priest.

Since then, no on-the-job fatality has occurred. Now, during every New Year's holiday, the management of that construction company journeys to the Grand Shrine of Ise to pay homage, express gratitude for the past year's safety record, and appeal for help for the year ahead.

On most rooftops of Japan's giant department stores I found shrines erected to house the spirit of the fox. They are called "O-inari shrine" — the shrine of the fox, the favoured deity of merchants. I was shown the O-inari shrine of the Sogo Department store in Yokohama by the then 80-year-old chairman Hiroo Mizushima, who was a personal friend of mine. It was situated on the rooftop. He and his directors who accompanied us paid homage to the shrine and prayed for a little while. Mizushima explained to me that nearly all department stores in Japan have O-inari shrines. He warned, however, that the shrine could bring bad luck if it is not properly cared for. The shrine has a Shinto type roof and four pillars, all painted red.

Since ancient times, the Japanese have thought foxes to be possessed of spiritual power and capable of bewitching people, perhaps because of the extreme deftness with which they escape danger. The story of a fox marrying a man by assuming the shape of a woman is found in many collections of tales, including the Konjaku Monogatari of the later years of the Heian period. The Chinese describe a cruel, crafty and witty woman as "Hu Li Ching" (the spirit of the fox) and many stories about the spirit of the fox can be found in the novel *Liao Chai* (one of the most popular novels in Chinese classical literature). In Japan, foxes also appear in innumerable other folktales and legends, in which they are described as having various occult powers and as being extremely clever.

In Japan there are different "gods" for different professions. For instance, merchants believe in Daikoku and Ebisu, the two gods of business, apart from the fox spirit. Singers, artists, and musicians believe in Benten, who is the patron of the arts. She is a woman. The intellectual classes worship Fukuamon and the travellers, doctors and missionaries pray to Bishamon. All these gods are grouped into one group called the Lucky Gods of the Seven. Perhaps one reason for this group worship is that the number of seven is sacred to the Japanese. Another reason, and this one is psychological, is that the Japanese people are fond of groups. This Lucky Gods of the Seven is very similar to the Chinese Eight Saints crossing the Sea.

The earliest mention of the Seven Lucky Gods as a group was made in 1420 at a place called Fushimi, where it has been recorded that a procession of the Seven Lucky Gods was held in imitation of the famed Daimyo processions. One of the many beliefs concerning the Seven Lucky Gods is that during the first three days of the New Year, the Seven Lucky Gods become sailors and command a ship called the takarabune, the treasure ship. It is said that the Gods steer the treasure ship from heaven into human ports every New Year's Eve. The legend is similar to the Chinese Eight Saints crossing the sea by boat. In the case of the Chinese belief, all the eight saints were real Taoist mystics with mystical powers who had lived in different dynasties. Seven is a lucky and magical number for Japanese and therefore chosen instead of eight, which has the same significance as seven in Chinese culture.

The Japanese have different gods to suit their needs. Japanese who are impotent or have no children go to the Kanayama shrine, which is situated in the shadows of a deep wood near the level crossing east of Kawasaki Daishi station. I visited this shrine one Sunday morning during the Kanamara Matsuri (Golden Testicle Festival). The Kanamara Temple is a small temple with a huge phallus in front of it. The temple is, in fact, a museum of hundreds of phallic symbols of metal, stone and wood of different sizes, shapes and colours.

The Kanamara Matsuri procession which I attended was led by a large banner with a penis drawn on it, followed by a mikoshi (portable shrine) containing a magnificent scarlet phallus. Hundreds of foreigners also took part. The musicians leading the procession played a distinctive type of music

The Kanamara Matsuri procession, where Japanese supporters carry the portable shrine called mikoshi in front of the Kanamara Temple near Kawasaki Daishi station. It is called the Golden Testicle Festival.

My family joined the procession of the Golden Testicle Festival in 1984.

Some of the exhibits inside the Kanamara Temple.

called the "hayashi", which was marked by warbling flutes and throbbing drums. There were two flutists blowing small bamboo lutes, one of higher tone and the other lower, accompanied by a drummer playing the deep voice drum and a few others hitting hand-held bells. The music was rich and beautiful. The supporters chanted mantras specially coined for that special occasion. The hayashi at the Kanamara Matsuri was performed by the members of the local Hayashi Preservation Society, which was steadily gaining in popularity among the young people. I saw many women rushing to touch the phallus while praying for pregnancy. Among those who went to touch the phallus were men, believed to be suffering from impotency. The shrine talisman (omamori) resembled a penis.

The festival is said to be efficacious in assuring good crops, curing sterility and impotence and guaranteeing business success and propagation of descendants. The worship of such deities is widespread in Japan and takes many forms. There are also roadside processions which are erotic in nature, sometimes representing a god and goddess in sexual union.

The unabashed sexuality of the Kanamara Matsuri was a happy turn-on. Here, religion and sex were welded joyously, not sundered by sexually repressive doctrines. In Japan there has been government interference at various times, but perhaps because of the comparatively tolerant attitude of Buddhism, there has never been anything like a similar severity of repression.

The Kanayama Shrine, popularly referred to as Kanamarasama, remains close to the hearts of the Japanese community. The date and circumstances of its founding are unclear. Government opposition to phallic worship, which had been severe in the late 19th century, gradually declined and these years saw heightened popularity and growing scholarly interest. The worst of the shrine's fortune was reached in April 1945, when massive bombing raids destroyed the building and almost all of the sacred objects.

Since Japanese believe in the existence of the soul, death is a very important matter in Japanese culture. Upon death, a person becomes a spirit. The spirit of a dead person is considered to possess individual characteristics for a certain fixed period during which memorial services are held for him as an individual. Then after seventeen, thirty-three or in some cases fifty years, the spirit of the dead persons loses its individual character and is merged with the symbolic soul which is called the "spirit of the ancestors".

The souls of the ancestral spirits are generally believed to gather at a high mountain where the descendants live. The Japanese believe that when the sakura blooms and the families gather under the sakura trees to enjoy their feast, the souls of their ancestors would descend to join them. That is why the Japanese never say to a girl "you are as beautiful as a sakura". Although sakura is beautiful, it is never associated with the beauty of women.

Like the Chinese, the Japanese have a "ghost festival", but the Japanese "ghost festival" is held according to the new calendar and not the lunar calendar. After the Meiji Restoration, the Japanese, in order to imitate the West, changed the lunar calendar to the Western calendar and started to observe all events according to the Western reading. The Japanese started celebrating the New Year on the first of January instead of the first day of the first moon. They also observe the "ghost festival" on July 13, 14 and 15 instead of the first day of the Seventh Moon. According to Chinese custom, the departed souls normally come back to earth on the first day of the seventh moon. When they come back to Japan, the Japanese have not offered anything for them and when they observe the ghost festival on 13 July, the ghosts have already gone away. Perhaps the ghosts in Japan have learnt to come back to earth later to suit the changing Japanese customs.

The Japanese call the ghost festival "O bon". They make a trip to graveyards and have them cleaned up. They also make trips to the Bon-ichi (Bon market) or kusa-iichi (grass market) to buy decorations, food and offerings during festival days. A visit to a Buddhist graveyard during Bon season will reveal elaborate decorations. Sombre branches of the Japanese umbrella

The Meiji shrine in Tokyo — an outside view.

The O bon mikoshi gathering in Akasaka Temple.

pine, koya-maki, can be seen alongside mochi (rice balls), fruits and incense.

On the first night of O Bon, Ueno Park in Tokyo features garlands of lighted lanterns, appreciated by milling crowds of millions around lakeside markets. Hundreds of stalls sell flowers, fruits, vegetables, crickets in cages, red fish, dwarf trees and bonsai and ferns. There are, of course, the inevitable fortune tellers and sellers of zodiac talismans for good luck. During the Bon season, presents are exchanged with friends and merchants give semi-annual gifts to their valued customers. A gay and extremely important part of Bon is the Bon odori, a dance intended for rejoicing. It is a dance that provides the most spontaneous outlet for the Japanese taste for music and rhythm. I have seen many such Obon dances in the streets of Tokyo.

It is a Japanese tradition and belief that the soul must be pacified and respected whether it is friendly or hostile. It is common to see Japanese paying respect to the souls of their enemies at funerals. They believe that once a person is dead, all his sins are forgotten.

The Japanese erected a huge memorial plaque near the sea of Kyushu to bless the souls of the invading Mongolians who tried to invade Japan in the eleventh century. On 15 August 1985, when I was still Ambassador to Japan, Prime Minister Nakasone created a storm in political circles when he officially visited the Yasukuni shrine in Chiyoda-ku where all the souls of the war dead were enshrined, including that of the war criminal Hidejo Tojo, Prime Minister of pre-war Japan who was responsible for the atrocities in China and Southeast Asia. Opposition members of the Japanese Parliament had suggested that Tojo's ashes be transferred to another shrine, but the temple authorities rejected the suggestion. One Japanese scholar explained to me that the controversy had arisen because of the lack of understanding of the Japanese deep desire to respect the soul, notwithstanding what the soul had done during his lifetime. Although Tojo had done a great deal of wrong in his lifetime, his sins were supposed to be forgotten and forgiven.

The Man-God Emperor

All the beliefs and practices that I have just mentioned are part of Japan's indigenous religion, Shinto (The way of the Gods). Shinto is written with two Chinese characters Shin (meaning God 'kami')and Dao (meaning 'The Way'). Shinto is a rich and complex system of religious practices, ideas and institutions which slowly emerged at the dawn of Japanese history, crystalised as a religious system during the Nara (AD 710–794) and Heian (AD 794–1185) periods, and subsequently was a constant and dynamic interaction with the other religious and philosophical systems of Asian Buddhism, Taoism and Confucianism. These combined schools ultimately merged in the Edo period (AD 1600–1868) and Japan finally developed Shinto into a religion where foreign influences were supposed to be absent.

This expurgated system was developed into a state religion at the end of the 19th century. The Emperor became the rallying point of the forces which sought to overthrow the Tokugawa Shogunate. When the Meiji regime came into power, the rulers made the Emperor the head of the nation, although there was little basis for the idea that the Emperor had always ruled the nation. The first article of the system declared that the Emperor had ruled Japan for ages eternal, and the third article declared that the Emperor was sacred and inviolable.

The founders of Meiji were content to manufacture history and they moulded the minds of the people to meet their own ends. Their aim was the establishment of a family state based on worship of the Sun Goddess, the extreme development of a chauvinistic renascent Shintoism. They amalgamated Confucianism into Japan's "kokutai" (a new Japanese wisdom fusing all good elements of Shintoism, Buddhism and Confucianism) into a State philosophy or "Japanese spirit" to be obeyed by all Japanese.

In other words, the Japanese nationalised Confucianism and included its virtues into the "kokutai" — the Japanese spirit or the Imperial way. The kokutai spelt out clearly that the Emperor was the "God" of all Japanese. The Japanaese regarded this move as vital to protect the nation against the rising tide of Communism in the early 1930s.

In the early 1930s, Communism spread to China and began to take root, a development which frightened the Japanese. They felt that the Chinese were slowly giving up their Confucianist way of life and accepting Communism. As China was a big neighbour, they were very worried that the influence of Communism in the mainland might spread to Japan.

To act against this trend, the Japan Ministry of Education issued circulars to all schools in the 1930s insisting that kokutai be part of the school curriculum. The students were taught never to set their eyes on the Emperor because he was "God". The warlords wanted to make the Emperor into a "utilitarian God" — a rallying point for the Japanese people to carry out ambitions they had in mind. The Ministry amalgamated Confucianism into kokutai emphasizing Confucian virtues of loyalty, obedience and filial piety. This amalgamation was a unique feature of Japanese culture. With this amalgamation, Confucianism has become part of Japanese culture.

Confucian ceremonies in those days had been carried out by Shinto priests in a manner ordinarily associated with Shinto ceremonies. There was also a tendency to worship Confucius as a Shinto god in some places. The Japanese are well-versed in assimilating foreign cultures into their own. For instance, Kukai fused Buddhist gods with Shinto gods and similarly, Meiji scholars mixed Confucianism with Shintoism. Such mixtures have become part of Japanese culture.

Confucianism became increasingly accepted as a basic element of the "Japanese spirit". One reason was that in the early period of Meiji Restoration there was a rush to learn from the West and there was tremendous copying of the Western way of life. That Western political and social ideas might take root in Japan presented a threat to both Japanese nationalists and conservatives, and could potentially rock the foundation of Japanese tradition culture. While willing to accept Western technology and industrial methods, the nationalist and conservative groups were apprehensive of the social, political and economic changes which were replacing traditional Japanese concepts with Western ones. Under these circumstances, Confucianism, within its strong anti-Western bias, recommended itself as a means of contrasting the avowedly superior spiritual civilisation of the East with the materialism of the West.

Another reason for fusing Confucianism as part of the Japanese spirit was a sugar-coating effect. Japan had ambitions to conquer China and tried to justify the invasion by saying that they went to China "for the purpose of restoring traditional spiritual values and redeeming the Chinese from the abyss of Western materialism and Communism". It was claimed that Japan had a mission to perform in protecting and developing spiritual civilisation in Asia, which was threatened by the egoistical and materialistic culture of the West.

When the leaders of Meiji Japan decided to make the imperial system the foundation of the nation and to construct the political order on the model of the traditional community, they were thinking of making Japan a divine land destined to achieve world leadership. They coined the slogan of "unity under the Emperor" and "tennosei fascism" (fascism under the monarchy). In its most extreme sense, Emperor worship led to the popular belief that the Head of the Japanese nation was a divine authority, the ruler of the universe. This view was officially sponsored through government propaganda agencies and led to firm conviction on the part of some of the Japanese that their nation was destined to rule the world.

After the defeat in World War II, Emperor Hirohito disclaimed his divinity and said he was no longer a "God" but an ordinary symbol of the nation.

MacArthur abolished the "kokutai" from schools. Some Japanese scholars however questioned the significance of the Emperor's proclamation that he was no more "God" because the Japanese concept of kami ("god") is not equivalent to the religious "divinity" known in the West. They said the concept of "living kami" has long been a part of Japanese religious culture, and even today some of the leaders of Japan's new religions claim (or have claimed for themselves) the status of living kami.

Emperor Hirohito could claim that he was the direct descendant of the deities who created Japan. But recent discoveries from ancient tombs in the Nara area have put those who supported the theory of a clear-cut blue-blood Japanese Emperor descendancy into some embarrassing positions. The number of Korean, Korean-like or even Chinese artifacts in the tombs have raised fears of what may be discovered when the coffins are opened. According to rumours, the authorities decided to postpone the actual opening of the stone coffins for fear that the Japanese ancestors were Koreans or Chinese after all. If the coffins are opened, the Japanese sense of cultural and racial uniqueness might be substantially damaged.

Shintoism

Shinto shrines are found everywhere in the country, from small stamp-sized fox shrines sandwiched between skyscrapers to the broad, wooded expanse of the complex dedicated to the Sun Goddess at Ise. Shinto is a basically pantheistic religion which believes in the kami's existence in practically every natural object or phenomenon. Often, particularly beautiful mountains or deep forest areas are venerated as sacred sites. Active volcanoes such as Mt. Fuji and Mt. Aso are considered sacred. The kami are thought to dwell in ponds, waterfalls, the confluence of rivers, giant trees and large or strangely shaped rocks.

During my stay in Japan, I visited many Shinto shrines in Honshu, Khusu Shikoku and Hokkaido. Some of the shrines were large, such as Toshogu at Nikko which consisted of a series of buildings forming courtyards staggered up a mountainside. The Itsukushima shrine at Miyajima in Hiroshima Prefecture stands along the island's edge and the buildings are completely surrounded by water at high tide. The worshipper knows he has entered a shrine complex because a large torri (gate) usually marks the sacred precinct from the residential neighbourhood. Stone lanterns usually mark the route. To maintain the purity of the shrine precinct, water basins are provided for worshippers to wash their hands and mouths. In Shinto shrines, the kami is housed by honden (roof) which has a gabled roof supported by large round posts. The roofing is of Japanese cypress tree bark. With the introduction of Buddhism, the nature of Shinto worship changed, including the shrine architecture. Many shrines were painted in Chinese red on the columns and white over the walls.

Shinto could well be termed a religion of ceremony. As a religion without official founders, Shinto has no tales of the conversion or revelations of early personalities, no official dogma, and no sacred texts. It does not even have classics of myth, ritual, and history. Thus, Shinto is a popular religion based not on doctrine but on elaborate ceremonial rites. Shinto places importance on ceremonial actions and on the transmission of ancient ceremonies, believing that in transmitting rites in their original form the power and dignity of the gods is made manifest.

When I visited the Yasukuni shrine in Tokyo, where all the souls of Japanese "heros" who fought and died during World War II were enshrined, I found a mirror standing before the inner sanctuary. That mirror was important because it was a gift from Emperor Meiji. There was the Gohei, which consisted of a wand with strips of paper folded in a zigzag fashion hanging at either side, standing in a central position before the doors of the inner chamber. It was a symbolic offering, indicating the presence of the kami. I saw a priest remove a purification wand (haraigushi) from its stand and start to purify the worshippers. He waved it first over his left, then right, and finally back to the left shoulder with a characteristic flourish before replacing it. Sometimes a small branch of sacred sakaki tree is used instead of the wand. I also saw straw ropes with short strips of zigzag cut paper stretched between the pillars.

Being primarily a ritualist, a priest must know how to conduct the rites, ceremonies and festivals including the preparation and intoning of the appropriate liturgy. This training can be secured either from other priests, by attending classes sponsored by the Association of Shinto Shrines and its prefectural branches, or by enrolling in courses offered at the Kokugakuin University or some seminary.

According to latest statistics of the Ministry of Education, there are 21,020 priests serving the 80,005 shrines. The priest's garb is modelled after the costume of court officials of the Heian period. It has no symbolic meaning and is not intended as a means of distinguishing the clergy from laymen. The simplest garb consists of a kimono, a formal divided skirt, a large-sleeved outer robe which hangs to the knees, a hat and shoes. The kimono is generally white, a colour that symbolises purity. The divided skirt may be in white or in colours which indicate the rank of the wearer and the formal outer robe likewise may be in white or colour. The formal robe is called in Japanese "kariginu", or "hunting garment", from the fact that the style originated as a hunting garment in the Heian period.

There are two types of headgear. The simpler form called "oboshi" is worn when a priest wears the low-ranked robe; the more elaborate called "kanmuri" is worn as full ceremonial dress or high-ranked robe within the shrine. The uniquely Japanese white socks "tabi" are worn on all ceremonial occasions. When a priest in ceremonial robes is outdoors, special black lacquered shoes made of a piece of hollowed paulonia wood called "asa-gutsu" are worn. The common sandals with white thongs are worn by the owner-class priests and by all priests as informal wear.

A Japanese friend of mine took me to a shrine in Tokyo. I had a glimpse of what he had to do as a worshipper. First, we had to take off our shoes, for Shintoism takes cleanliness seriously. Then, he had to purify his body and soul. He did it in the Seikan. (I have explained in the chapter on Xu Fu how Seikan came into being.) Then, he clapped his hands twice, calling the attention of the God and started to pray.

The offerings generally conform to very ancient tradition: the most simple ones are rice, salt, water and perhaps a sprig of "sakaki" (a type of tree branch). Offerings of cut flowers are also often seen. Four kinds of offerings were commonly presented: money, food and drinks and material and symbolic objects. Money gifts are made by tossing a coin into the offering box in front of the sanctuary, by presenting a small sum wrapped in formal paper as a gift for a special service, or by a donation in connection with receiving the shrine tablet, for the repair of shrine property or other special projects. Drinks offerings consist mainly of water or rice wine. Food offerings might be cooked or uncooked. Among food offerings are frequently rice, seaweed, vegetables, grains, fruits and cakes.

The ceremonial prayers that are recited at shrines by the priest are in classical Japanese, which was intelligible even when it was the prevailing language, but is not understood today by people unless they have made a special study of the subject. In ancient times, a great many historical and other important records were written in beautiful rhythmic poems in order to facilitate their transmission to posterity. Prayers were also composed in this style in order to convey the mystic feeling embodied in the manner of addressing the kami. Until the Meiji era, prayers were composed by the priests of each shrine in any manner deemed appropriate.

At the end of any Shinto ceremony, whether it be in a home or shrine, there is a sacred feast, called "naorai" which means "to eat together with the kami". In the case of worshippers, this consists of formally drinking a sip of rice wine served by a priest or one of the giri (protocol) attendants. In the case of shrine festival, the priests, prominent laymen and special guests gather together and partake solemnly of a few sips of rice wine, then enjoy a relaxing and even hilarious and entertaining meal at which much more wine is consumed.

At many of the larger shrines, especially during festival seasons, the sacred "kagura" dance is performed. The kagura dance is characteristically Japanese, emphasising posture and gestures rather than the motion of the feet. It was a dance to please the Sun Goddess when she was angry. The dance is always accompanied by Gagaku music, copied from music of the Tang dynasty.

The Shinto religion is very much associated with "mikoshi" or "jiaoche" (in Mandarin). Jiaoche originated from China. When I was young, I used to see "mikoshi" being carried by Chinese worshippers of little temples in Malaysia. During the birthday of the Monkey God, villagers used to carry the mikoshi of the Monkey God and went touring the village with drums and music. The carriers told me that the "mikoshi" was heavy because the Monkey God was inside it. It was difficult to handle the Monkey God "mikoshi" because the Monkey was restless.

It is difficult nowadays to see a "jiaoche" in China except perhaps at the museum. I saw one in Beijing's Forbidden City. But, the custom of parading the "mikoshi" has become very popular in Japan and has become part of an important event in Shinto festivals. Mikoshi serves as a rallying point for the Japanese to unite and have fun together. They are group conscious and also like fun. Any Chinese cultural activities the Japanese find useful, they preserve and blend them into their culture.

The average Japanese enjoys carrying the "mikoshi" of his shrine and parading the streets during a festival. I have watched numerous processions in most parts of Japan. This involves the transfer of the kami from the inner sanctuary to the mikoshi which becomes his abode temporarily. The sacred symbol of the kami is not removed. For the Japanese carriers, carrying the mikoshi is real fun. They put on colourful kimonos, wear fanciful hats and white pants. They sing songs accompanied by noisy drums and musical instruments.

The mikoshi is normally heavy and uncontrollable, for therein sits the soul of the kami who is easily excited by the crowd. The mikoshi therefore zigzags its way along the streets and the bearers sometimes find it difficult to control.

Shintoism has always been so intimately associated with the daily life of the people that the Japanese have found no necessity to formulate thought into any doctrinal system. The faith in kami and participation in its various rites and customs have become a matter of course among much of the Japanese community. In the transmission of Shinto from generation to generation, not much attention has been given to the philosophical or doctrinal expositions of the faith. Efforts have been made to preserve the record of shrine history and customs, but very little literature has been written to aid worshippers in understanding the nature of the enshrined kami and the meaning of shrine rites and practices. Generally speaking, Japanese are doers and are less inclined towards ideology and abstract thinking.

Shintoism emphasises sensory experience derived from mystic rites and natural phenomena rather than theological discourses. It is a way of life that is maintained through the observance of traditional ways rather than by overt propaganda.

There is excitement, a thrill of joy as one enters into a grove which surrounds a shrine, or stands within the view of a torii and sanctuary where a ritual is being performed.

Today, there are over 81,000 Shinto shrines in Japan and about 10,000,000 Shinto believers.

The Impact of Buddhism

According to one of Japan's earliest chronicles, the Nihon Shoki, Buddhism was introduced into Japan from Korea in AD 552 when the King of Paekche, one of the Three Kingdoms of Korea, sent a mission to the Emperor of Japan. He presented to the Emperor an image of Sakyamuni in gold and copper, several banners and umbrellas (both used in Buddhism rituals) and a number of sutras. The reactions of the Japanese were mixed. The Emperor was overjoyed and argued that Japan should follow the example of other more civilised countries like China. The Shinto supporters, however, were offended for they thought that their Shinto "Gods" would feel disrespected. Buddhism was accepted after the Emperor defeated those who were against him.

Buddhism became a state religion in the Nara period (AD 710–794). Official monasteries, "Kokubuni", were established in every province, and in every monastery an enormous Buddha "Daibutsu" (temple) was erected. During the Nara period, Buddhism reached its highest development. The early advocates of Buddhism employed Chinese architecture, costumes, rites and even conducted their services in the Chinese language. They made virtually no effort to adapt themselves to Japanese culture and the needs of the common people. For this reason they failed to exercise any influence outside the court circles. The whole Nara city was in fact modelled after Xian, the centre of Chinese Buddhism.

Under the favour and patronage of the court, the monasteries became wealthy and powerful in politics. Eventually, their priesthood became so corrupted by lavish living that they began to decline. There was then no proper Buddhist system of training, administration and rules. In order to streamline Buddhism, the Japanese Emperor decided to despatch envoys to China during the Tang dynasty, inviting knowledgeable Chinese monks to Japan to bring about Buddhist discipline. The Emperor wanted to establish the precepts necessary to regulate monastic life and establish in the capital an authentic ordination platform which the Buddhist clergy had lacked.

For ten years, several prominent monks were despatched to China to look for Chinese monks, without success. They had nearly given up the search for Chinese monks and were preparing to return home in 742 when they had an audience with Ganjin in Yangzhou. Already a widely known and highly venerated monk throughout China, Ganjin readily accepted their offer and sailed off to Japan. Between 743 to 748, he made five attempts to cross the China Sea to Japan but failed. These abortive attempts to reach Japan resulted in the death of a number of disciples and Ganjin himself was suffering from cataracts. In 752, the Japanese Government despatched another group of envoys to China to urge Ganjin to come to Japan. When he finally reached Japan, in 753, he had become totally blind. Three months later, in the spring of 754, he arrived at Nara and immediately established an ordination platform at Todaji. He was given the authority to ordain priests and to give instruction on Buddhist precepts. In 759, he established the Toshodaiji, where he resided and continued to instruct his students. Henceforth, Toshodaiji became the headquarters of the Ritse sect. Four years later Ganjin died, reportedly while in the meditation.

I visited Toshodaiji whenever I went to Nara. It is an impressive temple with cow horns on the four corners of roof-edges. The Chief Monk made special arrangements for me to have a clear glimpse of the image of the blind Ganjin in meditation which was hidden behind a panel of thick glass panel. The portrait was made of lacquer and painted in red. This portrait was taken by the Japanese from China during the Japanese Occupation. In 1987, on Ganjin's birthday, Japan made a benevolent gesture by taking Ganji's portrait to Yangzhou to enable Ganji to have a holiday in his hometown.

The lacquer portrait of Ganjin, founder of Toshodaiji.

The Toshodaiji in Nara.

The Japanese believe in the existence of the soul and they were trying to pacify the soul of Ganjin by this gesture. A replica of the portrait was also produced and presented to the Yangzhou Buddhist Association as a token of their appreciation for Ganjin's efforts.

I was also allowed to view the panels of precious paintings of Huangsan painted by Japan's most famous painter, Higashiyama, who took 15 years to complete the work. It was Higashiyama's masterpiece. They were really magnificent. Only VIPs and close associates of the temple were shown the wall paintings. It was painted to commemorate the arrival of Ganjin to Japan, for he liked Huangsan very much.

After Ganjin's demise, the Nara sect of Buddhism declined and was taken over by the more Japanised Buddhist sects known as Tendai Buddhism, the brainchild of Saicho (767–822), posthumously known as Dengyo Daishi, and the Shingon Buddhism founded by Kukai (774–835), posthumously known as Kobo Daishi. These two famous Buddhist leaders recognised the need for religious reformation and freedom from the orthodoxy of Nara. Tendai Buddhism reached the zenith of its influence in the ninth and tenth centuries. It materially aided the popularisation of Buddhism through attempts to identify Shinto deities with those of Buddhism pantheon, and it played an important role in educational and cultural developments.

Tendai's doctrine was based on the principle that every human being was entitled to become a Buddha. Tendai is still a rich field for philosophical research but, numerically speaking, it is one of the smallest branches of present-day Buddhism, its adherents numbering only slightly over one million.

Kukai's Shingon Buddhism

The case of Shingon Buddhism, founded by Kukai, is quite different. Kukai, who is regarded as "the greatest figure in the history of Japanese religion", is the country's well-known calligrapher, artist, educator and social worker, and other among other things a first-rate civil engineer.

Kukai's greatest innovation was his unification of Buddhism and Shintoism, which proved to be the most important factor in the popularisation of Buddhism. He made an attempt to identify the native gods with Buddhist dieties in the Nara period. The incarnation of Shintoism and Buddhism was his idea. Kukai even invented the name "Ryobu Shinto" and he is generally regarded as the founder of these two different faces of Shintoism.

A sketch of Kukai, the founder of Shingon Buddhism.

Kukai got the income for his Shingon temples by charging for funerals, memorial services and incantations of magic formulae for the acquisition of wealth, health and prosperity. Shingon is the Japanese counterpart of Lamaism in Tibet and Mongolia and is thus the best example of Tantric Buddhism and Hindu esotericism in Japan. Shingon has been one of the most alert branches of Buddhism in finding its place in Japan, and it can still claim approximately nine million adherents.

In the faith of Shingon, there are the well-known "pilgrims of Kukai" which are most popular in Shikoku, fourth largest of the Japanese islands. It is commonly said that Shikoku produces political leaders partly because in olden times it was a place of exile for troublemakers who were sent away from the centre of power and influence. The pilgrimage is almost a thousand miles, and for centuries there was no way to go but to walk, taking about two months. The ambition of Kukai's followers is to visit the 88 Shingon temples built by Kukai on foot because by doing so, they reserve their places in "heaven".

Whenever I visited Shikoku, I could not miss the crowd of Kukai devotes, wearing Vietnamese-like white caps, white clothing with long sleeves and carrying walking sticks. When they reached a temple, they would make sure that the registrar put the chop of the temple on a book which is called "nokyocho" which they carry along to prove that they have visited the temples. The temple official would write on one page "presentation" the name of the principle deity of that particular temple and the name of the temples. The record is completed by having the seal of the temple stamped on the page in red ink.

I visited one of these 88 temples, the most historical one called Zentsuji Temple, which has long been a centre of culture and recreation. It was surrounded by ancient camphor trees, bound with sacred robes. These trees have watched for two hundreds years as visitors came and went. Behind the temple rose five mountain peaks, presenting the appearance of a folding screen. In front of the Founder's Hall, there was a pond where, at the age of 31, Kukai looked at his own reflection in order to draw a self-portrait, a gift for his grieving mother on his departure for studies in China. It was on his return two years later that he began the construction of the Zentsuji Temple, modelled on the Ching Lung (blue dragon) Temple at Ch'ang-an or the present Xian, where his master Hui Kuo lived. As a memorial to Kukai's study in Xian, the people of Shikoku raised funds for the construction of a monument and information centre there. Nearby was an arched stone bridge, easily the oldest stone bridge in the world, from whence Kukai crossed over on his journey to China.

Under the Founder's Hall is the daidan meguri, an underground passage ninety to one hundred metres long. Midway through the passage was a chapel said to be located directly beneath the former site of Lady Tamayori's inner chamber. Except for the muted light of this one small room, the winding way was completely dark. I went safely through by holding my left hand against the wall as I followed the chanting priest. Although I could not see them, my hands passed over 88 representations of the Buddha, which symbolised guidance through the long dark passage of this life. The priest kept reminding me, "Please be mindful that a person guilty of wrong-doing will not be able to return from under the ground."

Kukai was credited with having devised a Kana syllable. He spent two years in Xian and within that short period of time, mastered esoteric Buddhism and brought back to Japan a wealth of written materials, art works and tirual implements. At the age of 43, he was granted permission to build a monastery for Shingon teachings on Mt. Koya, in present Wakayama Prefecture.

I visited the grave of Kukai at Koyasan, a site where most past Emperors were buried. It is a forest of tall and gigantic cedar trees. I saw many tombstones of past Emperors, every tombstone having a face, belly and feet. Kukai believed that tombstones must resemble human beings. Koyasan is the Mecca for all Buddhists. Different companies have reserved burial sites for their directors and important employees. Inside the main buildings hang thousands of stone lanterns contributed by devotees. It is a quiet and peaceful place, an ideal place of final rest for prominent Buddhists.

When Kukai reached the age of 62, it was believed that he told his disciples that he was going to Nirvana. He walked into another building which he had prepared, sat there crossed legged and spiritually disappeared from this earth. Most Japanese Buddhists believe that Kukai is still alive. Everyday, they prepare food for him and leave it on the doorsteps from where he entered Nirvana. Every year, on 21 March, his disciples donate clothing and leave it on the doorsteps for they believe that he is still alive.

The Japanese tend to worship human beings rather than an ideology or religious gospel. In China, the Chinese spend a great deal of their time and energy arguing on principles of ideology, and the rights and wrongs of religious dogmas. When the Buddhists came to Japan, the founders or leaders of Buddhism became the targets of their worship.

The Japanese tend to believe in persons more than scriptures and theories or teachings. They believe in Kukai more than Shingon Buddhism and its theories and teachings.

Zen Buddhism

The Japanese are practical and, apart from its esoteric aspects, see in Buddhism the utilitarian value of helping one to strengthen self-discipline and powers of concentration. Japanese companies and multi-national corporations, in order to increase production, have organised training programmes for new employees to undergo strict regimes of Zen meditation and lectures on self-development. The various forms of meditation are all aimed at enhancing the powers of concentration and awareness of the self's connection with the environment. Aside from the ultimate spiritual meaning of this process, many companies find that it is a valuable tool for training individuals to respond effectively in an environment that demands cooperation and adaptability.

The introduction of Zen into Japan is one of the most important events in Japanese religious history. Zen came from the Chan School in China and is perhaps defined as the meditation school of East Asian Buddhism. It did not develop into a major branch of Japanese meditation until the time of Eisai (1141–1215) and Dogen who took advantage of the increasing exchange between Chinese and Japanese Buddhism. Many Japanese Buddhist monks journeyed to China with the express intention of studying Zen there. Zen became established in Japan only by resisting attack from the powerful Tendai and Shingon sects.

Zen practice consists of mediation in the lotus position (zazen) and a study of koans, satori and poems. Meditation in the lotus position should be viewed first of all as a concentration exercise, calming body and mind. The master of zen coins a koan to ignite a spark in their disciples by an exchange of words. The significance of the koan, or stories, is a method to lead one to awakening.

A koan cannot be solved rationally. The practitioner is obliged to "hold" the koan constantly in mind, day and night. Concentration increases until the tension causes rational thinking to give way under the pressure and a breakthrough occurs. This is the "turn back to the roots of consciousness" that opens the mind to a new way of seeing.

The koans are intricately ordered according to circumstances. It was the Japanese master Hakuin who perfected the koan system. He added to approximately 1,700 koans the famous "sound of one hand clapping" which uniquely displays the paradoxical character of the enlightenment experience.

A koan such as "When you clap your hands together a sound arises. Listen to the sound of one hand" is paradoxical. The famous Chinese Zen master also has a well-known koan: "When the carts stops, do you whip the cart or whip the ox?"

There are also many Zen poems to make the disciple think. One famous poem by Basho reads: "An old pond. A frog jumps in — plop." The old pond corresponds to an eternity of endless space, while the frog jumping in causes the water to create a sound, breaking for the first time into a tune.

It is by bringing the mind to bear on the koan, poem or puzzle that the disciple's power of concentration is strengthened and thus it helps meditation. Some other streams of Buddhism stress on mumbling mantras (the sacred words of God) to help meditation.

All the different denominations of Buddhism in Japan have monks. They wear Buddhist religious robes and there is little difference in their attire from that of the Chinese monks. The only difference is that in China monks are prohibited from marrying, whereas the Japanese monks are allowed to marry. The monks and their wives live in temples. When Buddhism crossed the China sea and entered the land of pragmatism, all that was irrelevant and impractical was left out. The Japanese are practical and realistic people. They were able to distinguish between religion and sex. Man cannot do without sex. Why force the monks to give up sex? In the early period of Buddhism, monks were probihited from marrying but as time passed by, the Japanese have done away with such unnecessary restrictions.

Similarly, the Japanese were very much influenced by Confucianism. In China and in many other countries, the Emperors and the royal household used enunchs to help them administer. In Japanese history, enuchs never existed. This is another example of Japanese pragmatism and wisdom.

Nichiren Shoshu Buddhism

Of all Japan's so-called new religions, the Soka Gakkai (Value Creating Society) is the most popular and powerful. With 17 million registered followers and vast riches resting in banks throughout the nation, Soka Gakkai perhaps commands more economic, political and social influence than any religious organisation in Japan. The Executive Director of the organisation's international wing, Soka Gakkai International (SGI), is Daisaku Ikeda. His followers, to be found around the world, call him "master" and some members even assert that Ikeda is "divine".

In recent years, the SGI director has increasingly involved himself in international activities, holding meetings with leaders of the world and often travelling around the world. Ikeda's departure is always a momentous occasion at Narita airport. The VIP lounge is specially prepared for him, and hours beforehand senior executives of municipal banks come to the lounge en masse to see him off. If a bank president does not show up in person, a department chief is sure to apologise to Ikeda for his boss's absence. The assembled company bid Ikeda bon voyage, bowing deeply and imploring him to take good care of himself during his journey.

Something more than religious zeal draws these executives sixty kilometres from their Tokyo offices to see Ikeda off. Soka Gakkai has an enormous sum of funds distributed among different banks. Should any one give cause

Daisaku Ikeda, Executive Director of Soka Gakkai International, who is the leader of Nichiren Buddhism.

for offence, then Soka Gakkai might remove the sums entrusted to the banks' safe-keeping elsewhere, a nightmare for the officials.

Soka Gakkai's nature of activities include discussion groups, regional conferences, prefectural meetings, and even cultural festivals attended by tens of thousands of members. This large membership ensures that buses, railways and even airplanes are frequently chartered, making Soka Gakkai an eminently attractive target for travel companies.

The Soka Gakkai even has a media connection. Its newspaper, the Seikyo Shimbun, boasts of a 4.7 million circulation, a figure exceeding that of any US newspaper. In Japan, its circulation ranks fourth among the major dailies. Seikyo Shimbun is printed by a firm with very close financial ties to a major newspaper. It is an open secret that editorials on this paper are usually slanted in favour of Soka Gakkai.

Soka Gakkai is the epitome of a well-established relationship between religious organisations and politics. Japan's third ranking political party, the Komeito (Clean Government Party), grew out of Soka Gakkai. Komeito currently holds fifty-nine seats in the Lower House and twenty seven seats in the Upper Hose of the Diet. Although it is an opposition party in the central government, Komeito wields considerable strength.

What makes Soka Gakkai so popular is the simple way of reaching "God through Nichiren Shoshu Buddhism". The basic practice of Nichiren consists of chanting the phrase "Nam-Myhoho-Renge-Kyo" to the Gohonzen, a scroll inscribed with many Chinese and two Sanskrit characters. Myhoho-Renge-Kyo is the title of Lotus Sutra which literally means "Mystic Law of the Lotus Sutra". The word Nam is a verbal contraction of the written Sadharmmapundarikasutra and literally means "devotion". Thus, Nam-Myhoho-Renge-Kyo could be said to mean literally: "I devote my life to the Mystic Law of the Lotus Sutra." Nichiren Buddhism explains how chanting this phrase many times can both energise and harmonise the physical and spiritual aspects of life so that, for example, through chanting, one can cure oneself of sickness, uncontrolable anger or temper. The "God" of Nichiren is the Goddess of Mercy (Kuan Yin in Chinese and Kannon in Japanese). Whenever a believer is in danger, just chant the phrase and the Goddess of Mercy will be present and come to answer his or her call.

It is this simple all-cure method of Nichiren that attracts so many Japanese devotees. As I have explained, the Japanese are doers and are less interested in difficult theories and ideologies. Any religion that offers an easier way to reach "God" gets a wider following.

Nichiren was one of the Buddhist sects of the Kamakura period (1185–1333), founded in 1253 by the Tendai monk Nichiren. He managed to transform profound theory into practical action by discovering the phrase "Nam-Myhoho-Renge-Kyo", thereby enabling ordinary people within their own lifetime to reveal their highest state of life in the midst of day-to-day reality.

To become a member of Nichiren Shoshu, it is necessary to go to Nichiren's headquarters at the foot of Mt. Fuji and pray to the Gohonzon, which is placed inside the inner chamber of the building. I went to Nichiren's headquarters one Sunday morning in 1985 and special arrangements were made to take me into the inner chamber to view the Dai Gohonzon (the mother Gohonzon) which was enshrined in a place called Sho-Hondo. The word "honzon" literally means "object of fundamental respect" and "Go" means worthy of honour. Together they signify that the Gohonzon is the true "object of worship". When an aspiring member has prayed to the

Dai Gohonzon, he becomes a full member and is given a copy of the Gohonzon in the form of a scroll of rice paper which is inscribed by the high priest. This piece of sacred paper is printed under the supervision of the Nichiren Shoshu priest by means of a woodblock process. The Gohonzon is then brought back to the member's home and enshrined in a special cabinet called a butsudan (literally a place of the Buddha). Thus, the member can communicate with his God from the home.

I have met many Singaporeans who have become members of the Nichiren Shoshu and they all have visited the Taiseki-ji headquarters of Nichiren and brought home the Gohonzon. Whenever they need the Goddess of Mercy, they chant "Nam-Myhoho-Renge-Kyo", some as many as a thousand times. Most of them claim that they received miraculous results.

Taiseki-ji has a remarkable architectural style, resembling two wings of a crane. When I visited Taiseki-ji, cherry blossoms bloomed all around us. With a fine breeze blowing, visitors feel they are in heaven. There is a huge main hall and many quarters to accommodate visiting members.

The Taiseki-ji, the headquarters of Nichiren Buddhism near Fuji mountain — it looks like two wings of a crane.

The Soka Gakkai claims 20 million members in more than 115 countries throughout the world. Once year, there is a great festival rotating in different countries of the world. I was invited to attend a memorable one in Nishimiy City in Hyogo Prefecture, September 1984, held in a stadium near Kobe. It was packed with 56,000 spectators including 44,000 Japanese youths who demonstrated a magnificent show of harmony, skill and strength with their gymnastic acts.

At the beginning of the show, two helicopters flew into the field carrying banners and at the end of the show there was a big display of fireworks. Participants from 55 foreign countries brought with them various international dances performed by 3,200 representatives and the theme was "Silk Road of Peace towards the 21st century". All the foreign performers were members of the Soka Gakkai. The countries that participated included the United States, Canada, England, France, Federal Republic of Germany, India, Australia, New Zealand, Asean countries, Hong Kong and Latin American countries such as Argentina, Brazil, Mexico and Peru. It was one of the grandest shows I have ever seen. Only a tightly-knit organisation could have put on such a good show.

Its international leader, Ikeda Daisaku, arrived at the stadium with the high priest and his supporters loudly cheered them. Ikeda waved his hands and smiled to the crowd, walking straight to his seat. He behaved like a "God". Ikeda had a broad, smiling face, and was a little bald, short and stout. He is regarded as "God" by millions of members.

About six months before he visited Singapore, he invited my wife and I to the Soka Gakkai headquarters for a special dinner. Before the dinner began, I presented him with a painting of Taiseki-ji which I had painted during my last visit there. He sprang a surprise at me when he conferred on me a special award granted by the Japan Institute of Oriental Studies for my contribution to furthering the studies of oriental culture. I felt a little embarrassed for I did not expect such an honour nor did I think it was deserved.

After that dinner, whenever I mentioned that I had dinner with Ikeda, supporters of Soka Gakkai would give me special respect because I had dinner with their "God".

The Fate of the Christians

Japan is usually not considered to be a Christian country. This is apparent when one looks at statistics. Christianity probably reached its high points in the early 17th century when two or at most three percent of the population embraced the religion. Not long afterwards, even these small numbers were stamped out almost completely, and for two centuries Christianity was banned from Japan with thorough and ruthless ferocity. After it was tolerated once again not much more than a century ago, it did not regain proportionately the strength it had once possessed, remaining always less than one percent of the population.

Japan's first direct contact with Christianity was in 1549, when Francis Xavier accompanied by two other Spanish Jesuits arrived in Kogoshima, the southernmost prefecture of Kyushu. The foreigners brought with them not only religion, but traders with exotic commodities. Numerous local lords encouraged the propagation of Christianity in their fiefs and ordered their people to treat missionaries with respect and in extreme cases, embrace Christianity en masse. Sometimes, however, when no ships or traders came, these lords ordered their fiefs to revert to their former faith.

Christianity was making headway even with Nobunaga, who met with a sudden death. His successor, Hideyoshi, suddenly issued a decree in July 1587 expelling all missionaries from Japan. Then began a ruthless persecution of Christians, culminating in the execution in Nagasaki of six Spanish Franciscans, three Jesuits and 17 Japanese converts. I visited the museum to commemorate the Christian victims in Nagasaki. I also went to the boiling hell of Unzen where Christians were tortured. My guide, who was a Christian, told me that those arrested had their fingers and noses chopped off as a first step to induce them to admit that they were Christians. When they refused, they were taken to the Unzen and dipped into boiling mud water. The Christians sang hymns while waiting to be dipped into the Unzen. They were hung upside down before they were soaked into the boiling mud.

In Unzen, there is an Unzen Catholic Church, built to commemorate the souls of thirty Christians who were persecuted in Unzen Jigoku (hell). This church was at Fudanohara, located where the persecution took place. In the Shimabara Nanko Hotel where I stayed, I was allowed into a storeroom to see a painting of the Shimabara revolt which was quite impressive.

By 1587 there were already about 300,000 Christians in Japan including various daimyos and influential courtiers, soldiers and officials. When the Tokugawa Government took over, it proscribed Christianity in 1614 and ordered missionaries to leave the country. It was estimated that about 3,000 believers were put to death for their religious beliefs.

The persecution of Christians coincided with the Bakufu (the Black curtain, a term to describe the ruling authority) heavy taxes on the farmers in

Shimabara. The farmers, who were mainly Christians, revolted against the Bakufu, led by a young "messiah" Amakusa. This was the well-known Shimabara revolt, which was social rather than religious. The Shimabara uprising of 1637–38 could be described as a Christian revolution in Japanese history. The revolt was put down only with unexpected difficulty and the insurgents and their families, numbering about 40,000, were massacred. To have a clearer understanding of this revolt, I visited Shimabara and saw the place where Amakusa was slained. There was a stature of Amakusa in the garden I visited.

After the Christian revolt, Japan closed its doors to the outside world and severed its contact with the West. Only the small man-made islet of Dejima in Nagasaki harbour was open to merchants of the Dutch East India Company. No information was available about subsequent Christian activities until the final years of the Tokugawa regime. Signboards offering rewards for information about hidden missionaries continued to be displayed and Dutch ships entering Nagasaki were rigorously searched for disguised missionaries trying to slip into the country.

With the arrival of Commodore Perry in 1853 Japan's period of isolation came to an end and Westerners were again allowed to enter the country. The Treaty of Amity and Commerce of 1858 permitted American residents in Japan free access to their religion and similar agreements were also signed with other Western powers. From 1865 onwards, Japanese carried out their Christian activities in disguise. These Christians were called "Kakure Kiristan" or "hidden Christians" and they became active again in Nagasaki. These hidden Christians had preserved their religion in secret for more than two centuries. The Kakure Kiristan biblical account, called Tenchi Hajimari no Koto, is a remarkable document incorporating both Shinto and Buddhist elements. They also used the image of kannon (or Kuan Yin) to personify the "Virgin Mary" in the Bible. It was difficult for me to distinguish between the Goddess of Mercy and Mother Mary when I visited Kakure Kiristan churches in Shimabara.

It was not until 1873, largely as a result of the intercession of foreign diplomats and popular indignation abroad, that the Meiji regime withdrew religious sanctions and allowed Christians to practise their religion freely. After the defeat of Japan in World War II, there was a marked revival of Christian activity and this resurgence had the clear support of General MacArthur and the Occupation forces. The social upheaval and disillusionment caused by the nation's exhaustion from war and military defeat prompted many Japanese to turn to Christianity in search of meaning in their lives. However, the situation lasted for only about five years. There are various problems Christianity has to resolve before the religion regarded as a "foreign creed", preaching admirable ideals but still not suitable for ordinary Japanese people, is accepted. Christianity has yet to establish itself within the cultural setting of Japan and the Christian movement remains on the periphery of Japanese society. Apart from the Nagasaki region, it has yet to make any appreciable impact on rural communities and draws it strength from the urban, professional class. Christian monotheism versus traditional polytheism, the concept of a transcendent God versus the imminent deities of Japan, and absolute values versus a more flexible situation are issues which Christianity has to contend with.

There are many obstacles to the spread of Christianity in Japan. First of all, the Japanese find it difficult to understand the religious spirit embodied in the commandment "You shall have no other gods before me". There is no philosophical basis in the Japanese system of thought for the idea of the transcendence of God. The Christian God, an uncreated God who stands above and beyond human activity, differs from the Japanese "maki" who are various, immanent and human.

Secondly, the Japanese have a profound distrust of organised religion, particularly when it is Western-oriented. They almost fear that the West would use Christianity to subvert the country. For 300 years, Buddhist priests functioned, in effect, as part of a network of government control. Shinto, too, was made a state religion in the Meiji period and was used to foster militaristic ideology. Christianity, which is both alien and organised, is distrusted.

Thirdly, Christian churches in Japan are often more concerned with orthodoxy than with the relevance of Christianity to society. Japanese Christian thinkers have made few serious attempts to concern themselves with the role Christianity can or must play in Japanese society.

Buddhism, which is also an imported religion, has adapted its teachings over the centuries to be more in accord with the traditional Japanese outlook and temperament, and has in fact merged with Shintoism and Confucianism. It has succeeded in integrating itself into Japanese society. It is doubtful whether Christianity can achieve the same integration.

According to the latest statistics, Christians number about one million or about 1 percent of the total Japanese population. Some prominent political leaders have embraced Christianity. The notable one was Prime Minister Ohira Masayoshi. Ohira was a "no church" Christian, a movement initiated by Uchimura Kanzo, in which Christianity was passed on by university and high school teachers to their disciples without the intervention of any formal church organisation. Many of Japan's intelletual leaders have stemmed from this very Japanese branch of Christianity, including Ohira.

The fact that a Christian could become a prime minister shows that Japan has become a very tolerant society. Could it be that Japan was tolerant towards the "no church" movement because the belief was not visible?

New Religions

With the open door policy of Japan towards religions, many new religions sprang up like mushrooms. Many Japanese were fed up with traditional religions and began to look for religious outlets. There are about 29 different recognised religions. Among them, one of the largest ones was Tenrikyo or Religion of Heavenly Truth. Its founder was Nakayama Miki (1798–1887), who reportedly had a revelatory experience and began to communicate it to others. The main worship centre of Tenrikyo is built around the jiba and the sacred pillar (Kanrodai) erected on it. Tenrikyo believes that this is at once the spiritual centre of the universe and man's spiritual home.

Then there is the Mahikari, believing in One God. Its headquarters are situated in the Takayama city of Gifu. Mahikari is the Japanese word for Divine True Light, a spiritual or cosmic energy of purification. Mahikari no Waza is the method of radiating Divine True Light from the hands of its founder Kotama Okada, whom believers believe has supernatural powers to transmit light and had an important revelation from God.

The founders of Mahikari Okada claim that after his revelation he was the absolute centre of the universe. In Shintoism he is "Amaterasu-Omikami", in Buddhism "Sei Kannon Goddess of Mercy", in Christianity "yah Jehovah" and in Islam "Mohammed" and "Allah". He is, therefore, the grand original Divinity. The religion is all religions fused together. I was once invited to attend a three-day Kenshuj (gathering) when I was Ambassador in Japan but I could not find the time to attend.

The religion has branches throughout Japan and also in France, Belgium, Italy, Switzerland, The United States and Brazil.

There are other new religions such as the Seicho no Ie (The Growing Home), the Sekai Kyueikyo (the World Salvation), P. L. Kyodan (Perfect Liberty organisation) and numerous other religions.

The new religion of Michi-no-Tomoor "Friends of Truth Church" shocked Japan when, in November 1986, seven followers committed mass suicide in an apparent reaction to the death of their leader. It took place a day after their leader and founder of the religion, Kiyoharu Miyamoto, 61, died of illness. The seven women between 20 to 30 years of age doused themselves with kerosene and set themselves on fire. Their bodies were found by a resident who happened to stroll along the beach near Miyamoto's house. One of the notes left behind read, "We are only trying to keep our promise. This is not forced upon us." The seven referred to themselves as "brides of God" and had been taking care of Miyamoto during his illness. Police said that Miyamoto founded the group in 1950, based on the belief that Jehovah was to be worshipped as God. Followers were to seek ways to attain salvation in heaven. The group has 120 members and most of them were residents of Wakayama.

The Wakayama mass suicide brings to mind the 1978 mass suicide in Gyuana of more than 900 members of the "People's Temple", who apparently took poison on the orders of their leader.

Aum Shinrikyo

The tragic nerve gas terror that killed more than 10 Japanese passengers and injured 5,000 others travelling in the Tokyo subway at the end of March, 1995 drew the attention of the authorities to the existence of Japan's latest religion, the Aum Shinrikyo, led by a 40-year-old guru Shoko Asahara. The Government is convinced that Aum Shinrikyo was responsbile for the Tokyo subway incident and has taken drastic action to raid the sect's headquarters and various branches throughout Japan. Asahara, who was in hiding, announced through recorded tapes that his religion had nothing to do with the subway incident. The police raid on Shinrikyo's Osaka headquarters and its Mount Fuji branch found huge chemical stores which could be used to produce sarin, a dangerous chemical for nerve poisoning. Asahara once said that sarin would be a primary weapon in the "final world war".

Japanese newspapers have estimated that Aum's chemical stockpile could create enough nerve gas to kill 4.2–10 million people. There is no evidence that this was Asahara's intention. But, by some estimates he could have created 50 tonnes of the nerve gas sarin from his chemical stockpile and then achieved the kind of urban Armageddon that he has been predicting.

Sarin was discovered in the 1930s by German chemists seeking better insecticides, tested by Nazis in death camps and also used by Saddam Hussein to annihilate Kurdish villages.

The Aum Shinrikyo rose in the late 1980s when new religious sects and cults were cropping up throughout Japan. Young people turned off by Japan's materialism and searching for something to believe in found a home in the Shinrikyo. This is particularly so with young Japanese whose fathers were never home when they were growing up. Their first real father is found within the Shinrikyo group.

Shinrikyo's leader Shoko Asahara was born Chiuo Matsumoto, the fourth son in a poor family (his father made tatami mats for a living). Asahara had bad eyesight from birth and entered a school for the blind at the age of 6, although one eye has at least partial vision. In his early 20s, after an education in acupuncture and herbal healing, he joined a Buddhist splinter sect and opened a Chinese medicine shop. He sold a mixture of carrots, snakeskins and other ingredients that he claimed could cure neuralgia and rheumaticism; Japanese health authorities disagreed and fined him 200,000 yen for violating pharmaceutical laws. He and his wife subsequently opened a new business, "Aum", offering yoga classes and selling health drinks. In 1985, he suddenly announced that he could levitate and told an interviewer that he would be flying freely with a year.

An expert in marketing, he travelled to India and Nepal to study Buddhism and Hinduism and returned with photos of himself with senior Tibetan Lamas including the Dalai Lama. He used these photos to portray himself as an internationally respected religious authority, and his yoga school became extremely successful. He began to call his sect Aum Shinrikyo and appealed to Japan's prosperous but alienated young people to find meaning in life through his teaching. About 10,000 disciples have answered his call in Japan and he has opened up offices in New York, Bonn, Sri Lanka and Moscow, the spiritually troubled former capital of Soviet Union. Aum Shinrikyo claims to have attracted 30,000 new members in the past three years. Like other Japanese sects, Shinrikyo claims healing powers. But while others promised earthly happiness, wealth and other temporal benefits, Aum Shinrikyo offered a spiritual release from the secular world.

The strange feature of Aum Shinrikyo is that it is able to attract people with higher education. Doctors, lawyers, engineers and chemists have become faithful disciples. The group runs restaurants, a publishing company, computer-sales shops and a hospital. Asahara promised his disciples that he would lead them toward enlightment and the supernatural powers of levitation, healing vision and prophecy.

Asahara also promised survival. According to his teachings, disciples who successfully pass through four stages of consciousness to enlightment will not only develop superpowers but will number among the quarter of the world's population who will survive Armageddon — the end of the world. A political commentator Takashi Tachbaba, an expert on the movement, said that Asahara seemed to believe that he was the one who would trigger Armageddon.

Shoko Asahara has a fascination with other worlds. He claims to have reigned during past lives as king of the "heaven" where unidentified flying objects come from. He has announced plans to establish an "astral hospital" using "astral medicine from the astral world". The other world that seems to obsess Asahara most is the one after doomsday. In his speeches, he warns followers of his sect that he will act as their defence lawyer on Judgement Day — and that only if they redouble their devotion to their teachings can he save them from the apocalypse.

There have been persistent reports of Aum using drugs, probably primarily hallucinogens to evoke the supernatural. The sect demanded that followers live in communes and cut off relations with their families. This led to clashes and law suits with family members. There have been repeated cases in which Aum has been accused of harassing, attacking, kidnapping or even killing its opponents. Earlier this year, according to Japanese newspaper reports, a woman trying to drop out of Aum was told she would be allowed to do so only if she signed her property to the sect. She agreed, but her brother opposed the idea strongly. On February 28 1995, the deadline that Aum had set for the property transfer, he was kidnapped.

Aum Shinrikyo, like the Nichiren, is also politically ambitious. In 1990, Asahara and many of his aides ran for Parliament, but all of them failed.

Recently, a rumour spread that Asahara's health is failing. He is said to have a liver ailment, perhaps cancer, but it is not possible to confirm. In a recent broadcast, Asahara announced in a videotape that his body is considerably damaged. Some people suggest that Asahara's own illness and his confrontation with his mortality have encouraged him to move towards a more apocalyptaic vision of the future, and perhaps even towards technologies of extermination such as nerve gas.

Many of his teachings are drawn from Buddhism and the occult, but he also emphasises a Hindu god, Lord Shiva, whose role in Hinduism may bear an eerie connection to Aum's present interest in poison gases.

Shiva is a god of destruction and creation, and his job is to destroy so that life can be renewed.

It may be that the interest in the occult and supernatural phenomena which is growing among young people and children is evidence of the anxiety that they feel about the real world in which they live. The appearance of new religious sects may be a response to the demands of the times. It is said that the structure of some of the established religions and large religious organisations have become "bureaucratic". Young people seek the help of the new religions in the belief that they will be able to help them cope with their worries and distress. These religious organisations are bound by a strong communal feeling with the leader, who is regarded as their spiritual pillar. When such a religious leader is lost, there is utter spiritual collapse among the followers.

But, new religions have yet to test the passage of time. The survival of what in some sense is a minor local cult against the overwhelming pressures of great religions like Buddhism, Christianity, Shintoism or Islam is historically a very rare phenomenon.When I visited Rome and Athens, I witnessed the splendid relics of religions that had suffered extinction. The powerful and huge Roman Empire was struck down by a religious front put forward by Christianity. From a Japanese perspective, it is almost impossible to imagine that the local cults and religious associations that had kept the Empire vital had, by the arrival of Christianity, been allowed to fall into so brittle and vulnerable a condition.

Today, Shintoism still stays in the hearts of the Japanese people. With its surprising power of continuity and self-renewal, Shintoism remains one of history's rare miracles. How many Japanese are aware of Shinto's amazing achievements? Shintoism is an ancient local religion. It lacks a systematic theology. It has no tiresome strictures and continues to flourish. Perhaps the secret of Shinto's persistence lies in the unbroken round of seasonal festivals which inspire such loyalty in the communities where they take place. Shintoism links generations with its belief in ancestor worship.

It is vital to understand that it was precisely this easy adaptability and willing syncreticism that allowed Shinto to develop links with modern Japanese nationalism, and to meet the needs of the Japanese people.

The pragmatic and practical Japanese and their utilitarian approach to religion has helped Shintoism to survive. I do not think any foreign religion can ever take its place.

CHAPTER 6

Rich Country, Poor People — Japanese Characteristics and Lifestyles

Through the stamina and efforts of the Japanese people for more than 40 years, Japan has become the world's richest nation. Japanese banks and corporations dominate the lists of the world's top companies, and the strong yen has given its citizens the world's highest average income, US$28,642 in 1986 when I was still Ambassador to Japan. The per capita gross national product, a key measure of national wealth, overtook that of the United States in 1990 by about US$3,000 — Japan's GNP per capita income being US$23,472 and that of United States US$20,907. In 1990, Japan produced 9,948,000 passenger cars, the largest number of cars produced in the world. America produced only 6,069,000 cars, Germany 4,661,000, France 3,295,000 and Italy only 695,000. In the same year, Japan produced 274,000 robots compared to 41,304 produced by USA and 28,240 by Germany.

Japan's direct overseas investment was only just US$6.4 billion in 1985, the year after I arrived in Tokyo. By 1987, it had jumped to nearly US$20 billion, of which more than half was in the United States. And by 1990, Japanese investment in the United States alone was US$27 billion. In Japan today, there are 40 million credit card holders, one for every three Japanese. By 1987, it increased to 110 million, nearly one each for Japan's population, well below "buy-now-pay" later America and Britain, but roughly in line with Germany. Wealth began to ooze out of every Japanese, as Japan's companies and individuals began to buy up the world.

There have already been strong protests by Hawaii and Australia against Japanese purchases of their land and properties, and there are calls for legal or constitutional restrictions. There are even comments in America that Japan, having failed to beat America by bombing Pearl Harbour, has now decided to buy it: first the harbour then the whole of America.

Although Japan has become rich — Japanese companies making money and conquering markets — the Japanese are missing out on one important element which wealth should bring: the quality of life. Most Japanese still live in "rabbit hutches" and travel long distances in crammed shinkansen or trains to work. After their long hours of work in the office they enjoy very few public amenities such as parks, community centres and other places of recreation. Japan is rich, but the ordinary Japanese are not that well-off in terms of housing, recreational facilities and general quality of life. It is almost as if there were a scission between the country and the people — a rich nation and a poor people. Japan's wealth is a myth and the poverty of the people, a reality.

On the problem of housing, Japan is far behind the Western countries in terms of comfort. In Japan, 2.8 percent of its houses consist of less than two rooms, with more than two members living in a single room. Japanese houses are normally small, often oldish and dilapidated buildings or new but hardly modern apartment buildings. In both cases, the rooms are small, the ceilings low and the walls thin so that privacy becomes a luxury. There is little plumbing, central heating, air conditioning or other amentities. With 17 water supply units per 100 households, Japan lags behind Latin America. The diffusion rate of sewerage in Japan's cities today averages 26 percent, while the rate in other advanced nations ranges from 60–100 percent. In terms of parking area per city resident, Japan's living space was shockingly low. New York, London and Berlin had 20–25 square metres per person; Moscow, Amsterdam and Vienna 10–15 square metres; while Japan's leading cities of Tokyo, Yokohama, Osaka and Nagoya only 1.2–12.9, with the national average a meagre 2.7 square metres per person.

The Japanese are paying an exorbitant amount for their primary necessity of food. The cost of rice is five times that of American rice and seven times more than Thai rice. This is so because the government is paying high, guaranteed prices to farmers to ensure their continued votes. While I was living in Japan, I got my rice supply from Thailand, partly it because was cheaper and partly because I was not accustomed to Japanese rice. Japan believes in the policy of self-sufficiency in rice supply and the Government puts high tariffs on imported rice. Whenever the LDP Government talked about lifting the tariff and of allowing foreign rice imports, there would be strong protest and street demonstrations from the farmers association stationed in Tokyo. In the course of my duties, whenever I visited the Foreign Affairs Department, I often saw crowds protesting against the government for allowing foreign rice to compete with Japanese rice.

Locally produced wheat as well as bread is obviously even more expensive than that imported. Fruits and vegatables are sold at extravagant prices, a single papaya or bunch of grapes wrapped like a precious gift costing five times what it does in the country of origin. Fish and other seafood are equally expensive... sometimes I wonder how the ordinary Japanese can survive on their meagre salary with such high cost of living in Tokyo. Only the minority of well-to-do can afford to stay in Tokyo. The majority live two or three hours away from the capital, where things are cheaper by Tokyo standards.

The Japanese consumers are generally unaware of the power of the consumers' movements such as those in Western countries or even in Singapore. During my stay in Japan, I saw little trace of Japanese consumers forming themselves into consumer clubs to fight rising prices. They are more passive and few would dare take the lead, for it is not the Japanese tradition to stick one's neck out for anything.

The gap between the wealth of the country and the quality of life of the average Japanese has repeatedly been criticised by foreign observers, as well as opposition politicians. It was even taken up by leading LDP figures. When Kakuei Tanaka became Prime Minister, he offered an impressive plan to clean up and restructure the nation to give Japan a decent environment. This dream has burst. His successors also put forward other plans, less ambitious but also seeking improvement in the infrastructure and social overheads. The only problem was that too few were implemented and improvement was slow in coming. In April 1992, Prime Minister Kiichi Miyazawa talked about working out a long-term programme for the nation's economy and society. A dominant concern of the programme-in-the-making was the quality of life of the Japanese people. Miyazawa was mindful of the public's mounting discontent that the quality of their lives does not reflect the nation's economic prowess and corporate prosperity.

This sentiment of improving the quality of life of the people has grown to the point where the governmnent and business establishments can no longer ignore it. The average Japanese has lost patience with making personal sacrifices — working long hours, living in unsatisfactory housing, coping with inadequate social infrastracture, commuting long distances on crowded trains — for the sake of national and corporate prosperity. The feeling seems to be that the well-being of individuals is being unduly sacrificed for the sake of corporations. When the nation was less affluent, people went along with enriching companies (and the entire economy through them) before claiming their own share of the affluence. The current debate boils down to which should be given priority — the individual or the group?

It is a delicate question, one that relates to a fundamental difference between Western and Japanese ways of thinking. It is unusual that the government, on the Prime Minister's own initiative, is addressing this question because it will almost certainly be an ambitious undertaking, involving change at the roots of Japanese society.

Realising the feelings of the people, the Hosokawa administration strongly supported the measures initiated by his predecessor Miyazawa and took steps to improve on it.

In Japan, group harmony comes first in the Japanese system. The assumption is that individual well-being is assured only when the group has become prosperous. Rebellion against this way of thinking is strenuously discouraged. People are allowed to assert themselves only when the group to which they belong has achieved a certain level of stability and only insofar as they do not endanger that stability. However, now that Japan is rich, there is no reason why the people should not question why they should not deserve a better standard of living and quality of life.

The Labour Ministry under the Hosokawa Government, in conjunction with the Ministry of Trade and Industry, took measures to cut down overtime hours chalked up by its legendary work force. For the first time, the MITI presented a paper discussing trade and industrial policy from the individual's rather than the corporations' viewpoint, urging Japanese companies to channel some of their surplus resources into boosting the living standards of workers, instead of focussing more on production. It apparently recognises that more and more Japanese are clamouring to enjoy their rewards (including improved "social infrastructures" such as better and more affordable housing) now, not later. The MITI paper will hopefully mark the start of Japan's attempt to right all the "wrongs" as perceived by its trading partners — including the irony of competitive made-in-Japan exports flooding the world while the Japanese at home have to pay ridiculously high prices for products and services because of the country's well-insulated market.

At this stage, it is too early to tell if Japan Inc. will go down the route suggested by the MITI paper. Will the powerful corporations resist the government initiative once the world economy recovers and orders start pouring in again?

Meanwhile, in May 1992, the Ministry of Labour indicated that it was planning new guidelines to lop off excessive overtime for workers. The Ministry said the guidelines had already been implemented. The guidelines were widely adopted by Japanese corporations, including cuts of at least 20 percent to the current recommended overtime limits of 15 hours a week or 50 hours a month. The proposed cuts should bring down the Japanese workers' average overtime from 185 hours in 1990 to 147 hours, or a cut of a total work hours per year from 2,044 to 1,800.

The move should help fend off some criticisms levelled against Japan by its trading partners — that its enormous trade surplus results partly from the longer hours put in by the Japanese worker compared with counterparts in the US or Europe.

With the Japanese economy now on the brink of recession and not expected to improve so soon, the move to cut overtime could not have been better timed. Japanese corporations will find it more acceptable now, when orders are less buoyant, than during boom days. As for the Japanese workers, many of whom have now had the opportunity to travel and see how the rest of the world works and lives, the move to cut overtime should prove a boom, as far as a desire to greater leisure is concerned. This move should help check what the Japanese call "karoshi" or death from overwork which, believe it or not, is reportedly a growing problem in Japan.

The desire for a more leisurely life is particularly stronger for the younger generation who did not experience World War II. They are beginning to ask questions as to why their parents have to work so hard and get back so little in return for their efforts. Even the younger ones born after the 1970s have already seen prosperity and the sign of affluence — the sky-scrapers, the booming factories, the cars, restaurants. They have not experienced hardship, hunger and humiliation. They cannot understand why the government is not providing them with the social amenities enjoyed by other Western countries. They are not the type that saves in the bank. They hold credit cards and have developed the art of spending.

This younger breed of Japanese, aged between 20 to 30 years old, have been spoilt by their parents and have learnt most of the things about life from the television screen. They have become a consumer society quite different from their thrifty parents. They are not so eager to work overtime, but are keen on having fun. In Japan, they are known as the Shinjinrui, which can be roughly translated as "new humans". They are a real problem for the older generation. They are mostly juvenile delinquents induging in divorce, drugs, urban crime, laziness at work and are always seen loitering in nightclubs, bars and the busy streets of Ginza, Roppongi or Akasaka. Every Sunday, when I walked through the streets of Yovogi Park or Harazuku, I saw young Japanese dancing in the street and dressed as "punks" and rock-and-rollers with their new Shinjinrui hairstyles. Tokyo even has a bar and motorcycle club called "The Health Angels". Every night, the dark streets of Ginza and Ronppongi are crammed with young shinjinrui, well-dressed

The traffic in Ginja, the busiest centre in Tokyo.

The normal crowd in Ronppongi, the centre for nightlife in Tokyo.

looking for pleasure. The telephone booths are pasted with telephone numbers of call-girls and there is usually a long queue.

The term Shinjinrui was invented in 1985 by a weekly magazine called the Asahi Journal. In an article in the magazine, the editor-in-chief Tetsuya Chikushi talked about the standard bearers of a new breed. It was meant as a double pun based on the different sets of Japanese characters that make up the same sound "shinjin-rui" or new faces, and "shin-jinrui" or new human race. Chikushi was furious about the word's popularity, and explained that he did not think the new race was any different from the old. He argued that it shares the same basic values of being hard-working, apolitical, materialistic and preferring jobs in large stable companies. Chikushi may be right as far as the exaggerated claims for the new breed. There is not going to be a social revolution, nor is Japanese industry about to fall apart because of lazy workers. But, there is no doubt that the attitude of the shinjinrui is quite different from the older generation, for they do not have the same experience as their parents who had undergone hardship in a war, suffering hunger, starvation and deprivation.

The shinjinrui are dedicated followers of fashion. They are the ones who would rather sip imported wine in Tokyo's cosy Italian bistros than green tea at a sushi bar. They are the ones dressed in the latest designer fashion, the ones always going away on holiday. They keep up with trends in clothing, music, food, interior decoration and other ways of spending. In the Ginza, I often witnessed the shinjinrui loitering around the 1,200 cabarets and bars and the hundreds of restaurants and coffee and tea houses. They are also seen in Asakusa, Shibuya nightclubs and places of instant pleasure or mizu-shobai (water business-prostitution). They also stay single longer than their parents did and have fewer children. There are many "love hotels" where Japanese or foreigners can pay and have "quick pleasure", although these hotels now face restrictions from the authorities.

The shinjinrui shock their parents by discarding traditional values of obligation, self-sacrifice and deference. They can afford to be choosy when they look for work as there are more jobs available than job seekers. These fun-loving youths are gradually replacing Japan's older alcoholic generations.

As a result of the growing number of shinjinrui in Japan, Kyoto-based Murata Manufacturing Co., the world's top ceramics maker, has begun wooing researchers with promises that they can choose their own working hours and locations. Even Seibu Railway Co., renowned for its strict training and autocratic management, can no longer force young male recruits to shave their heads and work 16-hour days, six days a week. After years of cost-cutting, Toyota Motor Co. in 1985 had to put about US$880 million into making its factories and offices more attractive to young workers. It added showers to locker rooms, set up carpeted lounges and installed air-conditioners and sound-proofing.

Although many companies still offer "lifetime employment" to those who want it, sacrificing everything for the company is fast becoming a rare phenomenon. Companies that once recruited only fresh graduates now sometimes hire people in mid-career, who inevitably disrupt the seniority system that once determined pay and promotions. Scepticism about company loyalty is spreading to middle-aged workers. The number of job hoppers has begun to grow.

Despite a reputation for individuality and self-centredness, the shinjinrui are pragmatic when it comes to career and family, attesting to the profound conservatism instilled in them at home, school and the workplace. When the time comes to become an adult member of society, most boys still buy dark suits and embark on a lifelong career as the family breadwinner, although they are increasingly turning down job transfers and overtime for the chance to be with their families. It is not easy to disregard Japan's strong pressure of traditional ways of life and social environment, which have taken root over centuries.

Sake and Alcoholism

Japan has a problem with alcoholism. Most Japanese are fond of drinks. At lunch or dinner, they always begin with beer and then later indulge in sake and stronger shochew, a kind of sake with a greater alcohol content. They often get drunk in bars and restaurants or nightclubs. To the Japanese, getting drunk is not a crime nor a sin; it is a release for them.

According to Shinto mythology, the gods who created Japan were surpassingly fond of Liquid Solace, and the Japanese have never found any solid reason for not following their divine lead. During the Han and Wei dynasties, Chinese historians who visited Japan (before the Japanese had a written language of their own) recorded that "the people of Wa (Japan) are much given to strong drink". The Japanese have always been notoriously lenient and forgiving toward the inebriated ones, who can curse, cry, dance, cackle, sing, fight and talk dirty without much fear of punishment or even a mild scolding. Japanese themselves have said that their country is the "drunkards paradise". The ordinary Japanese believes that the best policy is to endure everything and do nothing when the other party is drunk. In Japan, the Eden of the drunkards, one may drink like a baboon and not lose an iota of respectability in the eyes of the people. In Japan, there is a strange convention by which ordinary human beings strip themselves of their dignity when they drink, exposing their weaknesses and baring their hearts, confessing the most embarrassing secrets. No matter how much they grumble, they are completely forgiven on the excuse they have been drinking. There have been many cases in the past of murderers being acquitted or getting off with incredibly light sentences on the grounds that they were drunk. Drunkenness is a major safety valve on the pressure chamber of a society which is so stressful and demanding. Clamping it down could cause the excess pressure to seek release through less desirable avenues.

Because of the demand for drink, Japan has some 3,870 breweries that produce 400 million gallons of sake, running into 5,000 brands. Good sake drinkers know how to judge the quality of sake; it is judged by how it looks to the eye, how it feels on the tongue, how it smells and what tastes it leaves in the mouth. Each brand has its own subtle taste distinction, and that too may change with the year as the rice crops vary with the weather. The Japanese drink 4.2 gallons of sake per person every year. At a Shinto marriage ceremony, the Japanese bride and bridegroom drink the san-san-ku (three-three-nine) sake when a ritual is performed. They bow three times to one another with sake. When new buildings are completed, sake is drunk to celebrate, and birth and funerals are also performed with sake.

Japanese drinkers do not have to worry about payment. Every month, the hostess bar sends the bill to the company as a "company expense". In the case of large firms, it might work out at millions of yen. For smaller clubs dealing with smaller firms, the system can sometimes cause trouble for the collectors, for the firms might not be able to pay.

I have drunk sake with my Japanese friends and in most cases I found them poor drinkers. After two bottles of sake, my Japanese friends would soon lose control of themselves and start to behave differently. In recent years, Japanese professors Harada and Mizoi studied the livers of 60 Germans and 40 Japanese and found that those of their countrymen did not have a certain enzyme that breaks down acetaldehyde in the blood. It is the chemical acetaldeyhde that reddens the face and leads to disorderly behaviour.

Eating Habits

Apart from sake, the Japanese are generally adddicted to Japanese food. Among the major civilised nations of the world, no other people crave

Feasting in Japan.

their own food to the extent that the Japanese crave theirs, and no other food is as distinct from other food as the Japanese is. Everywhere in the world, wherever there are Japanese there must be Japanese restaurants to cater to their needs. It is difficult for the Japanese to live without eating their own food, and Japanese food is one of the most expensive in the world.

In Tokyo alone there are thousands of restaurants catering to the millions of government officials and businessmen who have expense accounts. The Tax Administration Agency recently announced that Japanese firms spend one-fifth of their total income in providing osake, onna and ongaku (wine, women and music) for those whose goodwill they seek.

There are various types of restaurants, some for the rich and others for the poor. The poorer class can squeeze into tiny roadside cafes to have a bowl of soba or udon for only about ¥200, and the rich go to expensive ones such as the Seryna in Roppongi or Ginza to enjoy ishiyaki (steak baked in hot stone) for ¥12,000. In Japan, most restaurants are speciality restaurants. There are restaurants specialising in tempura, where prawns and other seafood would be fried in front of guests seated around a circle. There are restaurants which serve eels, or sushi, or sashimi, or teppanyaki, or shabushabu, or tongkatsu, a kind of pork chop. Designed to please the eye and the aesthetic sense, Japanese food is artistically laid out on exquisite china and lacquerware that may be polygonal, triangular, square or even look like leaves or fans. The colour scheme, the way the dishes are laid out, and the seasonal significance of certain foods stimulate Japanese appetites.

The more enterprising Japanese gourmets go for dishes such as vinegared sparrows of Wakayama, salads made with raw cartilage of pig's ear, sweet and sour sexual organs of ox or turtle-blood-and-sake cocktails. Or cripled snake meat, grasshoppers of Akita dipped in wine, or pickled cheery blossoms, horsetails, braised cow's hoof or urchins and snake urine soup. I once visited a temple and was served with fried maple leaves. The taste was not so bad. Such bizarre dishes are meant for the people Japanese call getemono-gui (exotic).

Japanese like to eat raw food. The most expensive raw seafood is the poisonous puffer or globe fish called "fugu", marketed under the name "sea squb". The fish stomach looks like a globe bloating up. Fugu has caused the deaths of many Japanese, including a famous Kabuki actor. I have been invited to fugu dinners many times and have eaten fugu — the meat is tasteless, but the soup was superb. Nothing happened to me and my family. Once I was invited by the Soga Gakkai officials when I was visiting Oita in Kyushu to study Nichiren organisations. My host took me to a famous fugu restaurant. The captain served us with raw fugu liver and assured us with these words: "In the whole of Japan, only in Oita can one eat fugu liver unharmed." Being innocent and daring, my wife and I took raw fugu liver. It tasted really wonderful, particularly when accompanied by sake. Nothing happened during the meal. But when I was walking out of the restaurant towards the car, I noticed that my lips had gone numb. They were almost paralysed. My wife had the same feeling. I told my hosts, who were really worried and suggested we see a doctor. I told them not to worry. A few hours later, the feeling on the lips came back and we were normal again. From that time on, I dared not touch fugu. It can be really poisonous.

Whenever I met Japanese friends thereafter I would ask them whether they had tasted fugu liver and invariably they would say no, adding with these words: "I would not risk my life." When I told them I had eaten fugu liver, they would look at me and say, "You are really lucky."

Japanese food is standardised, with little variation. Those who prepare fugu must know exactly what is required, the style of cooking and the proper recipe. Similarly, those who serve tempura, shabushabu or teppanyaki know their jobs. Every restaurant will specialise in one kind of food. Geisha houses, for instance, always serve their customers with a kind of food called "kaiseki", a typical traditional food of the Japanese.

Kaiseki originated when Zen Buddhism came to Japan from China. In the past, during the observance of rigorous Zen austerities, a heated stone was placed in the bosom of the disciple to lessen the pangs of hunger and to provide warmth. Kaiseki means "bosom stone". This word was used to designate the food eaten at such times and the cooks were admonished to avoid extravagance, offer simple foods and bring out the natural flavour. A typical kaiseki menu consists of an appetizer, clear soup, raw fish, boiled vegetables and vinegared vegetables. A keiseki meal is designated by the time at which it is consumed. "Shogo no kaiseki" means during noontime, "hango no kaiseki" is served at about three in the afternoon and "yoba no kaiseki" around six in the evening. Some kaiseki are even more fanciful. "Yuki no kaiseki" is eaten while viewing the snow, "tsukimi no kaiseki" is taken as one watches the moon and "asacha no kaseki" is consumed at daybreak. Geisha houses serve kaiseki because they want to preserve the natural flavour of traditional Japanese food.

Whenever I was invited to a geisha house I would be served the kaiseki dishes. To one who has been so accustomed to spicy food, kaiseki food was tasteless. There was no chilly or spicy hot element. Kaiseki did not actually satisfy my gourmet requirements, but tastelessness is exactly what the Japanese want. To a traditional Japanese, whatever is tasteless is a good taste. This is so not only in Japanese food, but in painting. A good painting to a Japanese is not the inspiring and exciting one, but the plain, tasteless and simple one. Japanese paintings are normally very plain. The Japanese consider a painting to be good when it is simple, not too flowery and not too crammed.

Geisha Entertainers

In a highly pressurised society like Japan, workaholics need to let off steam after their daily routines. The rich and well-off such as politicians and businessmen would go to the geisha parties and drink their fair share of sake. Geishas are women entertainers of a traditional type, who provide singing, dancing, conversation, games and companionship in certain restaurants. The geisha world is generally referred to as the "karyukai" (flower and willow world). One of the reasons why rich Japanese go to geisha houses is that geisha girls are always tight-lipped and are able to keep secrets.

Geisha girls — four activities.

Politicians will discuss schemes and secret plots in front of geisha girls without fearing that there will be a leakage. The only occasion when a geisha girl exposed her client's close relations was the Uno affair, involving Japan's former Prime Minister Uno. The affair bought down the Uno administration. It was also the first time in the history of the geisha profession that something like that had happened. I was told that Prime Minister Uno had had an affair with the girl, but had refused to settle the demand for money she made after he became Prime Minister, and this had led to the unfortunate affair. In fact, Uno was not the only Prime Minister who had affairs with geisha girls. It just happened that he was unlucky and that his supporters did not handle the affair amicably. I knew Uno when he was Foreign Minister — he belonged to the Nakasone faction and appeared sober to me. He was also an artist.

Akasaka is the favourite spot for LDP politicians to patronise geisha houses. Each political faction has its favourite entertainment districts where, with the help of sake and a relaxed atmosphere, members discuss plots and schemes for or against other factions. The fortunes of the various hanamachi (geisha houses) tend to rise or fall according to the state of the political factions which patronise them. Ocassionally, the press condemns the so-called machiai seiji or "waiting house politics". Although geisha are professionally close-mouthed, opposing factions seldom patronise the same geisha houses. However, geishas would be the best target to cultivate since they know so many political secrets.

Whenever a foreign VIP visits Japan, the hosts invite him to a geisha party. I have been invited on many occasions to geisha parties, sometimes with former Singaporean Prime Minster Lee Kuan Yew and other times with Minister of Trade and Industry, and now Deputy Prime Minister, Lee Hsien Loong and other VIPs from Singapore. More often than not, those geishas who accompanied us were old ladies, some reaching the age of 70. They served us Japanese "kaiseki", and sang or danced usually accompanied by the playing of "samisen", a three stringed instrument. They tried their best to entertain us and make us happy, joking and feeding the guests. Their duty was to make the guests happy. I always felt relaxed whenever I attended a geisha party — the geisha was always obliging and would always smile.

Geisha may continue to work to an advanced age. A love for the traditional arts seems to be the most important motivating factor for women who choose to become geisha, and while some social prejudice against them exists, they are respected as preservers of traditional art and culture. Nowadays, it is difficult to find young geishas because the younger generation do not have the patience to be trained. Moreover, they think that the job of the geisha is rather degrading. Aspiring geisha must take lessons in various traditional arts. Some arts are not directly involved with their work as entertainers, such as flower arrangements, calligraphy, classical dancing or playing the samsen. After the trial period called minarai, she sits for an examination at the local geisha registry office, presided over by senior members of the geisha union. The lessons become part of her life as a geisha and she continues to do the traditional arts as long as she works.

I once visited a high-class hanamachi in Kyoto, named Gion, where young geisha were being trained. I saw girls from the age of 13 to 18 undergoing trained as geishas. They are called "maiko" and they have no lips because they are not allowed to put on lipstick. The maiko are like little dolls with painted white faces. They bustle awkwardly along the date streets of wood, pigeon-toed on their high sandals. They are assigned to a full-fledged geisha of the house, to run errands for her and assist in her time-consuming daily ritual of bathing and dressing. Following throughly the geisha's routine enables the apprentice to absorb knowledge by watching and listening. These young geisha-to-be dress more elaborately and colourfully. They are taught to sing, dance and are required by law to attend middle school lessons. They normally graduate at 15, and at 18 become full-fledged geishas.

Nowadays, the geisha is considered an independent business woman. She is fully protected from exploitation by labour regulations and must be 18 years old in order to become a full-fledged entertainer. While older geishas may be driven to work in rickshaws — there are still a number of rickshaws in Tokyo, Kyoto and other places where there are geishas — the younger geishas may ride to work on scooters or even drive their own cars. Of the 402 geishas in the Shimbashi districts, over 200 have driving licenses. It is estimated that there are 3,500 to 5,000 geishas in Tokyo and roughly about 35,000 throughout Japan.

In the troubled times after the Meiji Restoration in 1868, the centres of political power and intrigue shifted with alarming alacrity. The clique in power today might be in disarray and confusion tomorrow. Under such circumstances, many politicians found their favourite geisha to be an oasis of calm and staility. Politicians often came to rely more on the geisha for financing, loyalty and confidential information. Three men who later rose to the highest political office in Japan, that of Prime Minister, married their faithful geisha in appreciation of their loyalty and assistance. They were Hirobumi Ito, Taro Katsura and Aritomo Hamagata and their geisha wives were Koume, O-Koi and Oimatuse. These were pre-war days.

When geisha marry, they quit their profession, but while they are working, their relations with men may be of several types. It is generally considered desirable to have a patron with whom she is involved emotionally, sexually and economically. In addition to the patron, every geisha tries to build up a clientele of dependable favourite customers whom she can count on to call her when she gives parties and to contribute to the expenses involved in her public performances of dancing or singing.

Social Clubs and Golf Clubs

The well-to-do upper class of Japan spend a great deal of their time in social and golf clubs. I was once invited by a Japanese friend, Yoshi, to the oldest club in Tokyo called the Tokyo Club. Yoshi was introduced to me by my Australian friend, the late Peter Russo, who was a graduate of the Tokyo Imperial University and an expert on Japan. Yoshi was studying at the Ichibashi University when Peter Russo was a teacher. After graduation, Yoshi was sent to New York for four years and when the war broke out, he was sent as a naval officer to Singapore in April 1941. He stayed in Seletar for three years and was then transferred to Penang, Malaysia.

The Tokyo Club is a prestigious club frequented by politicians and professionals. The food is good and cheap. One could get a glass of whisky with water for only ¥150. It has quiet surroundings and is located very near the city. According to Yoshi, the Tokyo Club was established by Ito Hirobumi (1841–1909), who was Prime Minister during the Meiji period. He was the Prime Minister who married a geisha. He was a prominent statesman who took part in the struggle for the overthrow of the Tokugawa shogunate. As the Chief architect of Japan's first constitution and as Prime Minister for four consecutive times, he guided Japan in its formative years as a modern state.

Ito Hirobumi was known for the part he took in signing the Korean–Japan Convention after Japan's victory over Russia in the 1904–5 war. He initiated a programme for economic development and introduced the police system in Korea. In the following year, he forced the Korean Emperor to abdicate and established a full Japan protectorate over Korea, paving the way to eventual annexation. In 1909, whilst travelling to Manchuria, he was assassinated by a Korean nationalist.

The Meiji Emperor wanted the Japanese to appear civilised. Many foreigners were murdered in Tokyo before the Second World War and there was not much mixing between foreigners and Japanese. Ito came up with the idea of forming the Tokyo Club with the purpose of encouraging more social mixing between foreigners and Japanese. In the early days about 30 percent of the membership were foreigners. Nowadays, its membership is mainly Japanese. Ito succeeded in bringing about a social dialogue between foreigners and Japanese through the club.

During the war, the former Japanese Ambassador to the United States had to hide from the Kempaitai in the Club. He disguised himself as a bartender and survived.

After the war, the Board of Directors decided on new rules and banned discussions about politics and business in the club. They also banned women from entering. Other rules stipulate that a member should not bring the same guest there more than three times a month.

Apart from visiting social clubs, the more well-to-do Japanese are crazy about golf. There are hundreds of golf clubs in Tokyo. As a golfer, I had the rare opportunity of enjoying golf in some of the most prestigious golf clubs such as Kogane, Hoodogaya, Club 300, Kasumigasaki and the National Country Club near Fuji Mountain. To be a member of the Kogane Club, for instance, one has to pay something like US$1 million. If I were to ask the Ministry of Foreign Affairs for permission to join the club, the officials might ask whether I was buying over the club. I had the pleasure of playing in these clubs because I was a member of the diplomatic corp.

There are certain strict but outdated rules which some of these older clubs still steadfastly observe. Certain clubs like the Kogane do not allow ladies to play on Sunday. On one occasion, a friendly match was arranged between the diplomatic corp and the Gaimusho (Ministry of Foreign Affairs). The leader of the team of Gaimusho was a lady, who happened to be the Deputy Foreign Minister under Shintaro Abe. When she arrived at the club, she was told that she could not play on Sunday as stipulated by club rules. She was flaberaggasted and the organisers appealed to the club authorities to be lenient because it was a match with foreign dignitaries. The club would not give way and the match had to go on without her. This matter aroused some publicity in Japanese newspapers. Even Prime Minister Nakasone raised the matter in the Parliament. But the Club would not change its rules. There are certain clubs in Japan meant exclusively for men and there is nothing which the authorities can do about it.

To play golf in some of these prestigious clubs in Japan is very enjoyable, but expensive. The golf courses are always well run, the service excellent — the caddies do not accept tips and will bow to their clients before and after the game — and the surroundings and atmosphere of these clubs is beautiful. It is always a pleasure to play in spring when the cherry blossoms bloom and in autumn when the player is surrounded by red maple leaves. Some enterprising Japanese even play in winter under thick snow.

I most enjoyed playing at the National Country Club near the Fuji mountain because I could have a close look at the snowcapped Fuji Mountain from almost every green. As this club is far away from Tokyo, there are no rush crowds and we took our own sweet time to enjoy the game.

To play golf in Japan means a whole day affair. One has to get up early in the morning, take a two or three hour drive to the club and another two or three hours back home. In the case of the National Country Club, it means staying overnight.

Bars and Nightclubs

Those who cannot afford to play golf or hobnob in prestigious social clubs go to bars, cabarets and nightclubs or tea shops for relaxation. In Tokyo, there are about 100,000 such places. Most Japanese live in crammed houses which are uncomfortable and prefer to spend their time after the office outside the home. As many of them have expense accounts, they spend their time drinking and dining away from home. It is an integral part of Japanese life. Expense accounts are the fuel that powers most of this nightlife.

Most of the Japanese clients in bars have their favourite bar girls. The Japanese are generally shy with strangers and prefer to converse with someone they have cultivated a kind of understanding and friendship with before they can open their hearts. The chosen bar girls gradually become their "girl friends" or unofficial "mistresses". After work, they go to the bar to have a yawn with their "chosen angels" and relax and drink.

Taverns and bars are vital to Japanese salarymen because they are the nerve-releasing centres for them. The concentration of bars on the back streets of the shopping centres of cities is extremely high in Tokyo and other Japanese cities compared to Western countries. When offices close, Japanese salarymen stop over at bars to drink with their close friends, who may be colleagues, schoolmates and classmates. They will remain drinking there until well after the last train before they go home. It is not the drink itself that attracts them, so much as the chance of relaxation after the tension and competition in the office. Bars are a means of soothing their nerves.

The layout and atmosphere of Japanese bars is quite different from the London pub which is always crowded, bustling and open. The Japanese prefer smaller bars where lights are dimmed, with a background of quiet music and smart hostesses to serve them drinks and listen with constant appreciation and ready sympathy to whatever they may say. It is a very personal atmosphere: no matter how stupid they may be, they are accepted. To soothe the tired nerves, a Japanese client would pour out his grievances to the bar girl who has become "temporary sweetheart" — about office politics and intrigues or even love affairs or troubles in the family. Much of the talk could be so stupid coming from the lips of educated adults.

It is a Japanese tradition that whatever is said in drink is excused and should be forgotten and forgiven. The bar has therefore become an important place to pour out frustrations and grievances. It is here that the Japanese can let off steam after a day's strenuous work, where tension is so demanding. Many Japanese would say without scruples, "I can't live without a bar." Bars and girlfriends appear frequently in hundreds of popular novels and TV stories in Japan. One would even say that Japanese salarymen are very much influenced by "bar culture".

The Japanese salarymen need bars because they are rather slow to speak out on formal occasions and feel considerable pressure from the rigid vertical system. When a formal meeting faces deadlock or when difficulties arise in personal relations, a chat over drinks in a bar often proves effective to releasing one's tension. A gathering of intimate and lifelong friends to drink together is one of the most enjoyable occasions for Japanese men. Here, they can find complete relaxation and can talk and laugh from the heart. The essence of pleasure in such bar conversation for the Japanese is not in discussion but in emotional exchange. It is not easy for the average Japanese to express his ideas and opinions during ordinary working hours. Bar conversations enable them to voice their different ideas and views, and it is here that they really have an emotional outlet.

The Japanese tend to always drink with the same group, gathered from sempai (senior) or kohai (same rank) who are similar in age and rank. Close doryo who stand in a relationship of rivalry are often excluded. The salarymen spends not only the working hours but many evenings of relaxation in the company of his colleagues. Such closes intimacy between working colleagues leads to the development of cliques and complicates the process of decision-making.

Pachinko

Japanese salarymen who cannot afford to visit social clubs and golf clubs or go to bars and nightclubs spend their time enjoying pachiko — the

A look at a pachinko parlour in Tokyo.

Japanese pinball machines which are becoming a national passion for millions. Devotees cram into crowded, noisy parlours just to watch ball-bearings flash past their eyes at a rate of more than one every second. The game is big business and makes parlour owners huge sums of money — the equivalent of three percent of Japan's total gross national product is spent on pachinko. Grateful owners, who are mostly Koreans and Chinese, reciprocate by awarding selected players the pachinko culture award. The 1985 pachinko winners included the leader of the Japan Socialist Party, Takako Doi, an enthusiastic player.

The name "pachinko" is said to derive from the sound of the balls ricocheting about the machine. A player buys a box of ball bearings and feeds them into the machine. The aim is to direct the stream of balls through a maze of nails into selected slots. The machine disgorges a load of ball-bearings into the successful player's tray, which can then be exchanged for a variety of prizes. The open secret is that players can change the prizes into cash as well, even though the law bans pachinko gambling for money.

A select band of professionals even manage to make a living off the game. They know exactly which machine produces the best results. But the overall winner is the pachinko owner. I know the owner of a chain of pachinko parlours, a Chinese who has taken up Japanese citizenship. His main profession is as an assistant professor of a university. Of course, the university does not know that he owns so many pachinko parlours. The professor once told me, "Most people come here because they want to get their money back. I think more than 90 percent of the players are losing money."

The number of machines in Japan almost doubled between 1981 and 1985, to well over three million. The gross income of the 14,000 garish neon-lit pachinko parlours in 1985 came to around ¥10 trillion, or about US$75 billion — more than four times the 1981 figure. But with new hi-tech machines, luck rather than skill has become a larger factor.

Pachinko first appeared in Japan before World War II, but in the past decade or so the game has become an important source of tax revenue for the government and a common spot for Japanese salarymen to while away their time and money.

I once ventured into a pachinko parlour to get a kick out of the experience. I bought some ball-bearings and within ten minutes lost about ¥1,000. The smoky air inside the parlour and the noise was too much for me to bear. I could not understand why so many Japanese salarymen were so intoxicated by pachinko. Probably, the noise and smoke dull their senses while the excitement heats their blood.

It is generally said that in Japan, except for Emperor Hirohito, almost every Japanese has at one time or other enjoyed pachinko.

Wives Who Hold the Purse Strings

Although Japanese husbands may spend their leisure hours after work in geisha houses, bars, nightclubs or the pachinko parlours and return home late at night exhausted, they are handicapped by a lack of money to spend. The wives have control over them by holding their purses. Almost every Japanese husband hands over his monthly pay to his wife. I have asked many presidents and chairmen of multi-nationals whether they hand their pay to their wives and invariably they would admit that they do so. In most cases, the pay is paid by the company direct into the wife's account. The wife of a Japanese is responsible for all the household spending such as public utilities bill, house rent, telephones bills, school fees for children and food. Some husbands would stretch their hands out every morning to ask for "cake money" from the wives. The Japanese have a phrase for this practice; it is called "kaka tenka" (the world of the women). Salarymen husbands who do not have expense accounts will have difficulty in finding extra funds to spend after office hours. The wives know that without money the husbands cannot go too far. But, the husbands do not hand over their bonus or whatever extra money they have earned. This is where the husbands can tap their resources for spending.

The "kaka tenka" practice seems to have originated from the days of the samurai because samurais were supposed to be "gentlemen" in the image of Confucius and money to them was dirty. They left the handling of money to their wives.

Although the wives control the purse, life can be quite pitiful for them. They seldom see their husbands during the day and they have become accustomed to welcoming an exhausted husband, whom they believe is exhausted because of work. The husband gets up early in the morning to catch the train, roughs it out in crammed trains, and then feels shy about coming back too early. In Japan, the husband's duty is to work and earn money and the wife looks after the family. This is what I call division of labour. Life goes on for ten or twenty years in loneliness. She seldom has any emotional dialogue with the husband and there is nothing much to talk about between husband and wife. She gets used to loneliness and goes for ikebana and tea ceremonies or looks for own enjoyment and excitment if she has the opportunity. When the couple go for a holiday, they find nothing much to talk about. This was told to me by many of my Japanese friends.

This is the normal lifestyle of most Japanese salarymen. At the end of 20 years, when the husband retires from the company, the wife suddenly sues for divorce. Some husbands cannot understand the reason and commit suicide. The wife thinks that she has fulfilled her duties as the children have grown up and she has done her fair share of looking after the home. It is time for her to gain her independence. After all, she has had no dialogue with her husband; she has saved enough money to stand on her own feet.

In recent years, there has been a growing number of Japanese women, frustrated by years of the husband's neglect, divorcing their retiree husbands. This was revealed by the Ministry of Health and Welfare statistics. Divorce papers filed with the ministry showed that the divorce rate among couples who have been married for 20 years or more has grown steadily from 5.3 percent in 1970 to 13.9 percent in 1990. In many cases, it is the retiree husband who suddenly finds himself without a wife when he finally returns to his long-neglected home.

In fact, the Japanese have coined a term — sodai gomi (big garbage) — for the retiree husband who sits around the house all day because he is at a loss at how to interact with his family.

One 63-year-old manager of a major company told me that when he returned home from a farewell party that his colleagues held for him on the day of his retirement, his wife greeted him with words of appreciation for the years of hard work he put in to support the family. But, when he suggested to his wife that they go out to dinner, she refused and told him bluntly, "I too am going to retire from work." The "work" she referred to was her duties as a wife and housekeeper.

While he had always provided well for his family, the manager was so absorbed in his work that he left childcare and other family matters to his wife: a common characteristic among Japan's white-collar employees. The wife, meanwhile, studied for a teacher's certificate in the art of tea ceremony and started teaching at home. Soon, she rented an apartment to hold lessons because her husband, careless about his looks, would appear before young female students in his underwear when she had her lessons at home. Since there was no dialogue between the two, she had to give lessons in the apartment. When she filed for a divorce, he could not understand the reason.

Of course, one cannot generalise. There are many Japanese couples who lead a healthy life according to Japanese tradition and they are still together when they get old. This is particularly so with the older generation. I have seen many old couples strolling in the gardens as if they enjoy each other's company. With the younger generation, this trend of closeness is fast disappearing.

Tea Ceremony

The Japanese wives spend a great deal of their leisure hours at tea ceremonies. This is a traditional art which is traditionally required of Japanese women and girls. Most Japanese women know either the art of the tea ceremony or flower arrangement. Such knowledge and experience are expected of ordinary Japanese women if they want to be considered as having been well brought up.

The tea ceremony, literally known as "chanoyu" (tea hot water), is a highly structured method for preparing tea in the company of guests. The Japanese always pay attention to form. They like to prepare food in front

The author's experience of a tea ceremony in Fukuoka.

of their guests, like Teppanyaki when the guests not only eat but enjoy the way the cook prepares the food. The same applies to the tea ceremony. Although the origins of the tea ritual came from Zen Buddhist temples of Tang dynasty China (618–907) in its final form, the tea ceremony is a Japanese expression. According to records, Bodhidharma, who left India and introduced Zen Buddhism to China in 520, encouraged the drinking of tea as an exceedingly beneficial practice to keep the pupils of Zen Buddhism awake. In Tang Buddhist temples, a tea ritual was performed using a set of bronze utensils comprising of a brazier with a wood fire, a kettle, a water jar, a waste-water bowl, a baselike stand for a bamboo ladle and pair of tongs and a cylindrical rest for the kettle lid. The tea was made by aging the leaves, fermenting them and pressing them into a brick. The powdered tea was added to the hot water in the kettle and ladled into ceramic bowls.

During the Nara period (710–794), when the influence of Chinese culture was great, Emperor Shomu (724–749) held a tea ceremony to which a hundred priests were invited. But, it was in the Heian period (794–1185), after the capital was moved to Kyoto, that the tea ceremony became part of Japanese culture distinct from the austere tea rites of the Chinese temples. Aristocrats, who collected the highly prized Chinese utensils, served tea in their pavilions. Very early in the Kakakura period (1185–1333), a Japanese priest Eisai returned from Buddhist studies in China with seeds from the tea plant and grew them in Japan. It became the source of much of the tea supply in Japan till today. Despite the Onin war which devasted Kyoto in the mid-15th century and the hundred years of civil war that followed, the art of the tea ceremony continued to thrive. Then, in 1587, the de factor ruler of Japan, Hideyoshi, gave the largest tea party ever held. Hideyoshi invited every devotee of the tea ceremony from all over Japan to attend, with the warning that anyone who failed to attend would be barred from participating in the ceremony again. On that occasion, 16,000 devotees attended the tea ceremony. It was the grandest affair in Japanese history.

My first experience with the Japanese tea ceremony was in September 1984 in the Sen-kian garden which was surrounded by hills. In a valley beside a beautiful pond with plenty of blooming lotus, there was an old building specially built for tea ceremonies. The whole garden was planted with old pine trees with artistic rocks, little streams and bamboo. There were many Japanese ladies with lovely kimonos loitering and chatting in various old-styled houses bearing the names of Ura Senke and Omote Senke — the two main schools of the tea ceremony — serving tea for guests. It was drizzling and they carried umbrellas.

My family and I entered this small house through a narrow entrance. There was a scroll — a simple painting of a flower — and a flower arrangement below the painting. We entered the room, examined the scroll and sat facing the kettle and brazier that heated the water for tea. A kimono-clad lady served us a bowl of greenish tea called matcha made from a light green powder mixed with hot water and swished it in the bottom of the cup with a chasen or bamboo tea-whisk. We turned the bowl clockwise until the face was on the opposite side and tasted the tea. We turned the bowl back to the original position and returned to the server. The tea ceremony was nothing but an elaborate ritual of when to bow, when to praise the quality of the tea, how to hold the cup, how to pass it on to the next guest and so forth. It was a geometric progression in forms and manners. Although the guests may talk, the emphasis is on contemplative quietness and peace and the achievement of a silent symphony of graceful but restrained motion.

Today, more than two million Japanese consider themselves full-fledged devotees of the tea-ceremony, about which Kakuzo Okakura wrote in his book on tea: "Teaism is a cult founded on the adoration of the beautiful among the sordid facts of everyday existence. It inculcates purity and harmony...

it is a religion of the art of life. The tea room is an oasis in the dreary waste of existence... The ceremony is an improvised drama whose plot is woven about the tea, the flowers, and the paintings. Not a colour to disturb the tone of the room, not a sound to mar the rhythm of things, not a gesture to intrude on the harmony, not a word to break the unity of the surroundings, all movements to be performed simply and naturally... such are the aims of the tea ceremony."

The Japanese tea ceremony is basically divided into two schools — the Omote Senke (1619–22) and the Ura Senke (1622–97). They are the leading schools in Japan today, with millions of students. The Omote Senke school belongs to the Aristocrat category and Ura Senke is representative of the commoners. Despite the difference, they share the same discipline and the style of buildings, tea gardens and utensils. The tea ceremony which we attended belonged to the Ura Senke school. The founder, Sen No Rikyo, officiated at the sumptuous tea ceremony held by Hideyoshi in honour of Emperor Ogimachi (1577–93) at the Imperial Palace. In 1591, Rikyo clashed with Hideyoshi and was ordered to commit harakiri. Sen No Rikyo had placed a life-sized statue of himself in the Kimmo Kaku, a structural addition to the main gate of Daitokuji that had offended the powerful Hideyoshi. But one of the main reasons for the imperial disfavour was that he refused to give away his daughter to the powerful ruler. He made the tea ceremony accessible to the common Japanese by reducing the size of the tea house to two tatami mats instead of four mats, which was the original size and he used simple objects as utensils. In one of his poems, he reminded his disciples that "the tea ceremony is nothing more than boiling water, steeping tea and drinking it."

Flower Arrangement

Another pastime which Japanese housewives indulge in during leisure hours is flower arrangement, known as "ikebana" in Japanese. Ikebana comes from the word "ikeru (to keep alive) and "hana" (flowers). Ikebana had its origin in early Buddhist flower offerings and developed into a distinctive art form from the 15th century, with many styles and schools. The most popular schools in Japan and overseas are the Sogetsu and Hara. My wife belonged to the Sogetsue school and a teacher came to the Embassy twice a week to teach her. I attended the first lesson and gave up because the teacher thought I was too inventive and would not follow her instruction.

Just as in calligraphy and painting, ikebana lessons are strict and rigid. Students are not allowed to improvise and must follow each rule strictly. After the first lesson, I made up my mind that ikebana was not meant for me.

Buddhist ritual flower offerings date from the 6th century when Buddhism was transmitted to Japan from China. Ono No Imoko, Japan's Ambassador to China in 607, introduced the art of flower arrnangement to Japan and this art became known as Ikenobo (derived from his name). The important aspect of Buddhist flower arrangements was the "three elements" offering placed in front of a Buddhist image or symbol, which consisted of an incense burner flanked by a candlestick and a vase of flowers. Buddhist flower offerings were arranged in a natural style called tatebana (standing flower) with the main stem, approximately one and a half times the height of the flower container, positioned vertically in the centre; two additional stems were placed symmetrically to the left and right.

There is no record of any systematised form of flower arrangement in Japan before the period of the civil war in the late 15th century. It was after 1462 when a Japanese named Sengyo created the rikka style with a new innovation depicting the mythical Mt. Sumeru of Buddhist cosmology and, by extension, the entire universe. Many masters of rikka succeeded Sengyo, and during the 16th century rikka became almost synonymous with the Ikenobo school. In the late 16th century, a new form of flower arrangement began to emerge for use in conjunction with the tea ceremony, an elaborate ritual for the preparation for the tea ceremony which was then introduced from China to Japan. Then in the 17th century, the Japanese shifted away from the aristrocratic and complicated rikka style and created the simpler shoka school of flower arrangement. After the Meiji Restoration, traditional Japanese arts underwent a period of neglect as a result of the general enthusiasm for Western culture and Japanese ikebana went into a temporary decline. During the 1890s, however, when the Japanese realised the foolishness of copying Western culture, Ohara Unshin created the style called the Ohara style which was then followed by Sogetsu.

Most housewives are members of either the Sogetsue or Ohara schools. I was once invited by the Sogetsu Ikebana Centre in Tokyo, which is a tall modern building of considerable size. Sogetsu has many branches all over the world. The branch in Singapore is run by one Mrs. Kim, a Japanese lady married to a Korean. When former Foreign Minister Dhanabalan arrived in Tokyo with his Chinese wife, we took them to the Sogetsu Ikebana Centre and had a lesson on ikebana. Mrs. Dhanabalan is a student of Mrs. Kim, who flew to Tokyo to attend the function.

In Tokyo, every major hotel displays a giant ikebana at its entrance and it is the showpiece of the hotel. Whenever I go for functions at a hotel, the first thing I do is to spend some time admiring the ikebana arrangement.

One thing I learnt from the Japanese is their deep sense of appreciation for things aesthetic. They have a good sense of artistic appreciation. They appreciate nature and things natural. Sometimes, I noticed Japanese spending hours staring at a bunch of flowers, at ikebana or at a simple painting. They love nature and would like to be with nature. They believe that everything must come from the heart.

Cherry Blossom Mentality

The Japanese love cherry blossoms. When cherry blossoms appear in spring, the Japanese gather together under the trees to enjoy viewing parties. The Japanese name for cherry blossoms is "sakura", which is generally used for those species of cherry appreciated for the beauty of their blossoms rather than those grown for their fruit. The sakura is foremost among plants mentioned in Japanese literature.

The sakura normally blooms for only ten days. It has become a convenient symbol of the Japanese asethetic sense, an ephemeral beauty. It is one of the oldest flowers known in Japan. The word appears in the Kojiki and Man'yoshu, an anthology of poems compiled in the late 8th century which contains about 401 poems mentioning the tree and praising its blossoms. At that time, they were called ume (plum) more often than sakura because Japanese culture was influenced by that of China.

The sakura has become intimately identified with Japanese culture. In a poem expressing an appreciation that is both horticultural and chauvinistic, Notoori Norinaga wrote, "If someone wishes to know the essence of the Japanese spirit, it is the fragrant cherry blossoms in the early morning."

After my stay in Japan, I began to appreciate what Notoori Norinaga has said. The life of the sakura is so short that it has affected the psychic of the Japanese. To most Japanese, sakura represents life which is very short and fleeting. In ten days, the beautiful sakura fade away and green leaves take over. Since life is so short, why not make the best of it and don't try to remember too many things? Make the best of the ten days and enjoy the asthetic beauty of the sakura to the fullest extent. When the sakura starts blooming, the Japanese bring sake, food and cakes and spread their

A cherry blossom viewing party in Ueno Park, Tokyo.

mats under the cherry blossom trees. Under the shade they would sing, dance and celebrate the rare occasion. Every year, as Ambassador, my family was invited to sakura viewing parties normally organised in the gardens. Such parties are always packed. Japanese girls come in colourful kimonos and the whole family gathers together to enjoy the delightful atmosphere. We were served delicious Japanese sushi, tempura, yakitori (Japanese satay), soba, udon and of course sake. The Japanese either meditate or talk under the trees until sunset.

The Japanese believe that when they gather under the cherry blossom trees to enjoy the occasion, they are together with the soul of their parted beloved, such as their parents or those who have left the earth. Once a year, these souls come to enjoy the cherry blossoms with them. In other words, they are united once a year with their closed relatives who have left them and spirits abound at cherry blossom viewing parties. The Japanese, therefore, do not use cherry blossoms to describe the beauty of women. A foreigner once praised a charming lady with "You are as beautiful as sakura" and this offended her.

Forget the Year Parties

Because life is as short as the sakura, the Japanese tend to be more forgetful. At the end of the year, Japanese have a special party call the "forget the year" party. Nearly every company, ministry and social organisation celebrates the "forget the year" parties. The purpose of the party is to enable the partygoers to forget all that had happened during the year. The Japanese like to forget the past — good or bad, bitter or sweet — and start anew with the New Year. They believe that if one keeps remembering the past, one would be burdened by the past and would not get on with the work for tomorrow.

I was invited to such functions almost every year. On one occasion, the host asked me to make a speech. Being frank and blunt as usual, I made a comparision between the Japanese and Chinese characteristics. I said the Japanese like to forget things, including the massacre of Nanking during the Second World War. I said this is proved by the blackout of such incidents in Japanese history books for their children. The Chinese, however, would dig out a corpse which had been buried 200 years ago and would whip it for 30 days in order to satisfy their thirst for revenge. There was a story that in ancient days that a Chinese took revenge on his enemy by digging up his grave, taking out the corpse and whipping it 200 times. This statement took the Japanese by surprise but they admitted that I was telling the truth.

Japanese normally forget and forgive their enemy and his sins once he has passed away. They even attend his funeral. They never talk badly about a dead person. However, they will never forget or forgive their enemy while he is still alive.

There is a famous story about the forty-seven ronin (a term derived from the 47 masterless samurai of the Edo period) who were ordered to commit seppuku (harakiri) for their vindictive slaying of a corrupt court official whom they held ultimately responsible for bringing about the death of their master, Lord Asano. This was an incident that occurred in the era of the Tokugawa shogunate and has been told and retold in various versions and media, from traditional kabuki drama to modern movies and TV. The story is probably known to every Japanese in the world who is over the age of seven.

The forty-seven romin were the retainers of a provincial daimyo (feudal lord), Asano Naganori, from the province of Ako. Lord Asano and two other daimyo were appointed by the shogun to receive an envoy from the Emperor at the shogun's court in Edo. One Lord Kira, a corrupt official, was supposed to be the expert on imperial etiquette and was asked to ensure that the three daimyos knew their manners. The other two daimyos gave Lord Kira lavish gifts but Asano felt it was unnecessary to do so. Lord Kira taunted Asano with so many insults and created so much trouble that Asano could not tolerate any more. On 21 April 1701, he lost his temper and stabbed Lord Kira in the audience hall of the shogun's palace. Lord Kira was only slightly hurt, but the shogun was so angry that he ordered Asano to commit suicide that the same day. Asano's 47 retainers heard of their master's death and called a meeting to decide what to do. The leader, Yoshio Oishi, prevailed upon them not to do anything to avoid falling into Lord Kira's trap. They dispersed for one year, while Oishi spent the year drinking and galavanting. As a result of his disguised behaviour, the authorities did not take precautionary measures against him. All the retainers misunderstood Oishi and despised him. But when the time was ripe, he led the 47 to surround the castle and took Lord Kira by force and killed him. They finally took their revenge on behalf of their master. This story has become a popular topic for Noh and kabuki as well as the modern cinemas.

I visited the burial grounds of the forty-seven ronin in Tokyo. I did so because they are considered as heroes by most Japanese.

The Japanese are forgetful but they are also revengeful. Their character is rather dualistic.

The Distinction Between Culture and Civilisation

Japanese characteristics are rather controversial. They like to wear new shoes, new clothings, drive new cars and use any new invention which comes out of modern civilisation. Any car that is three years old is considered old to the Japanese. They like anything that is new and fresh — blooming sakura, sashimi and sushi and newly brewed sake and wine. But, they also like the old cultural traditions and have the capacity to preserve them. They copied the Han dynasty sumo wrestling, which was a sport to amuse Chinese Emperors, and converted the sport into the present-day sumo and made it a national sport — the only place in the world where sumo is performed. They imported Tang music from Xian and kept it as Japanised "ga music" in the Imperial Palace. They made the Sung dynasty flowing costumes which once flourished in Xian and other cities in China into the Japanese styled kimono and still wear them today in the streets of Tokyo. They inherited many Chinese cultural traditions, "Japanised" them and turned them into Japanese culture. They have the capacity to preserve old cultures.

They are able to distinguish between culture and civilisation. What is good they will absorb and what is bad, they discard. For instance, the Japanese have borrowed Buddhism from China. They sent their best scholars to China from Tang dynasty times to study Buddhism. Chinese monks were not allowed to be married. Initially, Japanese monks also abided by the rule, but later they found the rule to be impractical. They discovered that it was against human nature to restrain monks from marrying. They discarded the rule of celibacy and today Japanese monks are allowed to marry and more often than not, Japanese monks marry beautiful wives. Some monks even have more than one wife. Japanese monks are also allowed to drink and get drunk. They are able to distinguish the difference between religion and sex.

The Japanese introduced Confucianism to Japan in the early days. During the Tokugawa era, the entire government was run according to Confucian teachings. The Japanese government relied heavily on Confucian concepts and trained its people to abide by Confucian concepts of morality, patriotism, loyalty, filial piety and cultivating the proper relations between Emperor and subject, superior and inferior, father and son, elder brother and younger brother, husband and wife, and friend and friend. Under Confucianism, China was well-known for eunuchs, who played the an important role in Chinese politics from the Han dynasty down to the Ching dynasty. The

Chinese invented the eunuch system to facilitate the Emperors who had many wives and needed someone who could be close to them and yet do no harm to their wives. When the Japanse introduced Confucianism to Japan, they discarded the eunuch system which they found to be useless. In Japan's political history, there has not been a single eunuch.

Chinese ladies bound their feet during the Ching dynasty. The Japanese have not copied this ugly aspect of Chinese culture. The Japanese had used Chinese characters as a base for their hiragana and katakana alphabets, enabling them to spell Japanese words. For centuries, the Chinese have not been successful in inventing alphabets, making the study of Chinese extremely difficult.

The Japanese were quick to copy the virtues of Chinese culture which they found useful. But, in their choice they were selective and took only the good ones and discarded the useless and harmful ones. Herein lies the genius of the Japanese mind.

Japanese Behaviour and Manners

Any visitor who has visited Tokyo for a short period will have witnessed the world's most polite people in action: the elevator girls in most hotels are neatly dressed, wearing a cap and bow hundreds of times daily, cocktail waitresses kneel to take orders, new acquaintances will always smile and do their utmost to make a person happy. Most tourists who have visited Japan will agree that the Japanese are the most polite people they have even seen. But, just ask a foreigner who has lived in Japan for a longer period and someone who has lived with the Japanese, and he will tell you a different story.

Japanese bowing is a myth, and Japanese politeness is only skin deep. Bowing and politeness is only a form which the normal Japanese have to perform to impress the world that they are polite people. The distance between private manners and public behaviour is appallingly wide. On many occasions when I had to travel in packed shinkanshen or second classs trains, my family and I were shoved around unceremoniously. In a book published in 1904, an author wrote: "Enter a second class car on a Japanese railway, and you will find the Japanese race unmasked. From a pleasant, polite, deprecating folk they are changed to unmitigated boors." The situation in Japan proves him right.

I once went to Yokohama for a quick holiday, incognito in a batik shirt. I had to answer nature's call. It was lunchtime and I thought the best thing was to go a restaurant. I wanted to have lunch in a Chinese restaurant and asked the Japanese waiter where the toilet was. Speaking in Japanese, the waiter told me rudely, " Go away, this is not the place for you to release yourself." I had a good look at him and then went to my car. He noticed that I was travelling in a diplomatic car and started to wave to me and bowed. It was too late. I made up my mind to go elsewhere.

On another occasion, I went to the New Otani Hotel for dinner. As I entered the lobby, a row of Japanese were waiting for the arrival of one important leader of the underworld and they were preparing the way for him. They shoved me aside and shouted, "Give way, give way." They almost man-handled me. I shouted back at them in Japanese, "This is a hotel, not your private garden." They saw that I was rather fierce too and left me alone.

From time to time, I came across the same rude behaviour when I travelled incognito in Tokyo streets.

I often watched Japanese TV showing samurai films depicting the evil man who went about bullying people. When the representative of the shogun appeared, he would first bow to him as a courtesy, but soon after he would draw out his sword and try to kill him. The respect he showed to the shogun's representative was only a formality, a courtesy and a myth. In reality, he wanted very much to kill the man he had just bowed to.

A Japanese weekly, Gendai, made a study of how often Japanese bow after they have grown up. For instance, the priests at the Honganji Temple in Tsukihi, Tokyo, bowed an average of 150 times a day. A conductor of a shinkansen bowed an average of 2,132 times because everytime he checked a ticket he bowed. The elevator girls in Ginza department stores bowed the most — a total of 2,560 times a day — because they have to bend from the waist to everyone boarding and leaving the elevator. So important is bowing to department stores that many have bought infernal machines that teach people how to bow. The Gendai went further, and found that women bow 35 percent more frequently than men, and acquaintances begin to bow when they come within about twenty metres of each other. Employees of department stores are taught that customers are their "masters": they should never lose their temper under any circumstance and they should always bow to their customers.

The sight of two older Japanese women exchanging bows can be quite amusing. The Japanese have a word to describe such a scene. They call it a battle of striking the foreheads against the floor, called koto-sen. The inferior either in age, sex or social status normally bows more often and deeper and longer than the superior. Her head is bent way over her eyes which are fixed on the ground, making it difficult for her to see just what the person whom she is bowing to is doing. She is supposed to hold her bow for five or ten seconds longer than the other party, who would not tell her when to straighten up. The rules of bowing are rather complicated. Some foreigners who do not understand the rules might well start bowing to Japanese friends, only to find the other side not responding. The Japanese friends might be standing stiffly erect with their hands extended to be shaken.

Tatemae and Honne

The Japanese normally maintain two faces. One is a face for the ordinary people who are considered outsider or strangers — this face is called "tatemae". When he meets a stranger or anyone who is not close to him, he puts on the tatemae face, a face that is respectable, polite, cool and yet not revealing any feelings. To hide one's feelings is a virtue in Japanese culture. They learnt from the Chinese sage Confucius, who said a "gentleman" is one who would not show either happiness or sorrow on the face. But when a Japanese meets a true friend, someone he can trust and understand, he shows the other side of his face, which is known as "honne" — the true self. He would then be his natural self. He would pour out his feelings, grievances or happiness without any constraint.

It is not easy to get a Japanese to show you his "honne" face. It takes time, especially for a foreigner to understand the real feelings of his Japanese friends. It means going out for long sessions of drinking together for a long period, getting drunk together or sharing a common interest, hobby or entertainment. It is a long process, but it is a process which is necessary for foreigners, particularly businessmen who want to do business with the Japanese. Normally, the Japanese will not do business with strangers. They need to know their partner well before they discuss business. They will dig into the character of your father as well as your grandfather and your character background before they do business with you. If a foreigner only sees his Japanese partners at the conference table, he will only see the tatemae faces. In my stay in Japan, I must admit that I did not see too many "honne" faces. I did not have the time to spend long hours with my Japanese friends in favourite bars and nightclubs.

The "tatemae" face is a myth and the "honne" face the reality.

Nakama and Tanin

The Japanese live in a world of "we" and "they". First of all, they distinguish between Japanese and non-Japanese. Anyone who is not a Japanese is referred to as "gaijin" and all Japanese are treated as "nakama". Then, they differentiate between their own family, friends and acquaintances. All those belonging to the same family are "nakama" and those outside the family "tanin". The schoolmates, classmates and bosom friends are "nakama" and those who are not within the circle are "tanin". The consider those co-members of the same club — be it for sports, calligraphy, painting or poker — as "nakama" and those who are not "tanin". They are always guided by this principle of "nakama" and "tanin" when they meet someone and respond accordingly in the manner of bows, conversation and behaviour. They will play their role accordingly when they meet different people. Thus, foreigners have discovered to their surprise that Japanese who can be very polite with friends and nakama can be extremely rude to tanin. When they meet tanin in trains, buses, subways, they push, elbow and cut into lines but when they see a nakama they suddenly become very polite. There is a Japanese proverb which says: "Tabi no haji wa kakissute", which means "the traveller's shame can be brushed off". Japanese who are away from home where they know very few nakama are tempted to be ruder than they are at home.

Japanese atrocities committed in Asia during the Second World War show the worst of the Japanese attitude towards tanin. The leering men who fly off on sex tours also explain Japanese attitudes outside Japan.

Close Japanese friendships occur with nakama whom they see often. It is among the nakama that friendships are formed and thrive, but without regular doses of contact they wither. Everywhere in the world, in the remotest corner of the earth, you will find a Chinese running either a restaurant business or laundry service. The Chinese have a strong survival instinct and can live without any companion. They are used to solitude and can take hardship well. The Japanese are different. They cannot live without their Japanese nakama, they always live as a group and find it difficult to live alone.

However, everything in the world is subject to changes. Nothing is stagnant. So are the characteristics of the Japanese. When the Emperor Meiji passed away, a large number of his followers committed harakiri to show their samurai spirit. When Emperor Hirohito died, no one commited harakiri. In the past, whenever drastic mistakes were made by a leader, he would slash his waist and have his head chopped off to take the blame. Harakiri was the way out for people who preferred to die than face humiliation and shame. This was what was called "shame culture". Nowadays, Japanese politicians who are found guilty of corruption and big scandals appear in the newspapers, but the persons concerned just bow out of office and say "Sumimasen" (I am sorry). They just retire and continue living. Times have changed and so too has the character of the people.

Every year, millions of Japanese men and women travel overseas. In 1985 4.9 million Japanese travelled overseas; in 1986 it rose to 5.5 million, a 12% increase; in 1987 the number jumped to 6.8 million, a 24% rise; and in 1988 it rose to 8.5 million, another 25% rise. By 1991, it exceeded 10 million. When these Japanese visit foreign countries, they see how other people live and are bound to compare living conditions and the behaviours of others. This naturally has an impact on their psychology and behaviour. Japanese women, partricularly, do not want to miss the boat or rather the plane. They have begun to travel to keep up with the Joneses. Travelling has become fashionable and this seems to be especially so with the Japanese who cannot afford to own land. They spend their savings on travel.

At the same time, many millions of foreigners visit Japan and bring along their manners and behaviour. Millions of Japanese too travel abroad for business or holidays. Their contact with foreigners must have some impact on their behaviour.

A second factor that is causing the younger generation to behave different from their parents, in other words gradually eroding the traditional manners, is the sudden increase in the price of land and shares in Japan. From 1986 onwards, a new asset-rich class of the Japanese emerged. Nomura Research Insitutue defines the new rich as those with the assets of over ¥1 billion, or US$8 million. It reckons there are about 200,000 of these "super rich" Japanese. George Fields, chairman of the Market Research Corporation in Tokyo, thinks that 1987's land price increases have brought about a situation where 2.2 million households with 7 million newly rich have been created. Who are the new rich? First, a small number of elderly people who used to own land in central Tokyo and have sold it and moved to the suburbs to live off the profit. Secondly, a larger group of young and middle-aged people whose parents own property that the offspring will inherit. These new rich are leading a fancier and more visibly opulent life, setting an example to the millions who have only moderate wealth. The effect of their riches is trickling down, affecting what people spend, what they buy and their ambitions. The old austere homogeneity of Japanese life is fast breaking down. Some of the new rich are reminding people what entrepreneurship can bring: they learn to take risks, save less and, who knows, one of these days you too can own a business worth billions of dollars and are able to drive in a Mercedes and live like a Lord.

Take a trip to Alihabara, Tokyo's electronic district with its fashion boutiques, Ginza shopping centres or the crowded ski resorts of the Japan Alps and watch the Japanese spend their money. Go down to Roppongi, the paradise for nightlife, and watch how the youngsters look for entertainment. In the winter, Tokyo streets are full of women and men in fur coats. Japanese skiers wear not only the best gear but also the most expensive. Japan is the second largest market for cut diamonds in the world. On the streets of Akasaka, foreign limousines and Rolls Royces can be seen.

The new rich have brought along a change in consumption habits and they widen the gap between the rich and poor. Gradually, Japan's egalitarian, meritocratic society will become less equal and will be based less on merit. The rich can afford to send their children to the juku schools, choose expensive kindergartens, schools which would lead them to the best universities. The poor are left to fend for themselves in the mad rat race. The new rich does not include the elderly people, whose numbers are fast increasing in Japanese society.

I told Emperor Hirohito once, when he asked me what my impression of Japan was, that Japan had managed to distribute its national wealth fairly equitably and there was not much difference between the rich and poor. That was when I first arrived in Japan. Things have since changed. When I left Japan, I began to see a gap between the rich and poor. What will be the impact of this discrepancy in the future society of Japan nobody can tell.

The Aging Society

Japan is ageing. The country which enjoyed the world's youngest population after the war has become the world's oldest. Japan experienced a baby boom that was even more marked than that in the United States after the war. The relative youth of Japan's population was a big advantage in the 1960s and 1970s compared with Eastern industrial countries. Only between 5 to 8 percent of the population was over 65, which meant that employees had to pay almost no pension contributions or social security taxes to support the elderly. But, Japan's demography has changed since the 1980s and Japan cannot dodge this development, short of an immediate and large rise in the country's birthrate, which is not likely because Japanese nowadays marry rather late. The birthrate has fallen sharply as Japanese have become more affluent and are less worried about producing children to look after them in their old age. The death rate has also fallen as health care improved and affluence permitted better sanitation and diet. The average lifespan of the Japanese is getting longer, having overtaken that in the United States in 1982.

I visited the Tokujima Island in 1985 and had a short conversation with Japan's oldest man, Izumi Shige, who was 120 years old. He had a long white beard, a bald head and long face. His tiny eyes looked blurred but he appeared to be still alert. He offered me a cup of shochew for which he was advertising for longevity. He sat still while I shook hands with him. His palm was warm. He asked me where I came from and I said "Singapore". He had not heard of Singapore and asked: "Is it Shonanto?" I said, "Yes, of course." It was an interesting experience to have a conservation with the world's oldest man. One year later, I read in the newspapers that Izumi had passed away. "What would happen to Japan if the majority of the people were to live to be as old as Izumi?" I thought.

Japan's social security and pension scheme is so rudimentary that not only must the Japanese spend their lives scrimping and saving for retirement, but they have to continue to work in order to survive when they retire. The ageing population will be a burden to the younger generation because they will have to pay heavier taxes and security contributions. In 1985, Japan's total social security costs, including medical expenses, acounted for 14 percent of GNP. By 2010, the government estimates that social costs will have risen to 29 percent of GNP. The Ministry of Health and Welfare believes that by 2010 the elderly will account for a little more than 40 percent of total medical costs, compared with a quarter in 1985.

The powerful MITI are turning their attention to the ageing Japanese population. They are working out a scheme to simultaneously ease the problems of an ageing society and the curent account surplus. They have thought of a scheme called "Silver Columbia Plan" which involves settling aged Japanese outside Japan, in countries such as Australia, Spain, Brazil and other countries which have lower cost of living than Japan. The Spanish coast for example is packed with retired Britons. Following the MITI's scheme, an affiliated agency called the Leisure Development Centre has begun working out feasibility studies with a hundred foreign and domestic companies on developing retirement communities abroad. The Daiwa Securities, the country's second largest securities firm, has already led the way by building a retirement community for its own employees just outside Melbourne. The land prices there compared to Japan are dirt cheap. The largest silver market of all is in financial services. Japanese banks and brokers are breaking into the management of corporate pension funds. However, I was told recently by a Japanese diplomat that the experiment has failed. The Japanese old folk have discovered that they cannot survive outside Japan. They are so used to the Japanese climate and they want to maintain their roots and prefer to die in their homeland.

Japan is fast changing. After the war, Japanese worked hard and saved. They had the spirit to overcome insurmountable difficulties. I have described how and why they managed to turn Japan from a devastated country into an economic giant within 40 years. They have grown rich. That was the era of growth. Today Japan is facing the era of decline. The factors that characterised Japan's rise have changed. Japan is fast becoming a society of consumers, of pleasure seekers, of importers, of investors and speculators. Most Japanese now believe in getting rich through playing shares rather than by manufacturing. What this means economically is that Japan's trade and current account surplus will disappear for a significant period. With them will go Japan's role as an exporter of capital. Japan's ratio of saving has also fallen steadily, from as much as 23 percent in 1975 to 16 percent in 1985. It is quite possible that by 2010, Japan's personal savings ratio could be as low (3–5 percent) as America's is now. The shinjinrui appear keener on consuming, borrowing and living for the present rather than saving, staying out of debt and preparing stoically for the future.

There is a Chinese proverb which says "Survive in crises and difficulties and die in security and comfort". It means that during difficult times of crises, people survive because they have to work hard and tolerate pain. But, when life becomes too comfortable and the environment is secure, people tend to relax and take things easily and they will die in an enviroment of comfort. This happened in almost every dynasty in Chinese as well as Japanese history. One group of revolutionaries gathers support in order to overthrow an unfair ruling regime. When they have succeeded, they relax and enjoy the fruits of their labour. They dissipate and enjoy, and the natural conclusion is that they fall into decay.

My fear is that Japan has become so affluent that the Japanese are starting to think of enjoying life more than working. They have become soft. They have lost their samurai spirit which they had once used to conquer Asia. When the younger generation loses stamina and loses touch with the traditional Japanese characteristics and sense of value, the country will ultimately suffer. Nobody can tell what will happen to Japan 20 years from now if no effort is made to revive the old traditional spirit of Japan.

CHAPTER 7

The Miracle of Japan's Economic Recovery

Before I went to Japan as an ambassador, I had one thing in mind: to find out how Japan, a defeated nation devastated by war, could have transformed itself into an economic giant within the short space of 40 years. After a four year stay in Japan, I came to the conclusion that Japan's success is by no means an accident. It can be called a "miracle", made possible by the collective efforts of a people determined to make a success of the nation's economic recovery. It was the result of the collective sacrifice of millions of Japanese, from the Emperor down to the lowest paid worker; the result of their time, energy and hard work in life. It is the unique Japanese lifestyle and their intricate system of organisation that has contributed to the miracle.

When all the best brains of a country are harnessed and channelled to serve a common purpose — to rebuild the country — something miraculous must happen.

The Korean War in the early 1950s was an important factor in Japan's economic success. The war, particularly the special procurements it required, catalysed full-scale economic growth. From 1951 to 1953, Japan supplied billions of dollars of food goods and services to the United Nations' forces, equivalent to the cost of about half her exports for the period. After the war ended, she continued to supply materials to reconstruct South Korea. As economic output rose, money was ploughed back into capital formation, setting off a virtuous growth circle that survived more or less intact for 20 years. Japan's GNP grew at an average of 8.6% between 1951 and 1955, at 9.1% between 1956 and 1960, at 9.7% between 1960 and 1965, and between 1965 and 1970, at 13.1%. The rate of growth was well above the target set by the government in its five-year plans. It was a well-balanced performance with the private sector formation supplying most of the growth momentum, which started from the textile industry and later developed into heavier and more technologically advanced sectors.

Of course, the Korean War and China's massive military aid to North Korea was a god-sent opportunity to Japan because the Americans needed Japan as the base to help prevent the Chinese Communists from overswarming Korea. The Korean War benefited Japan's economic reconstruction a great deal, as did the Vietnam War later on. But without the spirit of the Japanese people, the effects of the Korean War and the Vietnam War would have been meaningless. It was the Japanese determination to rebuild their country that was paramount.

Whenever I had a chance, I asked my friends in Japan what hopes they had for their children. Invariably, the answer was to send them to one of the prominent universities such as Tokyo University, Keio University or Waseda University. These universities cooperate with the Government and the multi-national corporations to produce and provide them with the best brains.

Parents choose the best kindergartens and schools that will bring their offspring to Todai, Keio, Waseda or any better university. When the children have been accepted by the universities, they reach a plateau. Their futures are made. They may not do too well in the university and I was told some even have plenty of fun during their university days playing the guitar, games or doing whatever they would like to do. But when they graduate, they are sucked into either the government departments or the multi-nationals. The luckier ones join the Gaimusho (the Foreign Affairs Ministry), the Ministry of Trade and Industry, the Ministry of Finance, or Mitsui, Mitsubishi, or other multi-nationals. They have to make up their minds carefully before they pick their jobs, for in Japan lifetime employment is a common practice. A Japanese cannot easily leave his job. Job hopping is rare and the multi-nationals often exchange notes about job hoppers and gang up against them.

Promotion is too slow for many bright employees. In Japan, there is no such thing as a blue-eyed boy who is promoted faster than his colleagues, as there is no such thing as an honours degree. Every graduate is treated equally when he joins the company. For the first six or eight years, a graduate is promoted simultaneously with other fellow graduates strictly according to the length of service. He has to scramble up the corporate ladder. The promotion of employees in Japan is like an escalator ride. No one goes by helicopter. Only near the top of the hierarchy are the less capable employees held back. The management takes pains to scrutinise the performance of each employee, not by their work alone, but also by how they react to their colleagues. The gift of human relations and of working as a team is vital to one's promotion. Those who cannot make the grade when they reach 40 are put aside to idle away their time near a window. They are called "madogiwazoku" (window seat tribe). They are recognised as the incompetents an American company would fire. Since Japanese companies do not normally fire their employees, strictly abiding to the principle of life employment, these "madogiwazoku" are made to sit near the office windows, read newspapers and are ignored. In hardworking Japan, it is a disgrace to be placed in the "madogiwazoku" category.

When all the slower employees are stagnated or made "madogiwazoku", the more efficient ones are carefully chosen, given special tasks to perform and are judged by the management for vertical promotion. In judging the candidates for higher promotion, efficiency alone is not enough. They have to possess leadership qualities able to inspire their subordinates to perform and can get along well with them. Through a natural process, the leaders would emerge and take on higher duties and thus be promoted to the senior management level.

This is the normal pattern in almost every Japanese company. In the winter of life, if one is lucky and smart enough, he becomes President or Chairman of the company and enjoys company privileges — car, company homes, expense accounts in entertainment and travels and, of course, the respect of his subordinates.

I had dinners and lunched with many presidents and chairmen of multinationals when I was the Ambassador to Japan and invariably, the manager who accompanied me was never invited or even dared to join in the dinners and lunches.

Mizushima, the President of Sogo, one of the leading multi-national supermarkets in Japan, once invited me to the headquarters for lunch. We became close friends and had dinners on many occasions. At the first lunch invitation, Mizushima sent a protocol officer to escort me to his office. When the officer sent me home to my residence, he thanked me profusely because it was the first time he had had a glimpse of his god. I asked him what he meant by "god" and he said it was the first time he had met the company president. In Japan, most employees regard their President or Chairman as a god. "You are very lucky to have the privilege of having lunch with my god," he said.

I have experienced similar sentiments expressed by my guides on other occasions, who accompanied me to see the presidents of their multi-national companies.

Mizushima is a President who has a big stake in Sogo and is therefore very well respected by his employees. However, even presidents who are mere salarymen receive equally high respect from their employees.

Salary-earning presidents are by no means rich and powerful in the sense of a Singapore millionaire or an Indonesian cukong (the power behind the throne) who has amassed tremendous wealth and fortune. These presidents get handsome pensions enabling them to retire comfortably. When they retire, they move back to their hometown, usually a two hours ride from Tokyo by shinkansen. Their cars are taken away from them and they have to contend with a humble life in the suburbs.

They are the lucky few who have climbed the corporate ladder. Those who are left behind slog for a miserable life under difficult conditions. They live in the suburbs, travel by shinkansen early in the morning at seven, more often than not pushed from behind by hired students into the passenger carriage because it is usually packed like sardines. Life in the office is stringent and disciplined. Normally, they do not leave the office until their managers or president have left. When they leave the office, they feel shy about going home early for fear of being laughed at by their neighbours as "left-outs" in the office. If they return home earlier than expected, their wives would ask them, "Have you been sacked?" The wives do not encourage them to return early for fear that they will become the laughing stock of their neighbours. They while away their time in pachinkos (a Japanese invention of jackpots), visit their favourite bar girls and get drunk when they return home. The next morning, they get up early to catch the shinkansen again.

Those who miss the train or shinkansen find acommodation in "capsule" hotels which normally charge the tenant only ¥3,000 per night. The "capsule" hotel is a phenomenon in major Japanese cities like Tokyo, and Osaka where there is a great demand for easy and cheap accommodation by salarymen who cannot afford to go to more expensive hotels. I visited some of them in Tokyo and Osaka. The "capsule" hotel consists of many lanes of one square metre dimension, providing accommodation for ten to twenty cubicles just wide enough for a human being "to slide" in and sleep for the night. Each cubicle is provided with a television and a sliding door if he wishes to have privacy. There is a large enough furo (bath) with hot water facility to bathe and relax. There is also a common room for relaxation and a restaurant for cheap food.

I would imagine that the tenant would feel miserable with the little space at his disposal. But that is the best way out for salarymen who miss the train and cannot afford a taxi to go home. At least he has a place to stay overnight with all the necesary facilities. This sort of "capsule" hotel was the product of the ingenius Japanese mind who solved the urgent housing problem for salarymen. It was an invented after the Second World War.

In Japan, life is nothing but a big sacrifice. The presidents down to the ordinary salaryman spend their whole life and energy in enriching the companies to which they are loyal. The companies get richer and richer through their efforts, but they continue to lead their miserable lives.

I say miserable because almost every one of the Japanese salarymen does not have comfortable living accommodation. They live in "rabbit hutches", small cubicles with the whole family squeezing together. Husbands and wives cannot afford privacy. Most of them have no modern sanitation. In 1983, only 57.9 percent of Japanese houses had flush toilets. This is one of the reasons why youngsters prefer to spend their time in Harajuku on Sundays — a place where people young and old can do whatever they like, either singing or dancing, mostly in groups. In Tokyo, I hardly see any community centres like those in Singapore where the young and old can let off steam and entertain or educate themselves. They take to the streets and that is why Tokyo streets are always crowded.

I once met the adviser of Ajinomoto, a 70-year-old Japanese who has climbed to the top position of the company and who loves antiques. He was introduced to me by a famous Chinese painter Fan Chen, the artist who had exiled himself in Paris. At a dinner, Fan Chen suddenly asked me whether I would like to visit the home of this Japanese gentleman to see his collection of antique paintings and calligraphy. Of course I was interested, for it was a rare occasion for a foreigner to visit the home of a Japanese. The Japanese adviser was taken by surprise and agreed that I should visit his home. That same evening, I received a telephone call from his secretary informing me that the Japanese adviser was not ready to receive me because I was an ambassador. The secretary said the antique calligraphy could be arranged to be brought to my embassy for my appreciation. The next day, he came personally to the embassy with his precious collection and apologised for not inviting me to his home.

If the adviser of a big company feels ashamed to invite me to his house, then there is little chance for me to visit a Japanese home, I thought. Then, another close friend of mine who was stationed in Singapore for several years in the Japanese Embassy and who had risen to the rank of Director General of American Affairs also invited me to his home for dinner. I had given him one of my paintings and he wanted me to see where he had hung the painting. I naturally accepted. A day before the dinner, he suddenly rang up and apologised that he could not make it. He did not give an alternate date and we never had dinner before I left Japan.

Perhaps he thought it over and felt embarrassed to invite me to his little home.

The only home I visited in Tokyo belonged to the President of Kajima Corporation, the biggest construction company in Japan with branches all over the world. It was a grand mansion with a waterfall and a small pond with Japanese carp. It was three storeys high and the internal furnishing was superb. But the total area of land space was smaller than my own home in Singapore. This was the first and only home I visited in Tokyo during my stay in Japan. I got acquainted with Kajima because his corporation had built the Singapore Embassy. Being a golfer, he often invited Asean ambassadors for golf and ended our game with a dinner at his home. Kajima was a thin and short person who spoke good English and was quite charming.

I also visited and stayed overnight at the home of Takahashi, a multi-millionaire president of a ball-bearing company, in Karuizawa, a holiday resort about four hours drive from Tokyo. It was a really magnificent villa, the grandest bungalow I saw in Japan. It was autumn and red maple leaves in the backyard made the house even more beautiful. Takahashi normally used a helicopter to transport his guest to the villa, but I preferred to travel by car.

I had no chance of visiting the homes of the middle class and poorer population. But I had an idea of how they lived because I visited the home of a lady artist from China who rented a little cubicle in Tokyo. Even that cubicle was considered comfortable compared to those dwelt in by most Japanese salarymen.

Rabbit Hutches

Several years ago, the European Community published a report attributing Japan's phenomenal economic growth rate to the workaholic Japanese and their low-standard housing which Westerners would regard as little more than rabbit hutches. The Japanese often call their homes "humble burrows" or "ramshackle cottages". The phrase "rabbit hutch" in the context of Japanese housing is attributed to Basil Hall Chamberlain, one of the foremost Western interpreters of things Japanese, who was employed by the Japanese Government in the early years of Meiji. In his book *Things Japanese*, published in 1890, the English educator and teacher of Japanese noted that since 1870 the Japanese had abandoned their own architectural style in favour of a foreign style, and had started building ferroconcrete structures and houses in the style of rabbit hutches and locker rooms for bathers.

One of the major reasons why Japan was able to recover so fast from the ruins of war was the collective sacrifice of millions of salarymen — from the president downwards to the company employees — who worked day and night under difficult conditions, all for the sake of the company and not to enrich themselves. At the end of the day, their energies were drained off, and they retired with a minimum comfort and a sense of satisfaction that they had done something for the nation.

Group Commitment

Japan's unique social system of ably and effectively tapping the brains and harnessing the energy of their human resources for the benefit of the nation is, I think, one of the main factors that contributed to Japan's miraculous achievement after the war. For centuries, the Japanese had developed a sense of group belonging. Group ties can be so close that members feel collective responsibility for each other's actions. Loyalty to the group and a willingness to submit to its demands are thus key virtues in Japanese society. It is the values of the group rather than abstract principles that serve as the guiding principle for many Japanese.

The land-intensive method of producing rice involved backbreaking and never-ending labour and plenty of willing hands. Going it alone was out of the question. So villagers were compelled to get along with their neighbours. Individual farmers could survive the uncertainties of the weather, meet the heavy burden of the samurai or daimyo's taxes and deal with other emergencies only if they submerged themselves into a group and put the welfare of the community before their individual desires. A sense of a village's vulnerability to unpredictable outside forces was prevalent.

This sense of group commitment grew into the Japanese psyche as they isolated themselves from the outside world for nearly 300 years during the Tokugawa Shogunate. Tokugawa banned all contacts with foreigners (except for a few Dutch traders on Nagasaki's small island of Nishima) on penalty of death when they found the spread of Christianity threatening the Japanese way of life.

After 300 years of isolation, the Japanese discovered that they were weak and backward when the American Commodore Perry and his black ship bombarded Japan. They discovered that they had to learn from the West the modern technology that enabled them to bombard Japan. After the Meiji Restoration, the Japanese began to embrace everything Western from scientific advancement to style of living, and at the same time they began to ignore Eastern culture, especially things Chinese. They coined a slogan "Forget the East, learn from the West". However, although they modernised, they did not forget that they were Japanese and never gave up the sense of group commitment.

It is this spirit of group commitment that makes the Japanese work for a company for life. They climb from the bottom of the ladder, devoting their whole energy and time to the interest and benefit of the company. Very few go to the top. Even the few who get to the top and who became chairmen or presidents remain "salarymen". When they retire, they get large gratuities and live comfortably, but they are by no means rich in the Southeast sense. In Southeast Asia, when a person is president or chairman of a powerful company, he really owns the company and lives a luxurious life even after his retirement. He owns many prestigious properties, luxurious bungalows and cars even after he retires.

It is this spirit of sacrifice, I think, that makes Japan's economy tick and made the country overcome her difficulties and turned Japan into an economic miracle.

In Asian society, everybody lives for himself and his family. Everyone thinks of becoming rich. In Singapore, for instance, an intelligent youth would join a company, learn whatever he could from his boss and if he masters the trade, set up a rival stall or shop in front of his former boss. Knowing this trend, his boss would not train him wholeheartedly and his company would not make quick progress. In Japan, every employee thinks of the company first and has cultivated the habit of trying to make his company the best in Japan, if not the world. His boss is his "god" and an employee will always obey him.

Group loyalty is evident and prevalent in every walk of life in Japan. The Japanese seem to focus their lives around one central group, whether it is a political party, university, a commercial department store, an office or a unity in a factory. Japanese who are not part of a tight group at work may become active in one of Japan's religious groups, or join a local consumer union or political association. The members of a group are a person's nakama, or buddies, and can easily become more important than the individual profession. The values of the group become the individual's values, and a large part of his leisure time is spent in the company of colleagues or other group members.

When a worker joins a company, he is first trained to become a member of the family before he can function effectively. The company does not fire an employee because he is seen as part of a functional group. The family character of Japanese organisations closely resembles that of parent and child.

The most extreme form of surrogate family group identity is found in the underworld gangs, whose members pride themselves in being the only modern Japanese to keep alive the spirit of samurai. Crime bosses are called oyabun (parent figure) and their henchmen are kobun (children figure). Kobun are supposed to be ready to lay down their lives for their oyabun or to mutilate themselves in atonement for any violation of the code of loyalty.

When former Prime Minister Tanaka was investigated for suspected involvement in the Lockheed affair, his chauffeur committed suicide rather than admit to investigators where he had driven the boss on certain crucial days.

The Pacific War was the most terrifying manifestation of Japan's sense of group feeling and interest and sense of destiny, when the people banded together against the outside world. The nation was one big underworld gang, with the Emperor as its oyabun. Millions of kobun died for their oyabun, and none so proudly and with a sense of fulfilment as the kamikaze pilots.

One author fancifully describes the Japanese society as a community of plants compared to western society which he describes as a community of animals. Plants grow up harmoniously with each other, look the same when they become a forest and do not clash with each other. Animals develop individuality as they grow. They roam about when they can run and fight each other and develop a strong sense of self.

In Japan, the baby is treated as an independent organism that must be drawn into the bosom of the family in an increasingly dependent way in order for it to mature. In America, the baby is seen as an independent creature that must be taught to stand alone. In Japanese classes, when a question is asked, one seldom sees any single smart kid stretching his neck out to show his cleverness, whereas in an American class, everyone would be clamouring to give his own answers. I once went to the University of Tokyo to give a lecture together with a Turkish professor. When we finished our lectures, one student stood up and asked me a question, "How can Japan be internationalised quickly?" I said, "It is quite simple if you really want to do it. Just make all Japanese pupils study English from primary one instead of beginning their studies of English in the secondary classes." Nobody argued with me on my statement. The Turkish professor, however, told me privately that it was not possible for Japan to teach English to primary students because that would soon Anglicise the whole population.

He said that if many Japanese were English educated, they would think of migrating to the West instead of doing the routine and tough work of novices in difficult conditions under Japanese management and supervision. For instance, an ordinary cook in a Japanese restaurant would have to undergo five years of washing dishes behind the kitchen or cutting vegetables and meat before he could emerge from the kitchen to serve the customers. They take on these jobs because they do not speak English. If they could speak good English, they would be thinking of migrating to America and other Western countries. It is because of the determination of the Japanese elite to prevent Japan from being too westernised that they do not encourage the Japanese to learn English at too young an age.

Japanese children often sleep in the same bed as their parents until they reach the age of five or six. When they get their beds they continue to sleep in the same room as their parents until puberty. Japan's housing scarcity and cramped living conditions was partly responsible for this habit. But, the Japanese feel cruel at leaving their children alone and are shocked to know that American mothers put their infants to bed in little rooms of their own.

Japanese parents discipline their children when they do wrong by excluding them from family activities rather than by punishing them physically. This practice of ostracising the child is "mura hachibu". In rural Japan, service to the village was enforced by the terrible threat of mura hachibu. The law of the land took care of villagers guilty of crimes such as theft, rape, or arson, and the village itself disciplined those who broke the law by doing a mura hachibu on them. That would mean the whole community would ostracise the guilty family who had failed to show loyalty to the group. It did not matter if only one member of the family was guilty. The whole family would suffer as a result of the guilt of one family member. Victims of mura hachibu, who had only the slimmest chance of being accepted into another community, often committed suicide. All these practices encourage group ties rather than a strong sense of individuality.

In a Japanese house, there is no private area for private leisure where one can shut himself off from the rest of the family. This is because Japanese houses are too small and partly because it has never been the habit of Japanese to want to meditate alone and cut himself off from the family. Privacy is a luxury in a Japanese family. A Japanese is always attached to a group, whether in feeling or thought.

The Japanese normally do not express their own individual thoughts, they always like to consult their group for an opinion before they express a thought or feeling.

The Turkish professor told me a story about his personal experience of teaching in Japan. It was one extremely hot summer day inside a Japanese classroom and he asked the pupils whether they would like to go outside the classroom, where it was cooler, to continue their lessons. There was complete silence in the room and suddenly the leader of the class stood up and asked for time to decide. The pupils got into a meeting and later came out with a consensus expressed by the same leader that they agreed to accept the professor's suggestion. This is typical of Japanese behaviour. It is ingrained in the Japanese character. From a very young age, Japanese are taught to obey the leader and not to stick their necks out to show their individual "true colours". There is a well-known proverb which says: "The nail that sticks out will be pounded down" (Deru kugi wa utareru). At home and in school, Japanese children are taught to fit in rather than stand out, and the habit of intellectual submission that they learn as students follows them into adulthood.

Generally, the Japanese have no private opinions, they only have group opinions. At a company meeting with foreigners, the Japanese are busy writing down what is spoken and only the leader will speak. Even the leader would not commit the company to a decision without returning home to consult the various department heads before a final decision is made. This sense of group supremacy makes decision-making a lengthy process. It took the biggest car manufacturer, Toyota, five years to decide whether or not to invest in the US. Often, the Japanese seem to prefer the company of their own kind and feel more at home when other Japanese are around. Japanese travel in groups wherever they go throughout the world. One can easily distinguish Japanese and non-Japanese tourists in international airports or places of interest in international travel. The Japanese group is always led by a flag-carrying guide with a whistle and they line up to take orders from the guide. Tourist brochures often show beaches crowded with bathers and mountains thronged with hikers. The press of humanity is reassuring to Japanese vacationers who might otherwise feel lonely. There are very few Japanese who would travel alone or with their families to seek quiet pleasure and places of private meditation. Japanese would feel uneasy without a crush of neighbours.

Japanese children are taught from a young age in school to conform rather than innovate. Every time I passed a street, I saw the same dull pattern of uniform worn by school children — usually black and blue for girls. It is seldom colourful like the uniforms worn by Singaporean school children. Children carry their books in identical book bags and eat lunch out of identical lunch boxes. There are still many schools that require nafuka (name tags) that specify their grades and names. Until recently, lefthanded schoolchildren in Japan were compelled to write with their right hand, so as to conform to the others. There is no double promotion in Japanese schools. No matter how bright or stupid they are, students never skip grades and are never held back. The group stays together. Children in the same grade cannot even be graded out in different classes according to ability. In universities, there is no such thing as an honours degree, everyone is treated as the same with an ordinary degree. Nobody excels and nobody is a blue-eyed boy. Although schoolchildren in Japan experience an examination hell when they compete to get into a university, once they get in, they have a long holiday and do whatever they like to do. Many of them never care to study for the university — is not the place to train them. They get their first training when they leave the university and join a multi-national company. There is no elitism in Japan. The country does not encourage the people to develop "helicopter brains" — meaning elite brains that can see events and things from the top of a helicopter.

Japanese conventional wisdom conspires to discourage Japanese from thinking for themselves. The Japanese are usually careful to take their cue from the crowd before they make a move of their own. When I was invited by the boss of a multi-national to have lunch or dinner, I observed that nearly every subordinate who accompanied the party would follow what his boss ordered. They dared not order food or drinks different from their boss. Japan is a nation where everybody believes there is a "right way" of doing things: a way to greet a Minister or an ordinary stranger; drinking a cup of tea during a tea ceremony; tying a belt of a kimono; arranging for teppanyaki; or swinging a baseball bat or stamping ones feet in sumo wrestling. Form comes first and function comes later. Much of Japanese teaching, especially in the traditional arts, is concerned almost exclusively with form. I once attended a lesson given by a famous calligrapher in Tokyo. The teacher wanted his pupils to copy every stroke according to his style. Students are not allowed to innovate. They have to copy. Anyone who had the guts to innovate would be thrown out of the class. The same applies to flower arrangement "ikebana" or schools of the tea ceremony. Every moment is strictly regulated and defined. Japanese society cannot function until every member of the group acts like a virtual blood relation. They can only survive as a group. They believe in "wa", meaning harmony. Wa represents the absence of conflict. It is love of consensus and a dislike of individuality. In most Japanese companies, the word "wa" is displayed prominently in the office. Language tells us a great deal about the importance of "wa". Japanese food is called "washoku", Japanese cloths "wafoku". The

Japanese nation itself is called the land of "Wa". The Japanese have succeeded in the miracle recovery of its war-torn economy because of this group spirit and the spirit of "wa". They have chosen to work together as one people, one heart, just as they had gone to war with one heart. The spirit lies behind the old ichi-oku expressions. Ichi-oku means "100 million", which was the population of Japan before the war. The pre-war slogan "Ichi-oku Isshin" means "100 million people with one heart" or perhaps "100 million hearts beating as one" — a poetic expression for national unanimity. The disturbing wartime expression "ichioku-gyokusai" (100 million crushed gems) meant Gotterdammerung in the Pacific (100 million glorious deaths). The same spirit which brought them to war was used by the Japanese to reconstruct their economically and spiritually devastated country.

The Samurai Spirit

The second important factor in the Japanese character which spurred Japan into rapid economic recovery is the traditional spirit of Bushido, commonly known as the "samurai spirit".

Literally, samurai means "one who serves". Also known as bushi (military gentry), the term also designates the warrior elite of pre-modern Japan that emerged in Japan's early history and became the real ruling class of the country from late 12th century until Japan's entry into the modern period with the Meiji Restoration of 1868. The privileged status of the samurai class was dissolved in the mid 1870s, but former samurai were by then firmly established as leaders in government and other sectors of a modernising Japan.

The Samurai originated from the early 930s, when warring clans in the Kanto region created disturbances and formed themselves into a ruling elite in both central and provincial areas throughout the country during the Heian Period (794–1185). The most fundamental reason for the rise of the samurai class was the failure of the central government in Kyoto, controlled by courtiers in the service of the Emperor, to maintain adequate administration of the provinces. Under such circumstances, it was inevitable that a military class would grow and thrive in the provinces. The first bushidan (organisation of bushi) were little more than family organisations of military units recruited from the same clans. These bushidan were maintained only so long as necessary to complete specific military campaigns. When campaigns ended, they returned to the management of their farming lands. By the

11th century, bushidan had developed into more permanent, feudal-like entities structured on lord-vassal ties between fighting men who were not necessarily connected by blood.

Leadership of the samurai class came to be assumed chiefly by men who were descendants of the Imperial family. Since Emperors were polygamous, they produced large numbers of offspring. It became the practice from the early Heian period to deprive of status the surplus members of the Imperial family and to give them surnames of either Taira or Minamoto. There was a struggle for power between the Taira (Heike) and Minamoto (Genji) which became immortalised in Japan's famous stories of "Genji and Heike". These were the serious conflicts known as the Earlier Nine Years War and the Later Three Years War, which actually spanned nearly half a century (1051–87). These conflicts ushered in an age of samurai dominance that was to last until modern times. The main victor in the Taira–Minamoto war was Minamoto No Yoritomo, who in 1192 established the true warrior government in Japanese history, the Kamakura Shogunate (1192–1333). The founding of the Kamakura Shogunate marked the beginning of the medieval age of Japanese history which concerned mainly the affairs of the samurai class. In 1338, the Muromachi Shogunate overthrew the Kamakura regime and Japan's feudal period began. Peasants were bound as serfs to the land and paid harvest rent to samurai, who held superior proprietary rights in the form of fiefs. The samurai themselves were organised into lord-vassal hierarchies and the values that governed their behaviour were military and feudal: honour, loyalty and manly demeanour, duty and self-effacing service for the good and the collective unit, whether family or military.

During the first half of the 16th century, a new class of samurai hegemonies called Daimyo arose and established territorial domains throughout Japan. Around the mid-century a competition began among the leading daimyo to unify the entire country. Unification was finally achieved by three successive leaders, Oda Nobunaga (1534–82), Toyotomi Hideyoshi (1537–98) and Tokugawa Ieyasu (1543–1616). These daimyos needed ever larger and more permanently organised armies. They recruited them from the peasantry. When the Portuguese arrived in Japan, Western-style rifles and later cannons were used by those daimyo to fight their enemies.

A fundamental policy of the Tokugawa shogunate that contributed to its longevity as a government was its isolationist policy of cutting Japan off from outside influence. Tokugawa was so afraid of the spread of Christianity that he shut the doors of Japan to the world outside and reduced it to little more than a limited trade with the Dutch and Chinese at Nagasaki. Then, in 1853, a squadron of ships commanded by Commodore Matthew

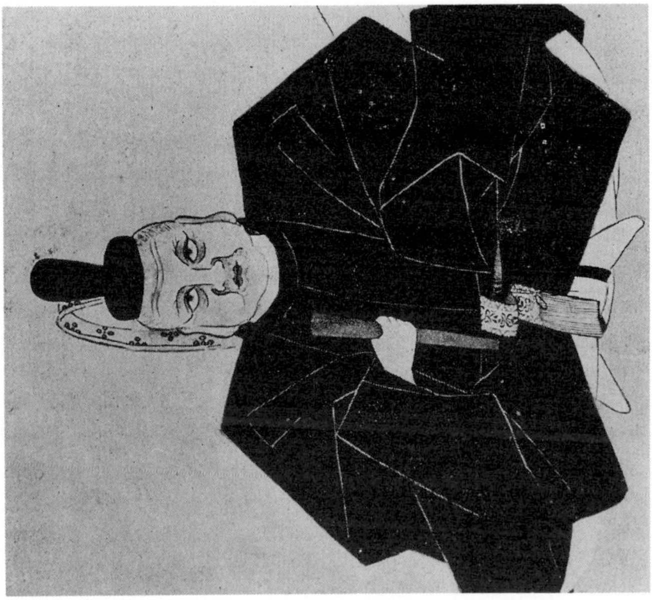

A sketch of Tokugawa Ieyasu (1543–1616).

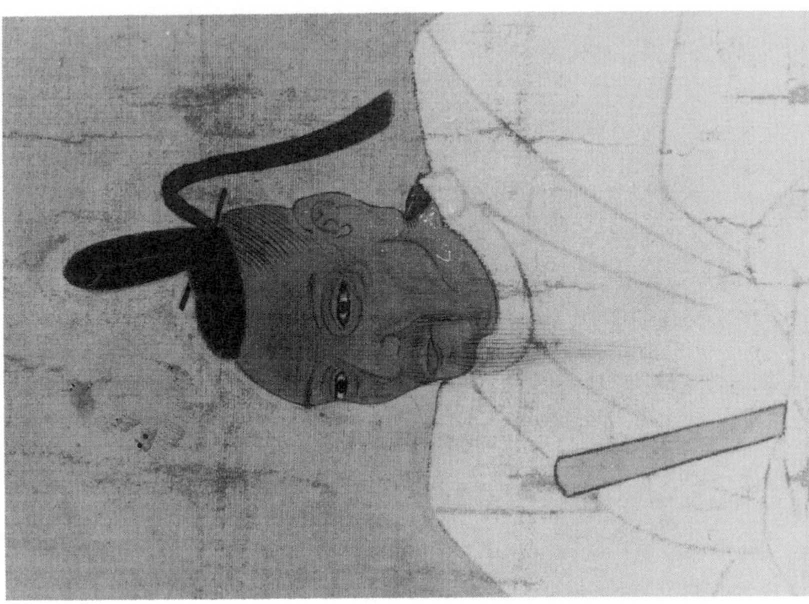

A sketch of Toyotomi Hideyoshi (1537–1598).

Perry of the United States pounded heavy cannons onto Nagasaki and brought the Tokugawa regime to an end.

The Meiji Restoration leaders stripped the samurai class of their privileges. The leaders who were themselves samurais realised with increasing conviction that there was no place for the privileged samurai status in a new Japan. They could ill afford continued payment of the hereditary samurai stipends. They also realised that continuance of the samurais elite warrior status was incompatible with the building of a modern conscript army. The Meiji period was an example of how the centuries-old warrior status was able to lead Japan into the mainstream of the modern world. The political leaders of the Meiji period changed the pattern of government, but they did not forget the spirit of the samurai.

Before World War II, almost every Japanese read Magakure (In The Shadow Of Leaves), properly titled Hagakure Kikigaki (Notes Of What Was Heard In The Shadow of Leaves). A manual for samurai, it consisted of some 1,300 short anecdotes and reflections completed in 1716. It is considered one of the classics on Bushido (The Way of the Samurai). This book, a bible for every Japanese, was dictated by Taishiro Tsunetomo in the late 17th century after Tokugawa Ieyasu had seized control of the whole of Japan following the turmoil of civil war. At the time of his lord's death, Yamamoto was thwarted in his desire to follow his lord by committing seppuku (harakiri) because this practice had been outlawed. Instead, he entered the priesthood to spend the remainder of his life in prayer for the repose of his lord Mitsushige's soul. He started to ponder over the duties of the samurai and took seven years to finish the Hagakure. In this book, Hagakure offers a panorama of do's and don'ts for samurais. It teaches the guiding concept "to die" as the very basis of samurai life. It is the philosophy of death. Basically, this philosophy applies to the samurai's ethic of shame.

The work's often-quoted first line "Bushido is a way of dying" expresses the theme that is elaborated upon throughout the work. It said that only a samurai prepared and willing to die at any moment can devote himself fully to his lord. This devotion is conceived of as an emotional bond. The desire to serve one's lord, Yamamoto declares, should be like the desire to please a lover — a homosexual lover. Indeed, the proper conduct of a homosexual relationship is given detailed attention, as well as conduct between husband and wife, between antagonists, and between fellow samurais.

According to the code of samurai, it is better to die than to live in shame. It was never the style of the samurai to mention money. There were sayings like "A hawk may be starving but he won't touch corn" and "The samurai may have eaten nothing but he uses his toothpick" to illustrate a samurai's feeling. A samurai prefers to go hungry than to ask for a bowl of rice.

Yamamoto teaches one to polish up, through everyday training, mental attitude for the time of crucial need. He perceives this world as "empty uncertain and floating" — contrary to the Confucian stand of existentialism. His philosophy is that man should live his life doing whatever he likes to do, and the greatest misfortune of a man of action is to fail to die after the final chapter of his accomplishments. In Japan, it is not uncommon to find a loving couple jointly committing suicide at the height of their romance. These incidences happen quite frequently in the beautiful surroundings of Mount Nikko. The couple normally fear that if they drag on with their romance, something sour might occur that might destroy the beauty of their romance.

The leaders and any other voluntary samurais who triggered the Meiji Restoration of 1868 were considered heroes who underwent the "revolved action bordering on insanity thereby answering the call of Hagakure".

It was this spirit of Bushido that inspired the Japanese to conquer China, to bomb Pearl Harbour and to march downwards into Southeast Asia. It was again this spirit that brought about the miraculous economic recovery from the defeated ashes of conquered Japan into a triumphant economic giant. It is the same spirit that is driving the Japanese to aim at conquering the world economically. Every Japanese worker would like to see his company achieve pre-eminence and collectively enable Japan to become the world's number one economic power. The devotion of the Japanese workers and salarymen to their companies springs from this samurai spirit. They have an intense pride in seeing Japan triumph over other nations, particularly the Western countries, in economic competition. Behind most Japanese minds is the determination to take revenge against the United States for having dropped the atom bombs in Hiroshima and Nagasaki. They want to show the world that the Japanese are a race to be reckoned with.

It was also this samaurai spirit that inspired several leading Japanese companies to engage in espionage to steal scientific technology from Western countries, paying high prices for them. Some were caught. Japan's leading multi-national electronic company, Toshiba, was caught selling US defence technology to The Soviet Union in 1986 and was punished by the Cocom (an organisation preventing American high technology from being exported to Communist countries). Under Cocom rulings, such advanced technology was banned from export to Communist countries. But, Toshiba did it in order to gain monetary profit. The President of the company, Saba, had to resign to take the blame. But, he is still very much involved with the company from behind the scenes. According to another source, another

Japanese multi-national, Hitachi, also fell into the trap of the CIA by trying to steal IBM technology by bribing officials.

The Japanese are ruthless and have no scruples so long as what they do will benefit their country.

Attitude Towards Work

One other important ingredient in Japan's success story is the Japanese attitude towards work. The individual worker brings to his job a set of attitudes and expectations that makes him the perfect company man. The cliches about the Japanese as workaholics have caught on for a reason. The Japanese probably love their companies more and work harder at their jobs than any other people on earth.

There is an established tradition among Japanese, be they an ordinary worker, a cook, a sweeper or a manager, to find ways and means of constantly improving on their jobs. This perfectionist tendency is found in every profession. They do this as a matter of habit and are not inspired by any material motives. In recent years for instance, the Toyota Motor Company's 48,000 employees came up with more than a million formal suggestions to improve quality or lower costs — an average of 27 suggestions per employee. The management accepted most of the suggestions and saved millions of dollars. In every company there are Quality Control Circles (QC), which was in fact an American invention that took root in Japan. Workers formed QCs and met regularly to figure out ways to do the job better. QC circles develop team spirit and pride in workmanship.

It is this natural habit to improve on their work that enables Japan to develop the "state of the art" technology on the shop floor. In no other country can production engineers so quickly take the very latest technology breakthroughs and build them into inexpensive consumer products. None can seriously compete with Japanese manufacturers of quartz watches, electronic cameras, stereo video equipment or pocket calculators. Although the basic technology for all these products came from the West, in some other areas Japanese technicians are already catching up.

I used to watch the Japanese at work. If it is in a restaurant, I find the cook preparing the food with complete devotion as if to make sure his customers will enjoy the things he cooks. He takes great pride in his work. Underneath the pyramid-shaped white cap, his eyes concentrate on the food he is cooking with exact precision in style and timing. It is not easy for him to appear before the customers. He will have spent five years qualifying to be exposed to the public. He is prepared to cook throughout his whole life, hoping that one day when he saves enough money, he will open his own restaurant.

I watched the chauffeur of an ambassador dusting the car with a hand brush. He took his job as seriously as a samurai carrying a sword. In the elevators of every department stall, the lift girls bow lowly at the customers, and say "Ohayo gozaimasu" and smile at them. They take their jobs seriously and bow ceremoniously. Sales girls would say "Arigato gozaimasu" (thank you) to customers even if they go in only to window shop.

Japanese workers have the lowest rate of absenteeism in the world. They apply themselves to their jobs with touching enthusiasm. Tokyo garbage men scour and shine their trucks every morning before they start work. QC circles celebrate their success by throwing up their arms to shout "Banzai" (Long Live). Workers stand right by their machines, bobbing and bending in unison to piped-music during their ten minutes break of calisthenics. After that they are back to work.

A generation ago, Japanese went into the battlefield shouting "glory to the Emperor". Now, the workers of Nissho-iwai spirit proclaim "glory to the company". A few years ago, a director of Nissho-iwai, a major trading company which was involved in the Lockheed bribery scandal, leaped to his death from the top of the corporate headquarters. He ended his suicide note with the words "Long live Nissho-iwai".

Japan has recovered so fast economically because all Japanese workers work hard and take the right work attitude. They do this for a number of reasons that are unique to Japan. They are conscious of the vulnerability of their rocky island without natural resources. They feel the threat of natural disaster. They have suffered the horror of nuclear war and they live in fear of trade war. All these problems have been pumped into their consciousness by daily lectures by their superiors. They live or die as a group. This sense of fragility imparts a special energy to their efforts to subdue all problems not beyond human control.

Japan has survived and is becoming prosperous because most Japanese are willing to submerge their own interests in their companies, to find happiness not as individuals but as a group.

Meritocracy in Japanese Corporate Culture

Another important factor in Japanese culture that helped Japan's rapid economic recovery was the structure of corporate culture. The Japanese are able to distinguish between management and ownership. Only those with ability are allowed to manage. They go for brains. Only the best can climb to the top and become presidents and chairmen. They are just salarymen but they hold the power of management. When they retire, they are not rich for they do not inherit the wealth of the company. The descendants or offsprings of the owners may inherit the wealth of the company but if they are not smart enough, they do not run the day-to-day administration.

The Chinese and Koreans are more clan-centred. The clan functions not only as a social unit but also as an economic unit, seeking to provide a livelihood for all of its members. In Chinese and some Korean companies, the owners usually appoint their sons or relatives to take over the running of the company despite the fact that they are unsuitable for the job. A Chinese company is usually run by members of the same family. Some of the useless members of the family occupy certain positions and are paid for doing nothing. In Japan, this is not the case. Ownership and management are completely divided. Japan's departure from a clan-centred society began in as early as the 13th century. In Japan, the philosophy is that people with ability will get ahead. There is a tremendous amount of vertical mobility in Japanese society. A person may begin at the bottom rung of the organisation, but if he proves himself capable, he can quickly rise to the top and become a jitsu-ryokusha (man of influence). Foreigners have often been misled by the appearance of non-competitive harmony, but meritocracy has been a Japanese tradition for centuries.

From the 13th century, some of the legal foundation for Japanese individualism were laid down. Thereafter, the Edo Period (1603–1868) and Meiji Era (1868–1912) and finally the present day individualism and pragmatism shaped Japanese corporate culture. In 1232, the Kamakura shogunate established a new law code entitled Goseibai Shikimoku (The Formula for Adjudication) which became the foundation for a whole system of laws called Busho (warrior-house law). At first, this applied only to the warrior class, but by the 15th century, it applied to the common people as well. The Godebai Shikimoku included a unique law in which the order of inheritance could be determined on the basis of the heirs' abilities. To prevent people of little ability from inheriting and subsequently squandering the family assets, the father determined who was best able to manage the family assets and wrote a letter of transfer specifically for that individual. The government recognised only this letter of transfer as proof of the right of inheritance. This policy remained unchanged until the dawn of the Meiji era. If a father had no sons capable enough to handle the estate, then a daughter would inherit the property with the condition that she marry and her husband be adopted as son and heir. In Japan, it is still true that both sons-in-law and daughters-in-law are adopted into the family. Having the option to adopt either person was a natural part of Japanese culture. When the son-in-law is adopted, he drops his own family name and assumes his wife's family name. Former Prime Minister Sato and Nobuuke Kishi, for example, were blood brothers but their family names remained different because Kishi was adopted into his wife's family. In the Edo period, Osaka was the economic and commercial centre of Japan. Among the Osaka business families, it was a tradition that the eldest daughter inherit the company and marry the ablest man in the company to carry on the family business. In this case, it was the wife who inherited the property and the husband inherited the family name. The wife had the property rights and the husband had the managerial rights — an early example of the separation of ownership and management.

In the Japanese tradition, the inheritance took place before the parents died. This practice enabled the parents to select the most capable heirs. It also freed them from their social obligations and enabled them to operate behind the scenes. Before a person retired, he evaluated all his sons to see who was most capable of handling the inheritance. To prevent the other sons from interfering, he even disinherited them or declared them incompetent. He can disinherit a son after he has inherited titular leadership. This is a decidedly merit-centred orientation. The most capable person is put in charge, even if that means the disinheritence of a son.

Many people have said that Japan is a man's country and that the husband has (or traditionally had) absolute authority over the wives and children. But in cases where the husband's only rights are to the family name and his wife owns the property and other assets, his authority is limited indeed. The popular perception is that women and nylon stockings have gotten much stronger since the end of the war. While this may hold for stockings, women were not such weaklings, even in the Edo period. For instance, there was a rule that rich wives who sued for divorce were legally bound to forfeit their wealth. As a result, they found ways to make their husbands angry so that the men filed for divorce, even though this meant losing access to their wives' wealth. The merchant tradition, in which the husband had the right to manage his wife's money but not to own it, differed from the samurai tradition in which the wife handled the money. Japanese wage-earners follow the samurai tradition in that their wives manage all of their hard-earned money. This was the influence by Confucianism, which considered rice honourable and valuable but saw money as unclean. Men earn money through their work but are not to handle that unclean money.

When European methods of forming companies were first introduced, Japanese organisations adopted them but at the same time held onto their deep-rooted traditions. This is one of the areas where foreign businessmen working with Japanese companies get confused. The Japanese companies look Western, but inside they are very Japanese. In other words, their similarity to Western companies is a myth and in reality they are very much Japanese in their content and approach.

The roots for most of these traditions go back at least as far as the 13th century legal reforms, with their emphasis on the nuclear family rather than the extended family. Since then, the notion of extended family or clan has gradually died out, and any organisation above the nuclear family had to be made artificially. First and foremost, such an artificial organisation is called Ikki, literally a plan, but meaning a contract. This is very different from the Western concept of contract. It is the establishment of a collective rule, in which the members of the collective are like family members. When Ikki were formed, one of the procedures involved was to draw a circle at the bottom of the contract and have all the members lace their signatures around the circle. The circle was drawn to symbolise the equality among all members of the Ikki group. In Japanese Ikki organisations, the top managers also often rely upon their subordinates to aid in the actual decision-making. There have been cases where Japanese company heads have in fact assumed greater powers, but it is still a general rule that no person is dominant in a Japanese organisation.

When a Japanese company president participates in negotiations, he usually tells the other side that he must take any new proposals back to his company before they can be answered. Westerners have found this rather confusing for they wonder who is in charge in the Japanese company. However, in the Ikki tradition, the president does not want to make important decisions on his own, for if he were to make a decision and later find that most employees did not support it, his decision would be worthless.

Although many rules were adopted by these organisations, most shared five basic rules. First, no-one in the Ikki is to stray from the others by making a decision or taking any action ahead of them. Second, every decision is to be made only in consultation within the Ikki group. Third, all Ikki members must maintain solidarity within the Ikki. Fourth, any complaints to be made to the shogun must first be endorsed by all Ikki members. Fifth, even responses to orders from the shogun must be approved by the Ikki. The Ikki therefore achieved a high degree of political power by preserving its solidarity in group decision-making.

The principle of ground decision-making is still alive and well throughout Japan. In the government, bureaucratic ministers may give instructions or orders, but nobody does anything until the director-generals of the various bureau in the ministry get together and approve it. In Japanese companies, even if the president gives an order, it must be taken up by the board before it is implemented.

Japanese companies resemble European companies as far as their outer manifestations are concerned, but inside they still adhere to a 70-year-old tradition. Rather than attempt to change the Ikki system, businessmen both Japanese and foreign find it better simply to understand, adapt and act accordingly.

The strength of the Japanese economic recovery lies in the sense of collective consultation for collective survival. In Japan, an effective decision is virtually never made without preliminary groundwork done by the proponents of a given course of action in order to ensure the support of their superiors, peers and occasionally subordinates. This practice of consultation is called "nemawashi", which means "preparing the ground". Any farmer would know that soil had to be tilled in order to get a good crop. Nemawashi is undertaken in a very structured way. The proponents will first identify everybody who is likely to be affected by the decision and then methodically "consult" with departmental heads, getting their support before an actual meeting is held. Normally, Japanese formal meetings are short. The decisions are already made. The attendants are there just to endorse. It is very much unlike Western business meetings, when one expects questions to be put and long debates to ensue.

Government Support for Business

One of the major reasons why Japan's multi-nationals made great strikes and achieved such unprecedented levels of penetration in world markets is the continuous backing of the government. There is a degree of truth in the accusation that the Japanese government worked hand-in-glove with the business world and the labour force to ensure that Japanese business continued to expand world-wide. The Japanese are generally spurred on by their belief in the vulnerability of their resource-scarce country. The Japanese government seldom acts as litigant against Japanese business; it prefers to exercise "administrative guidance" in advising companies on how to comply with the law. This means that it can be relied on to work with businesses and not against them.

Japan has a very strong and powerful Economic Planning Agency, which maps out industrial strategy for the nation. The national strategy is taken seriously into consideration when companies develop their corporate strategies. Business is generally happy with the government because there is a genuine spirit of cooperation between the two, a feeling that all are ultimately working for the good of Japan. The close and unholy alliance between government and business is so intimate that Western observers have coined a name "Japan Inc." to describe the relationship. One of the strongest Ministries that often provides guidelines for Japanese trade and industries is the Ministry of Trade and Industry, known as MITI, which is the direct descendant of the wartime Munitions Ministry. The Munitions Ministry was an institution so feared and respected that the very mention of its name was said to have been enough to hush a crying child. Today, MITI is credited with a major role in running the economy, and its bureaucrats have come to take wry pleasure in their overseas reputation as master manipulators. MITI tries to create optimum economic conditions by encouraging efforts in promising industries, seeing that the right technology is imported, urging mergers when necessary and generally keeping an eye on the needs of the economy as a whole. MITI plays more the role of organiser than doer. It is not the direct amount of money that MITI provides in its specific policies but just the government's suggestions about priorities that really matter. They also provide subsidies. For instance, when MITI decided that Japan should attempt to overcome the lead of IBM and other US computer manufacturers in the area of computer chips, the Ministry acted as the catalyst, spending almost a billion dollars over a five year period in organising and controlling the research effort. The result was that Japanese companies came up simultaneously with such advances as the 643K and 256K RAM computer chips. Thus, Japan's lead in the production of chips and computer ceramics can be attributed not only to industry expertise and perseverance, but to government support.

Before the war, Japan had to conquer Manchuria, China and Southeast Asia in order to obtain the raw materials necessary for industrial expansion. They thought they had to use force to get what they wanted. They were able to seize control of a number of important international markets and by 1926, Japan's share of the total international trade had reached a level of 4 percent (compared to 10 percent today). Under the flags of large trading firms like Mitsui Bussan and Mitsubishi Shoji, Japan was able to overtake Britain's lead in textiles in 1932. This period was known as the Japanese Trade Crusade. Goods were copied from leading western brands and sold at rock-bottom prices, often below cost, just to gain foreign exchange in order to buy armaments and raw materials essential for the military build-up. The Japanese coined the slogan "Export or die" as they were committed to a militarist policy, and economic targets were set with military objectives in mind. Millions of Japanese in small and medium sized companies were inspired to work under sweatshop conditions for the glory and survival of Japan.

A Fortune article in 1936 described the Japanese as the "yellow peril", as the powerful young Japanese industry went about underselling western industry and taking over its markets. The traders of the thirties are now gone, the men who desperately sought a place for Japan among the industrialised nations, carrying their simple bags all over the world in search of markets that would buy their goods. They sold products that were half-priced imitations of western goods (sometimes complete with logos such as "made in U.S.A."). Today, the old traders have been replaced by the smooth English speaking jet traveller who no longer needs to resort to imitation and gimmickry to gain entrance to any market. Although the modern Japanese salesmen are different from their pre-war days, both in appearance and substance, they are essentially the same in spirit. They have an intense pride in Japan along with a continuing fervent belief that the Japanese people have no choice but to "export or die". It is this mentality that has given the Japanese the edge over their rivals. The Japanese have always worried about the lack of essential natural resources, a vital component in their business strategy, and therefore have made up their minds to gain control over them.

Before the war, in the thirties, the Japanese had invaded China and Southeast Asia to take over the rubber estates in Malaya and Bauxite in the Dutch East Indies where other materials such as sugar, raw cotton, lumber and coal were available. Their terrible defeat in the war convinced them that mercantilism was no longer a viable economic policy in the modern world, but they have not relinquished the idea of gaining control of the sources of required raw materials. Today, they do it through overseas investment. Through economic rather than military means, the Japanese have achieved their purpose. Today, Japanese have invested heavily in everything from US farmland to Australian uranium and coal. Wherever there are raw materials that the countryside needs, Japan always figures out how to gain permanent access to it.

With the availability of raw materials, the Japanese have expanded their export trade. Everywhere in the world, whether it is the United States or European or Asian countries, Japanese cars dominate the streets. Window shopping tourist never miss Japanese TVs, cameras, video tapes or computer chips. Japan's prosperity has been built on mastery of high-quality products at reasonable prices. Japanese companies tend to enter a foreign market one after the other, in quick succession, using low price, high quality, heavy advertising and shrewd knowledge of customers and competitors gathered prior to penetrating the market. Japanese goods are no more the lousy easy-to-break products, an image which Japanese goods had created in the minds of pre-war customers. The new image of their products is lasting, cheap, redefining the product of a sophisticated industrial complex. The Japanese have so perfected their products that they began to despise goods made outside Japan, especially those made in Asian countries. Just to cite an example, the Japanese government's aid to developing countries (ODA) is linked to the purchase of goods from Japan, thus creating an early market share lead for Japan in the countries that receive the aid. In this way, the government actively encourages the expansion of Japanese business into markets in developing countries that would not merit the efforts of individual companies.

Perhaps the most important aid given to Japanese business by the government is what it receives from the Japan External Trade Organisation (JETRO). The major objective of JETRO is to help Japanese business expand and to work with any Japanese company that requests its assistance. JETRO is extremely active in lobbying on behalf of Japanese interests in the corridors of power of target markets such as the US and European Economic Council (EEC). Top law firms and out-of-power administrators are given handsome retainers to drop hints in the right places. Richard Nixon was one such top administrator who worked for Mitsui in the early sixties when he was defeated by John Kennedy in the 1960 presidential election. Toyota alone had 26 law firms in Washington under retainership in 1981.

The Japanese Sogoshosha

One of the major reasons why Japan has been economically successful is the way that the Japanese organise themselves. Japanese trading companies and banks are two important cornerstones of Japan's success. The role of the trading company is the more dynamic of the two in building business for Japanese companies, but the banks provide the essential financial support that has made it possible for Japan to forge ahead of the US in the expansion and growth of multinational business across the globe. Behind the trading company and the bank are the financially interconnected companies known as zaikai, many of which descended from pre-war zaibatsu oligopolists. The modern zaikai has remained every bit as strong as its zaibatsu predecessors, achieving this result by linking companies (through interlocking directorships and equity by participation) whose operations comprehend most of the major areas of Japanese industrial activity. The zaikai is one of the greatest strengths of the modern Japanese machine, because even though companies are not always normally related, the strong force of history and personal ties causes them to act in concert and to assist each other whenever possible.

Japanese trading companies are divided into two major groups. The more important is the sogoshosha or general trading companies. These companies, now nine in number, are each linked to large zaikai groups, and they typically handle 20,000 to 25,000 items each. The other group, semmonshosha, are specialised trading firms. Combined, the nine companies employ over 80,000 people, with an average sale per employee of between US$2 million to US$6 million. The total turnover of the sogoshosha in 1981 was just under US$400 million or over 30 percent of the Japanese GNP. If the sogoshosha is a business institution unique to Japan in modern times, Japanese banks are also extremely different from anything in the West. The Japanese bank is the centre of the zaikai spider web, and through its investments in group companies, it can control the assets and influence the boards of each zaikai member company. One key difference between American or European banks and the Japanese bank is that in Japan, the customer feels that the bank is putting service ahead of profits. My personal experience with a Japanese bank is that it gives you personal attention and is willing to serve you although what you ask has nothing to do with the bank. I wanted to open an account in a Japanese bank and just rang up the manager. The next day, the assistant manager walked into my office after making an appointment and expressed appreciation for my decision to open an account in his bank, promising that the bank would do its utmost to serve me. The relationship between zaikai member banks and the sogoshosha is solidly based on mutuality of interest. The Japanese banking and trading company network, closely supported by the government itself through the Bank of Japan and the Ministry of Finance (MOF), is a crucial element of Japanese business strategy overseas, and should not be overlooked in any assessment of why Japan is able to take business away from the US–European consortia.

The zaikai, better known to the West as Zaibatsu, gives Japanese business a powerful advantage. Most of the zaibatsu have their Monday or Friday Clubs where they assemble the top men in the various companies within the group, ostensibly to know each other, but in practice to discuss matters of common interest. Such discussions often lead the companies to combine forces in an effort to make the most of an opportunity that opened in either the overseas or domestic markets. The government is usually brought in as an ally once the strategy has been decided on by the industry concerned. In Japan, almost every week, the Minister or Director-General of the Ministry of Finance or the MITI would have lunch or dinner with businessmen to discuss business co-ordination, with one thing in mind: "How to make Japan stronger in the economic world and become No. 1 globally". In Singapore, for instance, it is unimaginable that Ministers or permanent secretaries would be meeting businessmen from time to time to discuss business matters. The Corrupt Practise Investigation Bureau would soon catch up with the officials to find out whether there was something fishy. It is this constant dialogue between businessmen and Government political leaders and bureaucrats that make business run smoothly with the government. This interaction feeds both parties with ideas and suggestions that enable Japan to expand so rapidly in business.

The Shunto and Strikeless Society

In assessing Japan's success story, one must not forget the tremendous sacrifices and contributions made by the blue-collar workers as well as the white-collar employees in the multinationals and other Japanese companies. In Japan, there are no illegal wild-cat strikes which are so common in western countries. As a result, there are few work days lost. And that means productivity is always at its peak. The Japanese have their own way expressing dissatisfaction and pouring out grievances. Once a year, usually in April or May at the beginning of the fiscal year, a spring wage offensive is organised. The spring offensive is sometimes called "scheduled struggles". This is a strategy of organised labour, designed to achieve a near-uniform adjudication of the annual wage increase throughout Japanese industry. It is a yearly event when trade unions conduct waves of industry-wide work stoppages of short durations as the means of bringing about basic wage settlements with employers for the ensuing twelve months. It normally lasts one or, at the most, two days. The strikes are merely symbolic. This Japanese distinctive approach and style of "based-up" agreements have comprised a major part of wage bargaining in union-management negotiations in the country. The Shunto is organised by the General Council of the Trade Unions of Japan, known as Sohyo. The Shunto settlements serve as a Japanese type of national wage policy.

From the employers' point of view, the Shunto helps them to effect considerable consultation, bringing in the government through the Ministry of Labour and the labour relations commissions to ensure industrial peace and progress. The Shunto helps both the employers and the government to keep an eye on industrial development. Japan's Shunto had its origin in early 1955 when the chairman of Sohyo, Ota Kaoru, and Secretary General Iwai Akira called for the coordination of wage demands of the various enterprise-level unions in order to ensure the unity and solidarity of the labour movement at a time when it was threatened with division or possible decline. They took this step because after World War II there were numerous strikes organised by left-wing unions, some for political reasons. The whole situation nearly went out of control, culminating in the call for a nationwide general strike scheduled for 1st February, 1947. The Allied Occupation Command had to step in to force organisers to cancel the strike for fear that it would constitute a threat to the Command's own security. After the Sohyo was formed, the trade union movement became more stable and the leaders were able to exploit the national sentiments of the workers. Today, there are virtually no strikes in Japan because of the harmony between management and workers through the fair intermediary of government departments. But life was not always as peaceful as it is today. In the 1920s, Japan was racked by violent labour disturbances and in the early post-war years there were several politically motivated strikes, culminating in the abortive general strike of 1947.

Over the next few decades, there were strikes involving violence, leading to deaths between pickets and police. Until the mid 1970s, the number of days lost in industrial disputes was higher than in most European countries. After 1975, the number of days lost declined dramatically. The Japanese workers realised that there could be no improvement in living standards without corresponding rises in productivity. It was the Japanese workers who were responsible for the rapid rise in Japan's productivity and the miraculous recovery of the country's economy. Today, Japan has not only been transformed from a war-torn and poverty-stricken country into a highly industrialised economic giant, but has become a great investor in the world economic market.

In 1982, Japan's new direct foreign investment was just US$4.5 billion; in 1985, it was US$6.4 billion; by 1987, it had jumped to US$20 billion, of which more than half was in the United States. Comments have been made that having failed to beat America by bombing Pearl Harbour the Japanese have now decided to buy it. Even in Asia, Japanese investments have increased tremendously. In 1985, Japan's new direct investment in Hong

Kong was worth only US$131 million; in 1987, it was US$1 billion. In Taiwan, Japanese investment rose from US$114 in 1985 to US$367 million in 1987; in Singapore, during the same period, Japanese investment rose from US$339 million to US$494 million and in South Korea, from US$134 million to US$647 million. All other Asean countries benefitted from increasing Japanese investment.

Japan has come a long way from the devastating post-war years. The spirit and sacrifice of the people for the good of the country, the laws ensuring that meritocracy prevails over inheritance, and the parental guidance by various government ministries to ensure economic progress have all combined to contribute towards the miracle of Japan's economic recovery.

Japan's economic recovery was not an accident, although the Korean war was a god-sent opportunity. Japan would not have developed so fast without the Korean war. The demand for goods and services to supplement the war gave Japan a chance to develop its industries and boosted Japan's economy on the whole. It was, however, the result of collective efforts on the part of the Japanese that made it possible for Japan to seize the opportunity to enrich herself. It was the Japanese genius to channel the energies of the people towards a common goal — to put Japan back on her own feet and to make Japan strong again, not as a military power but as an economic power. They have succeeded and they have produced a miracle.

CHAPTER 8

Corridors of Power

Who rules Japan? Who has the power to decide for the nation, and control the destiny of 100 million Japanese? I asked this question when I set foot in Japan as Singapore's Ambassador, just as when I arrived in Cairo and Jakarta as Ambassador. In Cairo, it did not take me long to realise that power rested with President Nasser, surrounded by a number of generals and civilian advisers who controlled the destiny of the nation. Similarly, when I arrived at Jakarta, I soon found out that President Suharto was and is still the "King" of Indonesia, supported by the Abri — the military which is still powerful in the country because of their involvement in the revolution. In the case of Japan, however, after four years I could not find an easy answer to my question.

In Japan, power is so defused that it is difficult to pinpoint who controls the country and who is the most powerful. Before the war, one could have said the war-lords, making use of the image of the Emperor as "Man God", controlled the country. Since the war, things have changed. Power is now concentrated in the hands of a power elite — the politicians, the bureaucrats and the zaikai or business circles. No single section of the power elite can decide on the policies of the nation without consulting the other sections. That is why Japanese decisions take a long time to materialise. In the Japanese language, this process of consultation is called "nemawashi". Everything in Japan is decided by "nemawashi" — a sort of consensus which must be reached before a final decision is taken.

An intriguing characteristic of the relationship among the three groups constituting the power elite goes something like this. Politicians give instructions to bureaucrats who can allocate funds for a project desired by the constituents and decide on policies affecting business. During an election campaign, politicians endlessly stress their ties with precisely those officials who can allocate funds desired by their constituents. Bureaucrats do the everyday business of governing Japan. Bureaucrats, especially those belonging to the Ministries of Finance, International Trade and Industry and Post and Telecommunications, wield a great deal of power, definitely more than they are theoretically authorised to exercise. They restrain and control the businessmen and provide spurs for the economy. They make nearly all laws, which is quite something, if not everything, in terms of measurable power. These laws are almost always rubber-stamped by the Diet (Japanese Parliament) and they proceed to use them as means to achieve their own cherished aims.

Top bureaucrats who became close friends of mine often told me that they were the "real power" in Japan. One of them once said, "The Ministers or even Prime Ministers come and go, but we remain." Businessmen are definitely afraid of the bureaucrats.

The bureaucrats in the Japanese society are highly esteemed by ordinary people. They have the power to license and to regulate. The bureaucrats are seen to be above politics; they look after Japan first, rather than themselves. The bureaucrats also believe this and describe themselves as kokushi or patriots. The heyday of the bureaucratic power was the period of the Allied Occupation, up to the end of 1960s. During the occupation, the Supreme Command decided to rule through existing bureaucratic structures just as the Manchurians used Chinese scholars and administrators when they occupied China. The only difference was that the Americans did not take the trouble of learning Japanese, as the Manchurians did, thus losing their own culture after ruling China for 300 years. The Americans reinforced the tradition of legislation being drawn up within the Japanese bureaucracy.

The third power elite is the zaikai (business world), who foot the incredibly high cost of the electioneering of the Diet members, particularly the various factions of the Liberal Democratic Party (LDP). Some businessmen buy specific political power from individual LDP members who play a pivotal role in stimulating or retarding bureaucratic decisions affecting them. Businessmen in Japan form business organisations, the most prominent being Keidanren, a federation of leading industrial organisations such as the automobile manufacturers association, the ship builders association, the iron and steel federation, the petroleum association and the chemical industry association together with trading companies, wholesale businesses, banks, insurance companies and securities companies. Next is the Nikkeiren (Japan Federation of Employers Association), which controls the labour movement and keeps the lid on wage increases. This is followed by the Keizen Doyukai (Committee for Economic Development) which is a forum in which elite zaikai members can formulate business politics, and lastly the Japan

Chamber of Commerce and Industry which monitors the world of the smaller corporations.

The economic community is an integral part of LDP politics. It has a powerful voice in the direction of economic affairs concerning their future. The actual or potential power of a politician has often been described to me in terms of the number of times he meets with the businessmen each week. They are often found in the entertainment districts of Akasaka and Shimbashi, which is the backdrop for many political talks. Ishikawa Tatsuzo, the famous author, had this to say about the secret talks between politicians and businessmen in his political bestseller *Corona of Gold*: "At dusk, in the streets of the Akasaka district gleaming black limousines quietly flow through the streets, pause, then silently move on again. Passengers, middle-aged and elderly, alight and step through the gates of their favorite restaurants. Brightly coloured shadows-flawlessly dressed geisha are sucked in through the back entrances.

"This silence is what separates this place from the entertainment districts of the ordinary people. The strumming of the samisen is hardly ever heard. Instead of coming for entertainment, most customers have come for discrete discussions. Schemes buried in their breasts, masters of the alchemy of trickery, calculation, and barter, they quietly sip from their sake cups. Here is the backstage of Japanese politics, the kitchen for the Japanese economy. Here, secret understandings are made, personal alliances are drawn. Japan is governed from Akasaka and Shimbashi — the districts of the willows and flowers."

In present-day Japan, it is impossible to sit in the chair of the Prime Minister without the support of the economic circles. The reason is that vast sums of money are needed in politics. To win the presidential election within the LDP, the faction leaders must regularly distribute huge sums of money in order to attract to their side a majority of the politicians, who are convinced that money is everything. Money has become, in effect, political power. In order to collect these sums of money, there is no recourse but to rely on donors from the business world.

Pressure Groups

There are two other pressure groups which from time to time exert their influence on Japanese politics. First, the underworld of yakuza which has links with the LDP. In the early days of the LDP, when it was in its formation period, a man well-known in the underworld was financing the LDP. He was Kodama, a close friend of Prime Minister Kishi, who had been co-mates in Sugama prison. Both were arrested and detained as war criminals, having been heavily involved in the war against China during World War II.

Kodama began his career as a right-wing terrorist leader in the twenties, being imprisoned for a total of nine years for threats against moderate politicians. After the war-lords took over, he was rewarded by being posted to China as a secret agent with special responsibility for procuring war supplies. He became fabulously rich when he returned to Japan after the war. When the American Occupying Forces occupied Japan, he was sent to prison for three years as a Class A war criminal. Inside the prison, he met other powerful Class A war criminals such as Kishi and became friends.

Kodama's immense wealth contributed to the success of the LDP under the Kishi leadership. Kodama donated massive sums of money to the LDP and set himself up as a "business consultant". His name was mentioned in half a dozen of Japan's biggest post-war corruption scandals. In 1958, he began his secret consultancy work for Lockheed and was arrested. Kodama died while on trial of corruption in 1984, together with Kakuei Tanaka, the most powerful Prime Minister after the war. He lived in the twilight world where politicians, businessmen and gangsters freely interacted for their own and Japan's benefit. In his heyday, Kodama's network of influence stretched everywhere from the mass media to the police force. In 1970, he kept a private army which he helped train and was prepared for ready action during the Security Treaty disturbances. He was then supporting the Supreme Allied Commands. Kodama had also sworn "brothers" in the underworld. One of them was Taoka, head of the Yamaguchi gang. In the political world, Kodama associated himself with the Kono faction which Nakasone once belonged to, and the two of them were rather close.

On his deathbed, he said, "I always thought I would be punished for the Lockheed business. I made the mistake of my life in acting as agent for a corporation from the enemy that killed our soldiers in the Great East Asian War."

Till today, the underworld still has some influence in Japanese politics. Their activities become more visible during election campaigns. Some dietmen depend on the underworld for funds which, indirectly, exerts some influence.

Another source of influence in Japan is the strength of the mass media. Among the power welding groups in Japan, it is generally recognised as the most powerful one influencing decision-making. Professor Kabashima Ikuo, an expert on mass media, wrote an article based on a survey carried out in 1986, which stated that most of the leaders from various walks of life thought that the mass media was the most influential factor in Japan. He said that Japanese newspapers had come to be recognised the world over for their high standards in editorial contents and production techniques. The high literacy rate in Japan is also one of the reasons for the high degree of influence that the newspapers have, because the big national newspapers' circulations run to about 8 million copies a day. Most newspapers also run TV stations and thus further strengthen their influence. One important reason for the powerful influence of the mass media in Japan is that the newspapers and TV stations are not public companies. The shares are all owned by employees. No outsiders, however rich they may be, can own shares in newspapers or TV. Thus, neither political parties, nor multi-nationals nor bureaucrats own newspapers. The newspapers therefore have the freedom to criticise or report anything about the country and people without fear or favour. There is no pressure from the government, parties or constraints from the business world or bureaucrats. That is what makes the mass media so powerful in Japan and that is why politicians, business leaders and bureaucrats try to establish close connections with editors who are well respected in Japanese society.

It was the newspapers and magazines that exposed the Tanaka Lockheed scandal and caused his downfall. The Japanese support the newspapers knowing they are powerful, but they also regret that newspapers have no teeth to implement policies. Newspapers, however toothless they may be, can influence decision-making through their influence in moulding public opinion and in criticising whatever policies they may think are not in the interest of the people. They are the conscience of the people and a counter-check in society.

Although there is no interference in press policy and coverage, the Japanese have a subtle way of controlling press freedom. They encourage the setting up of "press clubs" in all government ministries and business corporations, and have specially nominated reporters to cover news stories in these concerns. The authorities dish out information to such reporters and thus subtly control information. These reporters are very well treated. They are provided with news rooms, good refreshments and have special privileges. If they do not play the game, they are replaced. Nearly all the information given out by these establishments is the same. Only those stories favourable to the authorities are dished out. That is why newspapermen in Japan are generally considered as "toothless". To get a scoop like that of the Tanaka scandal, newsmen had to rely on magazines which were out of the control of the authorities.

In Japanese politics, politicians have the power of political decisions. The bureaucrats have the power to license and regulate. The businessmen are able to influence the making of national decisions by contributing funds to the political world. The mass media acts as a natural system of checks and balances. The right wing yakuza put pressure on political leaders by giving them financial and physical support during election campaigns.

There is also an understanding between bureaucrats and businessmen in terms of fringe benefits. When bureaucrats are in power, they give favours to certain companies and when they retire, they receive "amakudari", meaning "voice from heaven". They become advisers or consultants to companies they have given favours to and enjoy a comfortable life of leisurely retirement.

The Rise and Fall of Tanaka

When I arrived in Japan in the middle of 1984, it was the era of Kakuei Tanaka — an era of money politics. Yasuhiro Nakasone was the Prime Minister, but he led a small faction within the LDP. He was put in the Prime Ministership by Tanaka — "the King maker" — who headed the largest faction within the LDP. Tanaka controlled 120 dietmen (parliamentarians) who received financial support from him and were therefore loyal to him and not the party.

Tanaka was Prime Minister in 1976, but when involved with the Lockheed scandal, was arrested and thrown into jail for three weeks. He was later convicted of taking a ¥500 million bribe in 1972 to help secure the US jet sales from the Lockheed Corporation for a Japanese airline. He was sentenced to four years imprisonment. He appealed against the conviction.

I first met Tanaka in 1974 when I was Ambassador to Indonesia and he paid an official visit there. Indonesian students staged a demonstration protesting against Tanaka's visit. The demonstration resulted in riots and students burning business buildings connected with Japanese business. Tanaka had arrived at a time when the Indonesian people were harbouring animosity against the Japanese for having ganged up with Chinese "cukong" (Chinese business tycoons who manipulated Indonesians as front men to do business with Japan) at the expense of local indigenous Indonesian businessmen. The demonstration was to remind the Japanese that they should not ignore the indigenous Indonesians when choosing a business partner.

As a result of the demonstration, Tanaka's entourage had to be flown by helicopter from the airport to the Istana Negara (Palace in Indonesia) to avoid the angry students who had gone to the airport to threaten Tanaka. As the diplomatic corp had to be at the airport to welcome the Tanaka

A portrait of Kodama, Japan's underworld head who backed the LDP.

Kakuei Tanaka (1972–1974), the "king-maker" who dominated the LDP.

delegation, we were entangled with the incident. When Tanaka flew off to the Istana, our cars had to return to Jakarta. My car happened to be the first car to leave the airport. About five minutes away from the airport, I heard someone shouting loudly "Tanaka, Tanaka" and pointing at me. The students had mistaken me for Tanaka (from the side, I look a little like Tanaka). When some angry students were about to stop my car, other students who were more alert shouted, "No, it is a Singapore flag, not Japanese flag." All ambassadors' cars hoist a national flag in front of the car. I sighed a great relief. If nobody had noticed the Singapore flag, I might have been dragged out of the car and possibly beaten up.

When Tanaka left the airport to continue his visit to other Asean countries, I went to the airport, this time to bid him farewell. I shook hands with Tanaka. He looked rather nervous and I saw the muscle on his left face twisting. I knew there was something wrong with his health.

After his 1974 tour, Tanaka was charged with bribery. Although he had fallen in disgrace in the eyes of Westerners, he was still the busiest man in Tokyo. Almost every morning, buses started arriving before seven at the estate of the Tanaka residence. Dozens of Tanaka admirers filed into special waiting rooms, to be joined later by businessmen, politicians and government bureaucrats. For the next few hours, the scene was reminiscent of one of Louis XIV's royal levees. The visitors flowed through Tanaka's private office, seeking his aid in finding jobs and dealing with the government, or just paying their respects. Government officials sought support for budgets, personnel changes and other plans. Businessmen discussed investments or political contributions. An average of 400 people visited him every day.

He was not the Prime Minister, but he was the "king maker". In the Indonesian sense, he was the dalang — the man who manipulated the puppets from behind the screen.

Tanaka's parliamentary faction of the LDP, referred to as "The Tanaka Corp", was 50 percent larger than any other voting bloc, giving him a virtual veto over party decisions. Although the 78 year-old Tanaka had to resign from the LDP in 1984, since 1978 he had successfully backed three Prime Ministers into power — Ohira, Zenko Suzuki and Nakasone. His latest triumph was in October 1984 when he successfully prevented LDP leaders from kicking Nakasone out of the Prime Ministership. Tanaka had rallied his faction and blocked the move by LDP leaders to oust Nakasone. And when Nakasone formed his new Cabinet, the Tanaka faction got the biggest share by having six out of 20 ministers, more than any other faction and occupying several major party jobs.

Politicians in Tokyo likened Tanaka to the old feudal Japanese military rulers. They call him "the shogun in the shadows". His ability to cling to his influence reflects something curious about Japan. Although Japan's economy is the second most sophisticated in the world, its politics have not kept pace. Perhaps because business relies heavily on personal connections and gift-giving, Japan finds it difficult to control favours and corporation payments in public life.

The Japanese sometimes say that politics is shrouded in "black mist". It is often said that "one step backward and you are in the cliff". That is the way they describe politics. In the years since World War II, numerous leading politicians have been accused of taking bribes. But few have been convicted. Bribery and scandals have persisted until today. In early 1992, the Kyubin scandal involved allegedly questionable donations by the transport firms in the Tokyo subsidiary to scores of politicians. It has developed into the biggest scandal since the Recruit scandal.

Tanaka's personal contacts, combined with a seemingly limitless access to political funds, help explain his broad influence. He claimed to have the allegiance of 60 percent of Japan's provincial governors. In the national government, bureaucrats knew that despite his legal problems, they needed Tanaka's support to win parliamentary approval for their budgets. Businessmen and politicians, in turn, often sought his help in influencing the bureaucrats. He maintained especially close ties with the Construction Ministry, which oversaw the nation's extensive public-works spending. His snow-bound home region in Western Japan was largely ignored by the central government. Today, the thinly populated area boasts two super highways — one with a special exit to his hometown, along with a bullet train line, tunnels galore and other major improvements. Public spending per capital in the district was among the highest in Japan.

Tanaka, who was first elected in 1947, had a personal fortune based on construction. Critics claim he added to it through his knowledge of government plans. The Lockheed scandal had not even come to light when he resigned as Prime Minister in 1974, following a magazine article accusing him of questionable real-estate deals.

The shadow shogun's vast influence understandably stirred much resentment in Japan. The public outcry following his conviction in 1984 obliged Prime Minister Nakasone to call a special election. When the LDP lost seats, he issued a written statement promising to "eliminate Tanaka's so-called political influence entirely". Many of Nakasone's associates say he truly wanted to do that. But, Nakasone remained dependent on Tanaka's support and therefore went back on his promise.

It was Tanaka, again, who came to save Nakasone when he was nearly ousted as Prime Minister by LDP elders. In an effort to split the Tanaka faction, the LDP elders named Susumu Nikaido as the candidate to take over from Nakasone. Nikaido was confident of becoming the next Prime Minister because he had consulted a prominent soothsayer who lived near Hakone. This soothsayer had proclaimed himself as "the son of God — a messiah". He had predicted that Nikaido would be the next Prime Minister. This fortune teller, who was a dentist named Murakami, had predicted that Tanaka would soon recover from ill-health and would back Nikaido. Many leading politicians, including Nakasone, had gone to see Murakami. It seemed it was the first time Murakami had made a mistake. Nikaido failed to be nominated as Prime Minister because Tanaka had chosen to support Nakasone instead of him.

In fact, Tanaka was a little surprised that Nikaido had accepted the offer of nomination as Prime Minister by LDP elders. In the words of Nikaido, "It has always been a one-way street; I told him I wouldn't take a one-way street. But he is the boss, so I said OK."

Tanaka had supported Nakasone because he wanted to make a comeback as Prime Minister after his conviction. He strongly believed that he would be acquitted and he would be nominated again to be Prime Minister. Although Tanaka had backed Nakasone, he was never seen publicly with him. He talked to Nakasone by phone and sent messages through intermediaries.

While Tanaka rarely got involved in broad issues of public policy, he kept close watch on the nuts and bolts of party and personnel decisions. A normal day in the life of the shadow shogun began approximately at midnight, when he rose from a three-hour nap. He spent two hours writing letters, reading documents and making notes in red pencil. Then he retired for four more hours and rose again at 6 am. He read all the Tokyo newspapers, took a lukewarm bath, ate breakfast and started receiving his visitors. No problem was too large or too small to bring before him. He said his only real sin was in using Japan's political system too well. "People like myself who actually accomplish things tend to attract some opposition groups," he once said.

Despite his conviction, he won the largest vote in Japanese history in his constituency, while other LDP Dietmen lost votes.

Bribe-taking is a salient feature of Japan's post-war politics. About 40 dietmen have been charged for corruption since the end of World War II. In 1948, an economics minister was convicted for receiving ¥1.5 million from a chemical company. He helped the firm to obtain easy-term loans from a government bank. In 1954, three legislators were found guilty for taking ¥250,000–¥350,000 in bribes from the shipping and shipbuilding industries in connection with a government subsidy program.

In 1961, an ex-transport minister was sentenced for a business licence. In 1976, a former parliamentary transport vice-minister was convicted for taking a ¥2 million payoff from an airline company. He was one of the politicians involved in the Lockheed scandal.

Up until 1984, Tanaka topped the list of corruption cases in terms of the size of the bribe money. He was charged with accepting ¥500 million from a trading company. How was such a huge sum of money delivered? According to the ruling by the Tokyo District Court, the first batch of the money — a cardboard box containing ¥100 million in bank notes — was delivered on a street behind the British Embassy in Chiyoda Ward. The rest of the money was handed in three installments, each time at a different location. For example, a Hotel Okura parking lot was used for delivery of the third installment of ¥125 million. Kodama was the go-between for Tanaka and Lockheed. The two had strong connections.

Tanaka, who was too busy, made a mistake in the arrangement of handing over the money. If it was meant as a political donation for his faction, he could have easily asked the donor to sign a check in favour of his faction. But, there was a limit to political donations by business companies and he was anxious to outdo this opponents in other factions. The method that was arranged for the delivery of the money got him into trouble with the authorities.

Since ancient days, Japan has been beset with corruption and scandals. It was and is a common affair in Japanese politics. In early 1992 Japan was again beset by a series of unraveling scandals including the one involving a trucking firm, Tokyo Sagawa Kyubin, which promised to eclipse the 1988 Recruit Affair, which resulted in the resignation of the then Finance Minister Miyazawa. After Miyazawa became Prime Minster, his top aide Fumio Abe was arrested for corruption. In the Kyubin affair, more than 100 politicians including the "king-maker" Shin Kanemaru were said to be involved.

77-year-old Shin Kanemaru, Japan's most influential politician in August 1992, admitted having received ¥500 million ($6.4 million) from the former president of the Sagawa Kyubin trucking firm. Kanemaru, who played a key role in propelling Prime Minister Miyazawa to power in November 1991, had earlier denied reports that he was involved in the scandal. In August 1992, he admitted at a press conference that he had accepted the bribe, but said it was meant for the political fund of his faction. "I feel I should take responsibility for my mistakes," he said. Kanemaru stepped down as vice-president of LDP as well as chairman of Soseikai, the party's largest faction originally established by former Prime Minister Takeshita.

The Japanese media considered Kanemaru to be the "yatai-bone" — literally the "framework on which a stall is built" — of the Miyazawa administration. His admission that he had received the enormous sum of questionable political funds only months after the Recruit stock-for-favours scandal rocked the ruling party and embarrassed the government, just as it was renewing long-delayed efforts to push for political reform. A spokesman for the Tokyo prosecutor's office said that Kanemaru had not declared the money as political donations and that the office intended to see if the transaction violated a law controlling the size and receipt of such funds. Kanemaru was charged in court, but he was still free pending an appeal in the High Courts.

Kanemaru, a member of Parliament who for more than three decades represented an area outside Tokyo near Mount Fuji, was adamant that the donations had been given to him in good faith and not as a bribe.

Money and politics have always been inter-related. But it was Tanaka who first created money politics. He was the first politician in Japan to institutionalise the use of money to gain power. Because of his ability to gather money, he successfully bought over 120 Dietmen onto his payroll. How did he get the money?

He started to colonise the Housing Ministry when he was Minister. He was so powerful that even after he left the ministry, housing contractors and real estate agents went to him to get favours from the ministry. When he became Prime Minister, he colonised other ministries. Even when he stepped down as Prime Minister, he continued to expand his faction and became a "king-maker" for ten years, enjoying enormous power within the LDP and the ministries concerned.

In Japan, the various LDP factions divide the spoils of power. Whichever faction controls a certain ministry, that faction has power to decide on the giving of licences or regulating matters concerned with that ministry. Thus, businessmen generally know what to do when they need favours. A housing contractor naturally goes to the faction that controls housing. Normally, strong factions get lucrative ministries such as housing, telecommunications and defence which deals with the purchase of arms and weapons.

When Tanaka was Minister of Housing, he cornered most of the important real estate agents and contractors and used his power to buy up all valuable pieces of land, building projects out of them, thus making fat profits. Since then, the contractors' world was under his command. The Ministry of Telecommunication was also a ministry under Tanaka's influence. From 20 years ago, Tanaka regarded the Housing Ministry as the most profitable and tried to occupy the post of Minister for his faction. With the privatisation of the New National Transport and Telecommunication, Tanaka colonised the new N.T.T. (Nippon Telephone & Telegraph) and hoped to boost his future profit to well over ¥10 billion. Tanaka never stayed away from these ministries even when he was sick in bed.

The Ministry of Finance also came under the influence of Tanaka when Takeshita was one of his top aides. He also controlled the Ministry of Home Affairs because one of his right-hand men, Gotoda, became the powerful Minister of Home Affairs.

In addition to his influence in various ministries, Tanaka also had a hand in picking governors of various prefectures. He was particularly powerful in picking the governor of his own prefecture, Niigata, and he was responsible for getting a big percentage of the budget for the projects of Niigata. He managed to build a shinkansen (bullet train) from Tokyo to Niigata, a remote place with little population, when he was Prime Minister. It was generally considered a "white elephant", but he did do it.

Most politicians admit that Tanaka had a "brilliant mind" in making money and in election campaigns. Whoever was supported by him got elected. He would go out of the way to back a person when he had chosen him. He had a marvelous touch for human relations and his supporters really loved him and listened to him. They were loyal to him personally and not so much to the party or his ideology.

Then in 1985, a severe stroke left Tanaka partially paralysed and created a vacuum in his faction. By June 1985, nothing was heard about Tanaka's health, although his daughter Makiko was caring for her father and was planning for his political comeback. The general opinion in political circles, however, was that it would be a while before Tanaka could be active again. At the end of June, a picture appeared in the Yomiuri, a leading Japanese language newspaper, showing him reading letters in his office located at his private residence. He looked pale and his face was sunken. This was the first time his picture had appeared since he suffered a stroke. It was Father's Day. News came that the office of the ailing "king-maker" was shut down. This was an indication that Tanaka's days were numbered. Rumours spread that Tanaka's daughter began interfering with the finances of her father's office, which had long been controlled by Tanaka's aides Hayasaka and Sato, and a dispute erupted.

When New Year came in 1986, Tanaka did not make an appearance before the well-wishers who came to his large residence in Meijirodai, Tokyo. The number of well-wishers who went to extend the New Year's greeting had dwindled. In the past, Tanaka with a glass of whisky in his hand chatting with visitors was the usual scene. But this did not happen in 1986. No alcoholic beverage was served to the visitors and Tanaka did not come out of his residence.

When Takeshita, secretary general of the LDP, one of Tanaka's right-hand men, turned up at his residence to pay his respects, he was barred from entering the house. It was an open slap on the face of Takeshita. The misunderstanding arose when Tanaka favoured an elderly right-hand man, Nikaido, as heir to the Tanaka faction instead of Takeshita. Both of them wanted the post of prime ministership and Tanaka favoured Nikaido, but Takeshita refused to listen to his paralysed boss.

In the past, Tanaka handed out pay packets to dietmen of his faction in exchange for their support. But, for the previous two years, Takeshita had played the role of Santa Claus and thus new members were more loyal to the person who dished out the money. It was a mistake of Tanaka's to trust Takeshita with the job of dispensing money. Takeshita was not worried about the snub shown by Tanaka and instead strengthened his determination to form his own faction called the "Soseikai", splitting the Tanaka faction.

The absence of Tanaka on the political scene was seen as a momentous change for Prime Minister Nakasone, who had finally acquired a free rein to conduct government business without being conscious of Tanaka's shadow.

Prime Minister Nakasone was a genius in the manipulation of political power. After the twin elections, Nakasone took a Machiavellian tactic in the appointment of new Cabinet ministers. He brushed aside all recommendations of various factional leaders, including that of Tanaka, and appointed older dietmen who had served more than seven terms and whom he thought would support his ambition to extend his term of office as Prime Minister. He began to ignore Tanaka for the first time. He even went off to London for the summit meeting before informing Tanaka and had to apologise by trunk call to Tanaka when he heard that the latter was furious.

I met Esaki, the former Deputy Prime Minister belonging to the Tanaka faction and who was once a strong supporter of Nakasone. The Prime Minister had used him to mediate matters in the Tanaka faction. This was what he commented about Nakasone after he was unceremoniously dropped from the Deputy Prime Ministership: "He (meaning Nakasone) is actually like Kozen Hirokawa, the LDP secretary general during the Yoshida Cabinet in 1950, who was a genius in fixing LDP elders by keeping them upstairs. He has no respect for the senior statemen and offended all of them. Finally, the older ones ganged up and ditched him. They saw to it that he lost his election and disappeared from the political scene. I hope Nakasone will not suffer the same fate." This confided feeling shows the grievances of cabinet ministers when they are dropped from the cabinet.

In Japanese politics, and perhaps with other countries, politicians cannot afford to get sick. Although there is the tradition in Japan to respect the senior and especially the "Oya Bun" (father or leader), the situation would not remain the same when the Oya Bun was rendered immobilised by sickness. The example can be seen from the behaviours of both Nakasone and Takeshita towards Tanaka when he became paralysed. Whilst Nakasone began to take advantage of Tanaka's illness to move more freely, Takeshita had formed his own faction to challenge his Oya Bun.

Had it not been for his stroke, Tanaka would have remained the most powerful leader in post-war Japan, even with the Lockheed scandal. Historians would judge him as a tragic leader because of a stroke. Other less charitable critics such as Shuichi Kato had this to say about Tanaka: "His power derived from the collection and distribution of money in a brutal way. He has scandalised Japanese politics. He made corruption quasi-legitimate in Japanese politics."

Tanaka has become a legend in Japan's political history. He was born in a poverty-ridden farming village, which was backward in the heart of the Niigata prefecture. For generations, the Tanaka family had suffered high infant mortality on the male side. His father was a horse dealer whose chronic insolvency meant that young Tanaka frequently had to do the rounds of neighbours and relatives asking for financial help. The practical experience he gained of the traditional Japanese ethics of duty and obligation must have been a tremendous asset to his later political career.

After completing elementary school, Tanaka began work as a ditch digger in the local paddies when he was very young. At the age of sixteen, he left home to seek fame and fortune in Tokyo. Working from five to the morning until midnight, Tanaka soon made his mark in the Tokyo construction industry. At 19, he became shacho (president) of his own company. After brief war service as a private in Manchuria, he built his company into a sizable one which by 1943 ranked amongst the nation's top 50 construction firms. By the end of the war, he had accumulated enough wealth to finance his political career.

In 1946, he stood for election but failed. He tried again the following year and succeeded on the Democratic Party ticket. Within a year of entering parliament, he crossed over to the Liberal Party, the conservative mainstream, and at the age of 30 was appointed Vice-Minister of Justice in the Yoshida Cabinet. He made his way up after that, leading to his success as Prime Minister against Fukuda, his biggest political rival.

Factional Politics

Although the LDP has been the ruling party in Japan, it is no more a party than it is liberal or democratic. In fact, LDP is only a myth. In reality, Japan is ruled by the five factions within the LDP. The Tanaka faction was the largest when I arrived in Japan. A faction, the basic unit of Japanese political activity, is a clique centering around an elder statesman who has the capability to raise funds and in power broking and who usually has been a Prime Minister. The key determinant of the Japanese political scene is the interplay of the balance of power between these factions, which are engaged in a constant process of manipulation and maneuver, trade off and betrayal. The prize at stake is the control of the nation's high office, and particularly the money-making ministries. When I arrived in Tokyo, the balance power between the different factions after the 1986 election was as follows:

Tanaka	faction	—	120	dietmen
Suzuki	"	—	77	"
Fukuda	"	—	67	"
Nakasone	"	—	65	"
Komoto	"	—	36	"

Towards the tail-end of my stay in Japan, the Tanaka faction was split into two — the Tanaka faction and the Takeshita faction. The Tanaka faction was weakened and Takeshita took over a "king-maker".

The five factions constitute the LDP. Nearly all LDP parliamentarians and certainly anyone with political ambitions belong to one of these factions. The largest faction is numerically and financially stronger than the other factions. Over the years, the tendency towards larger and more powerful factions has been steadily gaining strength. At the formation of the LDP in 1955, there were eight factions and nearby 100 "neutral" members of the Lower House. Today, there are five factions, and only 20 of the Lower House members are unaffiliated to any faction.

A powerful factional leader can exert more influence than a Prime Minister, as exemplified by Tanaka. After Tanaka had quit the LDP, as demanded by law after he was charged and sentenced, he was still the "king-maker" of LDP. The "king-maker" can make or break Prime Ministers, by shifting alliances or encouraging splits in the opposing factions. In his heyday, Tanaka, although officially not even an LDP member, nominated three Primes Ministers in a row — Ohira, Suzuki and Nakasone. He once said that the Prime Minister was merely "a hat" worn by the governing party — presumably capable of being removed when no longer fashionable.

Factional politics is a main feature in the Japanese political world. The LDP is widely publicised for their intra-factional struggles. But factions also exist in opposition parties such as the Japan Socialist Party and Democratic Socialist Party. Even the Komeito Party, based on a religious grounding, has a kind of faction. The Japan Communist Party, which appears to be tightly knit, also has internal factions arising from ideological differences such as the pro-Beijing and pro-Moscow factions.

The factional tendency in Japanese politics was embedded in the Japanese character long before the concept of representative democracy arrived. In feudal Japan, a samurai owed absolute loyalty to his clan. In return, the clan provided him with security and advancement. If ordered by the shogunate to overthrow the government, he would do so without hesitation.

In modern Japan, factions exist in all walks of life, from the playground to the boardroom. In the tea ceremony, flower arrangement, karate, indeed all traditional sports and arts activities, different sects compete for supremacy. The urge to seek security in powerful groupings, which maintain their identity by fiercely opposing other similarly constituted groupings, is the fundamental characteristic of the Japanese psyche.

Factions became a major element in Japanese politics about two years after the LDP was formed. Scalipino, the American political scholar, in his study of the party movement in pre-war Japan, quoted the grand-master of Japanese Parliament Ozaki Yukio as having said in 1917, "Here in the Orient, we have political factions, but no political party." The same words can describe the present situation in Japan. There are only factions and no party.

The five factions in the LDP are formal political entities with their headquarters, regular meetings, known memberships, an established structure and a firm discipline of their own. The factions are in fact parties within a party. LDP activities do not make sense unless the interests of the factions are taken into account.

The LDP chooses its leader through the factions. Each faction raises its own funds and leadership including the president, secretary general and other party officials. Cabinet ministers and government posts are determined by the various factions according to their strength in the Parliament. It is also through the factions that an individual candidate gets most of the aid for his election campaigns.

The greatest stimulus to the growth in the LDP has been the party presidential elections. Politicians wishing to become party president and therefore Prime Minister have to rely on LDP parliamentarians. To do that the potential candidate, normally head of the faction, needs money to feed the dietmen who will vote for him only if he is paid a regular retainer expense and election campaigning expenses. This was where Tanaka had an advantage because he was the most generous giver of funds to parliamentarians.

Japan has spent more than a century trying to catch up with the modern world. To be judged old-fashioned is the political death sentence. The party has resolutely put aside all that is tinged with the past and is concentrating on creating a modern image. But the dietman feels uncomfortable with political modernisation. He talks new but thinks old, and continues to look to his faction for both comfort and support. They have adopted the social values, customs and relationships of an older Japan. The old concepts of loyalty, hierarchy, and duty hold sway for them. They feel very comfortable and at home when they step into the factional world.

Everybody in Japan condemns factionalism, but nobody is able to get rid of the system. Factionalism seems essential to the functioning of Japanese politics. Factional politics is an integral part of the conservative politics. They fulfil the functions which the party does not have. If the politicians really wanted the factions to be done away with, they would have long ago ceased to exist.

The LDP factions are basically divided into two streams — the "conservative mainstream" and the "non-conservative mainstream". The so-called "conservative mainstream" began with Prime Minister Shigeru Yoshida who concluded the Peace Treaty and the Japan–US Security Treaty after the war. The mainstream branched out in two directions. One tributary flows from Prime Minister Hayato Ikeda, who was succeeded by Masayoshi Ohira and who handed over to Zenko Suzuki. Then the present Prime Minister, Miyazawa, took over from Suzuki and became Head of the faction before he assumed the prime ministership. Another stream flows from Prime Minister Eisaku Sato, who was succeeded by Kakuei Tanaka, and now indirectly to Takeshita, the former Prime Minister. Both Susumu Nikaido, former Deputy President of LDP, and Takeshita claim that they arc the legitimate successor of Sato's mainstream tributary. Nikaido publicly stated that the ailing Tanaka did not want Takeshita as his successor, and urged the followers of Takeshita to leave the Tanaka faction and form their own faction. Takeshita, on the other hand, handled the problem skillfully and choose the date of the inauguration of his faction to fall on July 7 — the date when Tanaka spun off from the Sato faction 20 years ago — to bolster his claim to be the conservative mainstream.

When Eisaku Sato died, Takeshita served as the funeral service director, demonstrating his deep relationship with the Sato family. As he was not acknowledged as the successor of Tanaka, he was trying to appear as a disciple of Sato, the boss of Tanaka, and seemingly wished to make it a legitimate reason to form his own faction.

The other factions such as the Fukuda faction, Nakasone faction and Komoto factions are classified as non-mainstream.

The strength of the various factions varies from time to time. It depends very much on how strong their factional leader is in raising funds. If he is able to raise large sums of fund and is able to pull over more dietmen into his faction, he becomes the "king-maker".

Nakasone Faction

I will first write about the Nakasone faction because when I arrived in Japan, Nakasone was the Prime Minister. I will also describe briefly the backgrounds of the various factional leaders, their political styles and the impact they made in Japanese politics.

Although the Nakasone faction had only 65 dietmen, he was supported by Tanaka, for reasons which were obvious — Tanaka wanted to stage a comeback and he could not afford to nominate a candidate from his own faction to be Prime Minister. Normally, only the Head of a faction will become Prime Minister and if Tanaka were to nominate his subordinate for the position, he would have to give way to that person as Head of the faction.

In a country of mainly short people, Nakasone is six-feet tall. The weedy looks of most Japanese politicians are one of their biggest disadvantages in international company. Nakasone can look Reagan straight in the eye, and stare down at President Mitterand. With his broad brow, courtly manners and survival English, he could never be mistaken for anything less than a formidable politician. Only twice in the past four decades has Japan been led by a Prime Minister who captured the international imagination and projected an image of confidence to a world still resentful of the wartime horrors wrought by the sons of Nippon. The first was the forceful self-made man-of-the-people Tanaka and the second Nakasone.

Japanese leaders normally get to the top by cultivating the support of backstage political grandees, and then slumber in office while civil servants and industrialists get on with running the country. Nakasone certainly used the patronage system (his sponsor was Tanaka), but when he took over,

Yasuhiro Nakasone (1982–1986), the Prime Minister whom I first met when I arrived in 1984 and who reigned the longest, having captured the international imagination with his charisma.

everybody knew that Japan was about to be led by someone more than a machine politician.

As a young man, Nakasone presented a petition (written in English) to General Douglas MacArthur, complaining about the curbs placed on Japan by its American style constitution. When voting in elections under the constitution, he donned the uniform of an officer in the Japanese Imperial Navy (he saw service in the Pacific war in the pay corps). By the mid-1970s, Nakasone had held a number of important government posts and was leading a group of about 50 dietmen in his own well-financed faction of the LDP.

During his visit as Prime Minister to the United States, he announced that Japan's role was that of "an unsinkable aircraft carrier". Back home, there was uproar as critics accused him of using warlike language and reviving militarism. Since then, Nakasone's nationalistic bent had continued to land him in controversy.

In 1985, he visited a shrine of Japan's war dead, the Yasukuni shrine, that enshrined the ashes of hundreds of Japanese soldiers who fought in the World War II, including that of pre-war Prime Minster Tojo. It was the first time a Prime Minister had paid respect to the shrine in his official capacity. There was a hue and cry from the Buddhist community and opposing parties, as well as from China and Korea. A year later he made a slip of the tongue when he said publicly that the average intelligence of American was "still very low" because America had a mixture of too many races. He later apologised. In 1987, he led a drive and broke out of the long-standing 1 percent of GNP on defence expenditure and got away with it.

More controversially, he had tried to argue that Emperor Hirohito should be revered again as semi-mystical figure and a focus of national identity. Before he retired as Prime Minister, he ruffled many feathers by proposing that the Japanese should devote less time to work and more to leisure. In a country where most people are workaholics, this has been portrayed by his enemies as an assault on the traditional Japanese lifestyle.

Nakasone had a gift for diplomacy and human relations. He knew which countries were more important to Japan and which countries less. He got on well with the American Ambassador and all Asean Ambassadors. During my first three years stay in Tokyo, I received a well-packed roasted turkey with a note wishing me a "Happy Birthday" from Prime Minster Nakasone. I was pleasantly surprised and wrote a letter to thank him. I reciprocated when his birthday came about and sent him a calligraphy personally done by me. I later found out that only the American and Asean Ambassadors received such favourable treatment.

I met Nakasone on several occasions when Singaporean Prime Minister Lee Kuan Yew visited Japan. He took us to a geisha house and we enjoyed traditional Japanese food, listened to samisen played by old ladies and enjoyed the company of elderly geisha girls.

Nakasone had two competing successors. One was Uno Sosuke, who was Foreign Minister under Nakasone and later became Prime Minister after Takeshita, and another Michio Watanabe, formerly Foreign Minster and who had a chance of succeeding Miyazawa. Uno resigned because of the publicity he received for his involvement with a geisha girl who exposed their connections.

Nakasone was a genius in politician manipulation. Before he retired as Prime Minister, he manipulated the three contending successors for prime ministership — Takeshita, Abe and Miyazawa — to such an extent that all of them had full trust in him. It was strange that a Prime Minister from a weak faction who depended on the Tanaka faction for support could emerge as a "king-maker" for his successor. The three were his closest cabinet ministers — Takeshita was his Finance Minister, Abe his Foreign Minister and the secretary general of LDP. They gave up the idea of fighting it out and left it to Nakasone to make the decision, each thinking that he would be favoured by Nakasone. Finally, Nakasone chose Takeshita because his faction was the strongest within the LDP.

I met Nara (former Ambassador to Singapore who was close to Miyazawa) and he told me that it had been a mistake for both Abe and Miyazawa to put their trust in Nakasone. Nara said Miyazawa actually believed that Nakasone would pick him as Prime Minister. So did Abe. It is hard to believe that the Prime Minister of Japan was picked by one man and not through democratic elections.

In Western democracies, an individual could not become Prime Minister unless his views echoed sentiments popular to the electorate and among his political allies. That was not so in Japan, where the Prime Minister rises from the shifting sands of factional politics, not from any popular vote or mandate. In the case of Takeshita, he was chosen by one single person — Nakasone. Not by LDP Dietmen, nor by the Parliament, but one man.

With the fall of Uno, Watanabe inherited the Nakasone faction. Watanabe, who appeared on television quite frequently, made himself known for his trenchant remarks about politics. I met Watanabe many times when he was Minister for Trade and Industry. He is an outspoken extrovert and does not bother to hide his feelings when making statements. As Minister of MITI, he once said, "The opposition parties only talk about agreeable things, such as reducing taxes and construction bridges and highways. That's like fishing with a feather jig. Fish that can be caught with a feather jig don't have much intelligence." The opposition parties demanded his expulsion from his post.

Most politicians are interested in winning popular support, but despite the strong words it was couched in, Watanabe's statement was welcomed in political circles as straight talk. Watanabe was also a rare bird in the LDP in that he was openly opposed to the plan to expand the Shinkansen network, which would only result in deficits. He was managing his own study group called the Onchi-kai, in preparation for becoming the next Prime Minister after Miyazawa. He had collected 53 young dietmen from various factions and recently opened his own office, which was bigger than the office of the Nakasone faction to which he belonged. In 1990 a rumour was spreading that he was suffering from an incurable disease.

Takeshita Faction (A Split from the Tanaka Faction)

I have written in detail of the rise and fall of Tanaka and some details of the Tanaka faction. The person who inherited Tanaka's influence was Takeshita, who was Tanaka's representative to hand out money to his supporters.

Takeshita, a graduate of Waseda University, one of Japan's top universities, was the son of a provincial sake brewer. He made his political debut in the early post-war years as an assembly member in his native Shimane Prefecture. He was the first ex-prefectural assembly member who reached the pinnacle of the nation's political world. Although he served briefly as a substitute English teacher at a high school before turning to politics, he readily admitted to not being able to speak the language fluently.

Takeshita, who had served as Chief Cabinet Secretary, Construction Minister and Finance Minister, reached the premiership largely through patience and perseverance. He never forgot that there were two sides to every issue

Noboru Takeshita (1986–1988), the Prime Minister who was squeezed out of power because of the Recruit scandal.

and would always lend an ear to conflicting opinions and then devote himself to coordinating views and building a consensus. Lacking in personal charisma, Takeshita made up for it through down-to-earth organisation work. Bland and shy in public, he cultivated a "decent guy" image that drew droves of political sympathisers to his fold. Through his long years of political apprenticeship, first with the late Eisaku Sato, the longest serving post-war Prime Minister, and later with Tanaka, Takeshita developed his organisational skills. He was able to mobilise political force to overcome entrenched and often clashing interest within the bureaucracy and powerful lobby groups that frustrated many of Nakasone's efforts.

Above all, Takeshita had mastered the single most important prerequisite essential to a successful career in LDP politics: the ability to raise big money. He had become one of the most efficient fundraisers among politicians in Japan, partly because he had been Finance Minister for a long period. For instance, at one ¥30,000 (US$200) per ticket fundraiser held in July 1986 he netted ¥2 billion (US$13 million) for his political war chest. This one-shot bonanza came on top of hundreds of millions of yen in regular political donations canvassed each year from a nationwide network of political supporters. This ability enabled him to become Head of the biggest faction within the LDP and thus become the new "king-maker", after he was forced to resign following the Recruit scandal.

As king-maker, he managed to put up two candidates for Prime Ministership — first Uno and then Kaifu, the former belonging to the Nakasone faction and the latter the Komoto faction. Prime Minister Miyazawa was also dependent on his support. He was waiting, like Tanaka did, for the day when he would return to take over the prime ministership. But, events have moved so fast that the possibility of a political comeback is remote. However, he would remain a king-maker.

Takeshita's strongest behind-the-scenes boss was Shin Kanemaru, 77, the most powerful "king" of "king-makers" in the LDP. Kanemaru's son married Takeshita daughter and they were therefore related. Both of them emerged from the construction industry. Kanemaru had held several Cabinet and party positions before he was appointed Deputy Prime Minister in the Nakasone regime. He was still the strongest figure in the Takeshita faction and was responsible in encouraging Takeshita to split from the Tanaka faction as he was the mainstay within the Tanaka faction.

In late 1986, when Kanemaru was hospitalised because of a chronic diabetes and had to undergo an operation, rumour spread that he would not be able to return to politics and that it would have a big impact on the future course of Japanese politics. Lately, when he admitted that he received large sums of money from the Sagawa Kyubin trucking firm, it caused an earthquake in LDP politics. A strong move from normally apathetic Japanese voters clamoured for Kanemaru to quit Parliament. On October 14, 1992, Kanemaru was forced to resign from the Parliament, sending shockwaves through the ruling LDP and the Miyazawa administration.

Billed as the "king-maker" who was said to have brokered the rise of last four Prime Ministers, he was also seriously hurt by disclosures of his links to organised crime.

After Kanemaru had quit the Parliament as well as the Deputy Leadership of the LDP, a serious breakup occurred within the LDP. A fight for leadership began between the acting chairman of LDP, Ichiro Ozawa, and the mild-mannered aide to ex-Premier Takeshita, Keizo Obuchi. Both of them belonged to the younger generation of LDP leaders who do not believe in seniority rules and patience. Both of them have followers within the LDP. Hitherto, the LDP had wielded decisive power in the making and breaking of Prime Ministers and dictating key policies because of the strength of its size and iron unity within the LDP. This split could be a political earthquake in Japanese politics. It might throw out the delicate balance of factions and will have tremendous repercussions in Japanese politics.

Suzuki–Miyazawa Faction

The Head of the Suzuki faction inherited the leadership from his mentor Prime Minister Ohira, so far the only premier who was a Christian. Ohira died of a sudden heart attack and Suzuki was picked as Prime Minister by Tanaka. One of the nicknames that Suzuki earned as Prime Minister was "tape recorder" because for meetings that could not be avoided, the bureaucrats always tried to shield him carefully from foreign dignitaries and editors. Yet misunderstandings could not be avoided. On one occasion, Suzuki sat back and with eyes half closed, recited the answer he had memorised, which sometimes sounded odd since some correspondents had rephrased their questions. He became an international liability for Japan when he denied a statement included in a joint communiqué signed together with President Reagan. He was a big headache for bureaucrats when he had to attend the summit meetings. Japanese newspapers were stating uninhibitedly that Suzuki was not intellectually equipped to think seriously about matters that would come up for discussion. However, Suzuki was the ideal Japanese Prime Minister, judged by standards often presented as ideally Japanese. He was self-effacing and believed above all in "consensus".

I met Suzuki once when he visited Singapore, at a cocktail party given in his honour. We spoke for a few minutes. He was talking about his hobby of sword practice, the Japanese style, and about calligraphy. He said he would give his calligraphy freely to his constituents whenever they asked for them.

Recently, Suzuki was reportedly involved in a scandal and had to appear before a parliamentary sitting.

Miyazawa took over the Suzuki faction when he was fighting for the prime ministership. Miyazawa came from a "blue blooded" political family, but he is regarded as lacking deftness in backstage political maneuvering.

A Finance ministry bureaucrat turned politician, he hails from a family that had produced some prominent politicians. His father was a member of the House of Representatives and his maternal grandfather was a Minister of Railways before World War II. His brother, a former governor of Hiroshima, is a member of the House of Councillors.

Through marriage, Miyazawa's family ties extend to former Prime Minister Ichiro Hatoyama and Zenko Suzuki. Despite such an impressive family lineage, Miyazawa for many years remained aloof from "cloakroom and teahouse politics". That was one of the reasons why he faced an uphill battle against his opponent Takeshita and Abe when they competed for the prime ministership when Nakasone was about to retire. When finally he became Prime Minister, he was already 72 years old.

Fluent in English, Miyazawa took part in negotiations with US Occupation Forces in the reconstruction of Japan from the ashes of the war. Miyazawa had been Minister of MITI, Foreign Minister and Chief Cabinet Secretary. He displayed his talent in the international scene and became friends of many prominent world political figures such as former US Secretary of State Henry Kissinger, former West German Chancellor Helmut Schmidt and Singapore's former Prime Minister Lee Kuan Yew.

On several occasions I was the intermediary between Premier Lee and Miyazawa when I was Ambassador to Japan. Singapore wanted to invite Miyazawa to give a lecture. He had declined because he was too busy. I first met Miyazawa in New Delhi in 1962 when we both attended a seminar organised by the Indian Institute of International Affairs called "Democracy in South and Southeast Asia". I later met him in Tokyo with S. Rajaretnam, Singapore's then Foreign Minister when Miyazawa was Foreign Minister. We got in touch again when I was posted to Tokyo as Ambassador.

Miyazawa is by nature quiet and reserved, but speaks a lot when he drinks a little to much. He was strongly criticised when he begged Shin Kanemaru to reconsider resigning from the post of Deputy President of LDP when the latter had admitted receiving a large sum of money from the Kyubin scandal. His position was dependent on Kanemaru who is the "king of king-makers" in the Takeshita faction.

Fukuda–Abe Faction

Fukuda was a prominent Tokyo University (Todai) graduate who had reached the apex of the Finance Ministry and then turned politician. He was a bitter rival of Tanaka and had a low opinion of him because the latter was not a graduate of any university. In 1948, there was a big stir in political circles when Fukuda was indicted in connection with the Showa Denko scandal.

He played a major role in stirring up the scandal over Tanaka's "money politics". One of the strongest feuds in recent history was the fight between Fukuda and Tanaka. It was so famous that it was known as the "Kaku–Fuku ten year war". It would be difficult to identity any ideological difference between the two — it was merely a personality clash. The feud started when Tanaka's boss, Prime Minister Sato, was favouring Fukuda as his successor when Tanaka should have been the natural choice as he belonged to the Sato faction. Tanaka had to break away from the Sato faction in order to challenge Fukuda. Fukuda had never respected Tanaka, who had no university education, while Fukuda himself was as a top scholar, a graduate from Todai. Both as a personality and as a political animal, Fukuda was the antithesis of Tanaka — reserved and patrician in style, very much the product of his elite training at Tokyo University Law faculty and as a top official of the Finance Ministry. Tanaka was no match to Fukuda in terms of education. The infuriated Tanaka had formed his own group within the Sato faction in 1972 and stood against Fukuda and defeated him.

In Japan, Fukuda was a more popular choice because he was closer to the people and had charisma. When Fukuda became Prime Minister, he concentrated on building good relations with Asean countries and established an aid system to help those countries. His scheme for Japan to help Asean countries economically has come to be known as the "Fukuda Doctrine".

Takeo Fukuda (1976–1978), a rival of Tanaka, who initiated the "Fukuda doctrine" when he became Prime Minister.

Shintaro Abe, Foreign Minister (1984–86), who could have become Prime Minister if he had survived his illness.

He also promoted a foundation to bring about closer relations between students in Asean countries who had studied in Japan.

I first met Fukuda when he attended the Asean–Japan dialogue in Bali which hosted the Asean Summit meeting. I was then Singapore's Ambassador to Indonesia. He was a short, slim with sharp eyes with attractive Chinaman's V-shaped eyebrows. I met Fukuda many times in Japan at conferences organised in Tokyo restaurants by the Alumni of Asean students. He was dynamic and energetic despite his age, and he was immensely popular among Asean students who studied in Japan.

When Fukuda retired, he handed over his faction to Shintaro Abe, who was Foreign Minister when I arrived in Japan. Abe generated a "Mr. Nice Guy" image, appearing amicable, frank, uncomplicated and outspoken, giving one an impression that he was a good and honest man. Bespectacled Abe was taller than most Japanese and would look into the eyes of his American and European counterparts. Like Miyazawa, Abe came from a family of politicians. His father was a member of the Diet and his father-in-law, Nobusuki Kishi, was the right-wing Prime Minister from 1957 to 1960.

Abe, a graduate of the University of Tokyo, was once a reporter for the Mainichi Shimbun. After his marriage, he became Kishi's secretary and was elected to the House of Representative for the first time in 1958. He was dubbed "Prince" in the Fukuda faction as Fukuda was Kishi's protégé and Abe, the son-in-law of Kishi.

Abe held such Cabinet posts as Minister of Agriculture, Forestry and Fisheries, Chief Cabinet Secretary, MITI Minister and then Foreign Minister. He was present when I first presented credentials to Emperor Hirohito. When I last saw him, he was the chairman of the LDP Executive Council. He made his name when he became Foreign Minister and made a mark in diplomacy as Japan's Foreign Minister.

Abe competed for the prime ministership against Takeshita and Miyazawa and missed his chance of premiership. He died of cancer before I finished my assignment in Japan. Abe had been kind to me when he was Foreign Minster. I met him on many occasions to discuss matters of common interest between Japan and Singapore.

Komoto–Miki Faction

The Komoto faction is the smallest faction within the LDP. Komoto was a follower of Prime Minister Miki, who became Prime Minister in 1974 by an accident of history. Tanaka had stepped down under a cloud of criticism and the Lockheed scandal touched off a bitter succession struggle between Fukuda and Masayoshi Ohira. With rumours of a party split in the air, his party vice-president and elder statesman, Etsusaburo Shiina, came forward as a self-appointed mediator. He went back and forth among the major contenders and faction leaders and finally came out with the choice of Miki as a compromise candidate because he was known as the "Mr. Clean". Miki's selection was intended to improve the image of the LDP. Both Fukuda and Ohira accepted the compromise because rejecting it would have put the LDP into a situation of conflict.

Miki had held several Cabinet posts before he became Prime Minister. He had served as Foreign Minister, MITI Minister, Minister for Posts and Communication Minister for Transportation, Minister for Economic Planning Agency, Minister for Environment Agency and later Deputy Prime Minister.

When Miki became Prime Minister, his task was to try to reorganise the party and to do away with party factions. He tried to introduce control over the contributions towards the various factions and to put a new image for LDP. But all his efforts were in vain.

I met Miki when he visited Singapore to meet scholars. We met at the Shangri-La Hotel and a meeting was organised by Professor Lau Teik Soon, Member of Parliament for Serangoon and Head of the Political Department of the University of Singapore. During the meeting Miki started snoring. When it came to my turn to talk, I said I had nothing to say. I would not speak when someone was snoring. Suddenly, he woke up and gave a short comment. This was the impression I had about Miki and it was not a very pleasant one. I was then Ambassador to Japan. Miki passed away soon after that.

Komoto was a follower of Prime Minister Miki and when Miki retired, Komoto took over the faction. Komoto, who was the largest shareholder of Sanko Steamship Co., was on the brink of bankruptcy with accumulated debts of ¥168.2 billion at the end of March 1985. Having inherited in his youth the obscure shipping firm from his brother, Komoto has developed it into one of the world's largest operators of tanker fleets. The company has been the main source of funds for Komoto's political activities.

Komoto became Deputy Prime Minister under the Nakasone administration. Although it is the smallest faction within the LDP, it produced two Prime Ministers after the war, firstly Miki and then later Toshiki Kaifu, who was Prime Minister until Miyazawa took over. Kaifu, another "Mr. Clean", made an impact in Japan and overseas when he took over after the Recruit scandal.

Money Politics

Despite all efforts to do away with money politics, the LDP is still very much influenced by it. After the resignation of Shin Kanemaru, one of king-makers within the LDP, who admitted receiving money from the Kyubin scandal, the LDP government and the party have agreed to press for early passage of stop-gap election reform measures. In a meeting with Prime Minister Miyazawa in August 1992, officials decided to start compiling a plan for more sweeping political reforms. The LDP had made similar promises ever since the Takeshita administration was forced from office, but had not delivered any strong programme. The programme would reportedly consist of a re-apportionment of seats in the Parliament and steps to control the flow of money into political coffers that was the norm.

The need for political funds is mainly responsible for the development of the factions. Before the war, land, particularly farm land, was held by a small minority of landowners. The farmers depended on the landowners for their livelihood, but the owners also looked after the farmers to satisfy their needs. After the war, the US Occupying Force stripped the landowner of his economic powers by putting ownership of the land in the hands of the farmers themselves. By so doing, the US Occupying Forces did not institute a system to compensate for the social services the landlord had provided them. With the removal of the landlord, the farmers turned to their dietmen.

The demands of the farmers are great. The elders want to purchase fire fighting equipment. The village may need a playground, a swimming pool, piano or nowadays, TV sets, computers and agricultural tools. The shopkeeper expects flowers from the dietmen when he opens a new store. Somebody must pay for the activities of the youth and ladies of the village. Before the war, a wealthy landowner could comply to these demands without inordinate strain on his purse. Present-day politicians cannot afford to do so. They therefore need finance from their factional heads. The party is not rich and can only pay a small amount.

Tanaka was popular and powerful because he was resourceful in collecting funds. He paid each dietman an average of a retainer fee of about S$2 million a year. In time of election, a candidate would need at least another S$2 million. Otherwise, he would have no chance of winning an election.

Kato Ryogoro, a dietman who had spent 50 years in Japanese politics including service as Speaker of the Lower House, had this to say about the voters in Japan:

"They force the politicians to spend money on them. For instance, anytime anything happens, they immediately demand a wreath... . When they come to Tokyo from the provinces, they demand a lunch box... . What's more, they act as if these demands were a natural right. They lead the politicians around by the nose. But I can't waste any sympathy on the dietmen. As soon as they run out of money, they go crying to their faction leader. This is what makes the factions strong."

That was the reason why Tanaka was strong, because he always looked after his 120 dietmen. For that he needed a lot of money. The more money he gives to his dietmen, the more he becomes popular and powerful. Tanaka always prided himself on a modern office, kept more than 20 secretaries employed in serving his electoral district and many more when he was secretary general of the LDP.

One method adopted by politicians to collect funds is to hold parties for one reason or another. Enterprises and organisations are asked to buy tickets to these parties. Another method which is still commonly used by politicians who are Ministers in the Cabinet is to utilise the favours they are able to bestow on businessmen in exchange for funds. This method of raising funds which is known as "Tanaka politics" is still being carried out brazenly.

The reason for the adoption of the first method of collecting money is that the Regulation of Money for Political Activities Law has been revised. The total amount of political donations by enterprises has been restricted. It has become necessary for politicians to make public the method of procuring funds and their use. The law has restricted the donations from individuals to a politician to ¥20 million and that of enterprises and trade unions to that of ¥100 million.

Japanese business circles are unhappy that many tickets to raise funds for politicians are forced on them. One prominent tycoon, who prefers not to be quoted, told me once: "It is a nuisance when we are asked to buy 200 to 300 tickets for ¥20,000 of ¥30,000. These politicians demand that we buy them. We cannot afford such an expense. Considering the complicated relations between Japan's political and business world, it is difficult for business circles to refuse to buy such tickets."

Political parties and other political organisations and individual politicians collected a total of ¥116.7 billion in political funds in 1984, according to a Home Affairs Ministry report published during my first year in Japan. Of the major political parties, the Japan Communist Party (JCP), topped the income list with ¥21.7 billion. More than 90 percent of its income came from the sale of its organ and other publications. The ruling LDP reported a total income of ¥13.2 billion, followed by the Komeito with ¥9.2 billion, the Japanese Socialist Party (JSP) with ¥6.3 billion, the Democratic Socialist Party (DSP) with ¥1.7 billion, and the New Liberal Club (NLC) with ¥420 million.

Within the LDP, the five major factions raised a total of over ¥4 billion in 1984. The faction headed by Takeo Fukuda topped the list, raising ¥1.17 billion, and Prime Minister Nakasone was second. Within the Tanaka faction, Takeshita, being the Finance Minister, raised more than ¥92 million, an increase of 11 percent on the previous year.

The largest funds to LDP came from business enterprises who are mainly members of the Keidanren, a leading business organisation representing all big businesses in Japan. According to official figures, it amounted to ¥10,924 million, indicating the party's reliance on business firms for political funds. But, LDP received much more funds than the official figures had shown.

In Japan, political funds can be donated direct to the party, individuals or factions and they are deductible from income tax. Each faction within the LDP receives political donations on its own and does not hand over such donations to the party. According to official figures, Tanaka received the least political funds because he was convicted by the courts for corruption, and Takeshita, who has been collecting political funds on his behalf, received large sums of money.

The various factions collected political funds under different legal organisations which are authorised to collect funds. In the case of Tanaka, he had seven organisations to collect political funds, the most famous one called Echizen-kai (越前會). It collected ¥959 million, 60 percent of which came from the Finance Minister Takeshita who raised ¥831 million. The Suzuki faction collected political funds under an organisation called Kochikai (高智會) which received ¥1,423 million. The Suzuki faction has one other organisation to collect funds. The Fukuda faction has six organisations to collect funds, and the most famous being Seiwa-kai (清和會). All the six organisations in total collected ¥1,614 million.

There was an increase in the collections of funds within the Suzuki and Fukuda factions because Suzuki was planning to hand over leadership to Miyazawa, and Fukuda to Abe, because both the new leaders were contending to be President of the LDP and therefore the Prime Minister.

The Nakasone faction raised money through four organisations. The principle one was Shinseiji Chosakai (新世紀). This faction raised ¥1,979 million. As Prime Minister of Japan, the factional leader invariably raises the large sum of money because of his position. The Komoto faction, which is the smallest faction, collected the least, totalling only ¥1,528 million, because he was without an organisation to collect funds. All donations were made under his own name.

On an industry by industry basis, the banking industry (23 banks) donated the largest amount, followed by the construction and real estate industry and then the electronic and telecommunication and manufacturing industries.

Koenkai

Apart from donations from the business world and organising parties to raises funds by the factional groups, each individual dietman has his own individual support organisation. The Koenkai, as this organisation is called, is the main concern of the dietman. Anything that benefits the koenkai receives the attention of the dietmen and anything which does not benefit the koenkai are left undone. Prime Minister Sato Eisaku once said, "If you ask why we are in this present state with no party organisation, the answer is that the koenkai rather than the party is the important body in the election districts. No matter how hard the party labours, it can't seem to build itself up as it wishes to... ."

The koenkai is a post-war creation. When the American Occupying Forces purged the old political leaders and landlords, their monopoly in the countryside was broken. Land reforms removed the economic underpinning for the dominance by local landlord families. The introduction of the diversified farming and new agricultural techniques, coupled with the flow of younger population to the cities, disrupted ancient customs. The high fluidity of conservative politics — sixteen political parties appeared and disappeared in the first decade after the war — meant that no single party was able to fill the organisation gap. Each candidate was left to look for his own resources. There are also other reasons that caused the emergence of the koenkai. By 1952, the dietmen had created the koenkai to serve their own purpose.

Kakuei Tanaka, the "shadow shogun", said when he was secretary general of the LDP that there were ten million people throughout Japan who were members of the koenkai. The koenkai serves as a social and cultural role in the community and it has come to be the fundamental political organ in the countryside. Localism is still a powerful force in Japanese politics. Most politicians are natives of the district from which they run for office.

Social pressures can still be mustered to push the great majority of the inhabitants of a village into voting for a given candidate.

On one occasion, I had the opportunity to speak to Nakasone about koenkai when he was Prime Minister. Nakasone told me that he did not originally intend to become a politician. He had graduated from Tokyo University and entered the bureaucracy of the Home Ministry. In 1946 he was worried about the communist damage to the nation in the aftermath of the war and decided to resign from the Ministry and go into politics. His family owned a lumber concern in Takasaki and he was quite comfortable as far as living was concerned. He was 28 years old.

When he returned to Takasaki, he was surrounded by young men who shared his political ideals. They supported him during the elections and these young people became the backbone of his koenkai. His headquarters were located across a busy street from the lumber yard in Takasaki. One of Nakasone's modest private homes there was a low Japanese style building which housed the secretaries in a jumble of desks, telephones, tabular steel chairs and overstuffed sofas. On the other side of Nakasone's home was a large two-storey building which on its ground floor had offices and small conference rooms which could hold 50 people. There was a formal auditorium with a small stage on the second floor. These were all the physical equipment of his koenkai. He also organised the married women into a club to help the koenkai.

Nakasone said that he was called upon by the towns and villages to assist them in obtaining funds from the government for the construction of new facilities, paving the roads, building of bridges, laying water pipes and sewage systems, or constructing school gymnasium or train stations, or the installation of an intra-village communications system. His job was to put pressure on the appropriate government departments in Tokyo. He was also expected to lend his name and give financial assistance to the functions of the communities, such as village celebration, funerals and weddings. He sends followers to the opening of a new store and wreaths for funerals. He also serves as the intermediary in gathering capital to establish new businesses or refinance an old ones. He is also obliged to assist in getting the constituents' children into schools, or getting graduates jobs in business firms. Whenever such requests were made, he always asked them to join the koenkai.

A koenkai is something which is personal to the dietman. It is his service station and has nothing to do with the party. Why cannot the koenkai be incorporated into the party structure? This idea has concerned the party leaders since it was broached in 1963. Kuraishi Tadao, who was enthusiastic about the idea, announced to the party that it would increase party membership by three million within the span of a year when he was appointed chairman of the National Organisation Committee in 1966. He said: "I'm not blowing off hot air. If the party branches and the koenkai of the dietmen cooperate, and if the members of the koenkai can be induced to join the party, we shall soon gather about 3,000,000 members. All that's needed is a little effort."

Kuraishi's argument is impeccable. But the hitch lies in persuading the members of the koenkai to join the party. They just want to associated with the dietman. The reason being that the party does not do much for them whereas the dietman does. They owe their loyalty to the dietman and not the party.

One major reason why the koenkai cannot be drawn into the party structure lies in the popular attitudes toward the politicians and the parties. The Asahi Shimbun once reported: "When a voter is urged to join the party because he supports a conservative candidate, he answers, "I only support Mr. A. I don't have any desire to join the party." The Japanese has no sense of party. He looks only at the politicians' personality. The Japanese is inclined to vote for the man rather than the party."

I met the koenkai supporters of many Ministers and had lunch with them. I remember having lunch with the koenkai leaders of Shintaro Abe, the former Foreign Minister when he was alive. Abe was with us at the lunch. They were all prominent Japanese businessmen. They had formed the koenkai in order to support Abe. Each of them paid roughly ¥1 million so that they could have lunch with Abe once in three months. At the lunch, they would try to put their problems to Abe for help. Abe had numerous koenkais comprising of businessmen. He had to employ a chain of secretaries to deal with his koenkais-fixing lunches and answering their calls for services. But, koenkais are definitely a good source for political funds.

Election Campaigning

Election campaigning in Japan is the noisiest affair I have ever seen anywhere in the world. Japanese elections mean noise, unbearable noise. Politicians wearing white gloves signifying purity stand in front of railway stations or bus stops and bellow their speeches at the rush hour crowds. Their propaganda vans go ahead blaring loud noises informing the crowd of the time and place speeches would be made by candidates. When two opposing vans closed in on each other, the result was a bawling cacophony of ingratiation. On polling day, low-flying aircraft buzz over the suburbs exhorting the people to their citizenry duty.

Nothing occupies a politician more than an election. Ono Bamboku, the late vice-president of LDP, once declaimed, "When an ape slips and falls out of a tree, he remains an ape. But let a member of the Diet lose an election, and... ."

Japan has some of the most stringent and detailed electoral laws compared to Western countries. Door-to-door campaigning is forbidden, no signature campaigns may be conducted, the number and size of campaign posters is limited, a candidate can have only one automobile and one set of loudspeakers. There are also restrictions on the amount of money that can be spent in a campaign. But, laws are laws and they are meant to be broken. The great burdens are thus placed on the police, who are supposed to enforce the laws. The police, more often than not, look the other way when most of the minor infractions of the law are committed. Nakamura Kijuo, a scholar who has stood for elections himself, explains how the election laws were being broken:

"Ask why there are so many cases of bribery in the elections and the answer is that many people look at the elections as festivals. In Japan, there are festivals, which occur regularly throughout the year. At each of these festivals, bags of money are distributed, the celebrants gather in one of the buildings in the temple compound to feast and drink, the children carry portable shrines through the streets and are happy by gifts of candy.

"Elections are the same. There is a steady stream of people into the candidate's election headquarters to eat and drink. They warm themselves around the braziers on the mats and excitedly gossip about past elections. Others show up promptly at meal time, talk a bit, eat and then go home. Election headquarters are supposed to serve only light refreshments, but that restriction is not always observed. When one looks behind the scenes, more stimulating refreshments are served. The mood at the election is no different from that during the festivals when people gather at the temple compounds to drink it up."

Hold a political rally without refreshments and you can be sure nobody turns up. Next thing you know, the voters are calling you cheapskate and beginning to doubt your ability to serve them. To supply food and drinks during the election period involves large sums of money and candidates without sufficient funds cannot afford to stand for election.

Japanese politics is a one-trillion yen industry — one third of the size of the defence budget. It is growing at 20 percent each year, even at times of economic slow down. When favours are asked and obligations assumed, cash often changes hands wrapped up in a brown paper bag, delivered to an assigned spot. "Political money" was a rumour, but never substantiated. Japanese campaigns are renowned for the envelope-passing customs. Campaign workers take busloads of voters to the polls, then on the way home, stop off at a restaurant for an early celebration of the "sensei's" victory. Politicians in Japan are known as "sensei", a term with a wider reference than "teacher", translated literally. Doctors, writers, lawyers, university professors and many other people of authority are called sensei. The politician is a sensei not because of any wisdom but for the good works he has performed. He is at the centre of the complex interchange of favour and obligations through which most important transactions are settled. The campaign worker would distribute boxes of seaweed or fancy cigarette lighters to commemorate the occasion. The senkyoya-san (professional election fixer) will buy up voting vouchers beforehand, then distribute them to teams of substitutes.

But, the real "sensei" are those who go for "hard votes" (koteihyo) — special votes that go consistently and repeatedly to a particular person as a consequence of personal ties. The term "hard vote" is common to both popular and academic writings on politics in Japan, but few scholars have attempted to analyse its meaning systematically. In discussing the concept of "hard vote", Japanese lay great stress on the role of "giri" or obligation in the political system. A voter will cast his vote for a certain candidate in order to return a favour received from that person or to repay an obligation to a third party who is supporting the candidate. Votes become "hard" for the politician who reaches the voter through a web of personal relationships. A dietman who continues to serve year after year gradually builds up personal relationships with a large number of voters in his districts and with local politicians, business leaders and others who in turn have intimate ties with numbers of the electorate. Such relationships are established through the help of the koenkai.

At election time the persons brought into this personal relationship are expected to vote for the politician at the web's centre. This behaviour is something uniquely Japanese. On the whole, Japanese are very self-conscious about the influence a supposed "feudalistic" senses of obligation has on voting behaviour. Such "hard votes" are not easily bought with bribes because of a sense of traditional obligation.

Although Japanese elections may be noisy, there has been a complete absence of strong-armed tactics in post-war elections. The atmosphere is often festive: much sake is consumed and many beneficial relations established. Apart from the evil of money spending, no one can complain that Japanese elections are unfair and undemocratic. The Japanese electoral system does the job which is asked of it and provides considerable entertainment into the bargain.

Status Position and Money More Important than Power

Japanese believe more in form than substance. The life of a Japanese politician is not easy, as I have explained above how he has to satisfy the needs of his constituents. He has to raise the necessary funds and spend most of his time and energy serving the people. Yet, many Japanese have chosen politics as a full-time job.

What does a Japanese politician hope to achieve by going into politics? I have spoken to many politicians and also Japanese political scholars, and I came to the conclusion that the Japanese go more for status, position and money than for the sake of power. Every Japanese politician hopes to at least become a Cabinet Minister, if not Prime Minister. In Japan, a prospective minister will have to be elected to the Diet at least five times before he can be considered as ministerial material. When the Prime Minister is chosen, the first duty is to consider a list of names presented by the heads of each faction as candidates for his new Cabinet. Normally, the head of each faction will not recommend those who have not been successful in winning elections at least five times. This is an unwritten tradition in Japan. Priority is given to those who have not yet served in a Cabinet. The length of time a man has been in the faction carries great weight. The intangible considerations of whether a man has the ability, experience and stature to serve as a Cabinet Minister are also evaluated.

Once a dietman has succeeded in being appointed Minister, his life's ambition is fulfilled even though he may warm his seat for only one day. He is already a Minister and he has achieved what he wanted to achieve in life. Whether he inherits any political power when he become a minister is secondary. What he wants is status in society, a position where he can be seen as a VIP and, of course, the money that goes with it. For instance, Prime Ministers like Uno and Kaifu may just have been puppets of the

Takeshita factions because they came from the smaller factions, and were put there by stronger factions. But, they were happy that they had at long last become Prime Ministers and whether they had real power did not matter.

Japanese politicians are paid extremely well by modern standards. In a country where the average salary is ¥4 million, an ordinary dietman is given ¥15 million, plus ¥7 million in expenses, free housing, two secretaries and free ride on every train. The top LDP leaders are rich men in their own right, possessing large holdings of land and securities and usually several gold-club memberships. They deal actively and profitably on the stock exchange, making excellent uses of their business connections. But, it is not an easy matter to be a Japanese dietman. I have visited the Japanese Parliament many times and I always found every dietman extremely busy. Politics is a full-time profession. All their secretaries were also busy dealing with their voters. I never found any dietman who could afford to idle.

In Japan, the life of a Prime Minister and Ministers is also not easy. Their terms are short-lived. Normally a Prime Minister serves only two years, so do Ministers. There is a long queue of dietmen who have served more than five terms waiting to be nominated as ministers. They rotate so frequently that sometimes it is difficult to recognise who are the ministers. They are new to their jobs and have to spend all their time boning up on answers to questions in the Diet. By the time they are experienced, they are out of office. The result is that the bureaucrats are the real power behind the throne. The Yomiuri Shimbun once published an article on how bureaucrats look at their ministers: "... From the point of view of the bureaucrats, there are two types of ministers. One is the 'chapeau minister' who during his term of office, simply wears the hat of the ministry. He does not interfere with the formation of policy or with administration. His only task is to grant affirmatively to explanations and reports of the bureaucrats and try not to advance any ideas or thoughts of his own.

"The 'muscle man minister' is just the opposite. He has complete and direct control over the high officials. He uses two methods. First, he uses the power to appoint, transfer and promote personnel... . Second, he has a close understanding of policy and administration, and through his ability, he controls the bureaucrats. Most of these Ministers are dietmen who are former bureaucrats."

The bureaucrat in Japanese society is highly esteemed by ordinary people. In the mind of the public, the bureaucrat is seen to be above politics; he looks after Japan first rather then himself. The bureaucrats also believe this and describe themselves as "kokushi" or patriots.

The heyday of bureaucratic power in Japan was the period of the Allied Occupation up to the end of the 1960s. During this period, the Supreme Command decided to rule through existing bureaucratic structures, and this reinforced the tradition of legislation being drawn up within the bureaucracy. Until 1970, government officials had much more power than politicians. They could act on their own initiative, because the economy was expanding and so was the government's budget. The end of Japan's rapid economic growth coincided with a number of other important developments. First, there were a number of scandals involving lower-level bureaucrats which made the government change their jobs every two years. This creates the generalist who has a broad knowledge of his department. But, until the early 1970s, the second tier bureaucrat never changed his job; he stayed in the same division until retirement. The second tier was, in a sense, the collective memory of the department. Having worked in a single area for 20 years or more, it was this bureaucrat who knew the past history of policy and could advise his superior. When the government made these people change jobs every two years, the accumulative knowledge of these people dispersed.

The second major development was a function of the LDP's growing experience of government. To compete with the bureaucrats the politician had to specialise. To do this he joined a policy division, of which there are 17, of the LDP's Policy Affairs Research Council, and these divisions mirrored the bureaucracy.

The top leaders of these PARC divisions are called "zoku" and these men were the power-brokers of the 1980s. Zoku means family or tribe, but in the political world it can apply to an individual politician or a group of senior politicians with a common administration interest.

The zoku are the key politicians in Japan — no legislation that relates to their interests is put before the Diet until they approve it — and some could one day be Prime Ministers. They are men with many years of parliamentary experience and moreover, they have become specialised in fields of government administration.

Prime Minister Tanaka took great pains to foster the zoku, having exceptionally strong connections with various government ministries, especially the Ministry of Posts and Telecommunications and the Ministry of Construction. As zoku have their power-base in specific departments of the ruling party's Policy Council, the leaders heading such departments came to have tremendous power.

It has been estimated that of the LDP's total parliamentary representation of 399, about 50 are zoku. In Prime Minister Nakasone's former Cabinet, there were a number of top zoku in charge of their administrative speciality. Nakasone was the first Prime Minister since Tanaka fell ill who advocated that the politicians should be the policy makers and that they should lead the bureaucrats instead of the other way round. He told his ministers to give instructions to their bureaucrats, instead of being led by them.

The whole involvement of politicians in the political process is to generate political funds, and they do this by giving their supporters what they want. The ability of politicians to put down roots in certain policy making areas enables them to ensure a supply of money and contacts to help them win elections.

Now, in a sense, the politicians have caught up with government bureaucrats. In the past, politicians were not good at planning because they did not have the resources to make those sorts of decision. Now this has changed. Bureaucrats change their jobs every two years, but a politician will stay in the same PARC division for ten years or more. During that time he can get information and resources through his particular specialisation.

In Japan, it has got to a situation where if the bureaucracy designs a programme or a law which could impinge on the interest of zoku, then it has to get the ruling party's approval first before it is presented to the Diet. There is certainly a shift in the balance of power toward the politicians, but it cannot entirely deprive the bureaucrats of their normal power. The senior bureaucrats have developed strategies to counter the power of the influential zoku. These groups do the utmost to persuade other important groups, such as businessmen, or enlist other forces such as foreign pressure to try to counter top zoku if their policies were not acceptable.

Other bureaucrats who are more opportunistic have developed advanced techniques for coping with politicians. They are highly adept at making subtle adjustments in response to the changing pattern of action alliances. As they often say, "Bureaucrats must move their antennae like those of an insect in the direction from which power emanates." Bureaucrats will not openly criticise, let alone openly defy political leaders. Politicians can afford to talk down to bureaucrats and scold them in public. They will sometimes do so to demonstrate their superiority, but such superiority is mostly illusory. The bureaucracy can create problems for politicians by not keeping them informed of what is necessary.

As this continuing tussle between centres of power within the Japanese government becomes institutionalised, it must itself slow down the process of change in Japan.

Opposition Parties — The Japan Socialist Party (JSP)

The LDP, or in actual fact the five factions under the name of LDP, ruled Japan for nearly 45 years. What happened to the opposition parties? Why was it that the Japan Socialist Party, the strongest opposition party, did not have a chance to rule Japan? Can the socialists seize power in Japan in future? These questions have occurred to me from time to time.

This was partly due to the fact that the JSP has experienced intra-party struggles concerning the ideology of the party as well as factional disputes, thus dissipating the energy of the party. The opposition parties could not find common ground for a united effort to oust the LDP. In other words, the opposition parties were also split.

One major reason is that the majority of the Japanese people find the capitalist system quite beneficial to them. Ninety percent of the Japanese people profess to consider themselves middle class. There is little gap between the income differentials amongst the high income group and the lower income groups. Life under the capitalist system may not be perfect, but it has created a dramatic rise in living standards within the memories of most people. It was difficult for the JSP to persuade the Japanese voters of the benefits of socialism. The JSP's failure to move away from Marxist theorising made it impossible for the party to make any headway. The left has turned its back on the dominant characteristic of modern Japan.

Whereas in the 1960s Japan was still in the process of developing heavy industries, in the 1970s it overcame the difficulties from the oil crisis and found itself as one of the most successful economies in the world. As a result, a majority of the Japanese voters regard themselves as part of the affluent middle class, and there are many among unionised workers who support the conservative or centrist parties, rather than the JSP or the Japan Communist Party.

The history of the JSP has been a succession of missed opportunities. It started out with a massive store of electoral goodwill, being a pre-war proletarian party with the strongest opposition to the war-lords. It was a natural vehicle for the millions of workers who flowed into the cities from the agricultural districts. It was during this period that the party made a mistake in organising a mass demonstration against the Security Treaty that culminated in chaos and disorder in Japan. It lost a great a deal of support because of the unrest.

The JSP has a close and long lasting relationship with the labour movement, both the party's greatest sustenance and its fatal weakness. Compared to their European equivalents, Japanese unions are simply not powerful enough to form a national party. The unionisation rate in Japan is low and falling, now barely half its post-war peak. The enterprise union system acts against the formation of class consciousness.

The JSP had failed to make serious attempts to meet the social change until Ishibashi was installed as chairman of the party in the fall of 1983. Until the end of 1985, there were still about one third of delegates who refused to say "sayonara" (good-bye) to Marxist Leninist doctrines.

In early 1986, Ishibashi was happy that at long last the JSP had unanimously adopted its "new declaration" at its National Convention, pledging its effort "to pursue every possibility of cooperating and uniting with other parties for the establishment of a socialist administration". This "new declaration" stipulates that the party will discard the Marxism Leninism followed by the Soviet Union and East European nations, and adopt a practical policy line of social democracy.

The JSP draws its strength mainly from the Korokyo (Council of Public Corporation Workers Union) which has a membership of 830,000. The core of Korokyo is the Sohyo (General Council of Trade Unions of Japan) which is confronting a major crisis with the prospect of losing 300,000 members due to the privatisation of two public corporations. Over the years, the JSP's membership began to drop. The party is less concerned now with expansion than it is with preventing further decline.

One factor behind the decline of the JSP is its method of recruiting candidates for election. In the 1983 election, almost half of the successful candidates were people with union backgrounds while another half were locally recruited government servants. Whilst the LDP were recruiting candidates of former bureaucrats and university graduates, the JSP were recruiting candidates of lower educated unionists. Another reason for the weakness of the JSP was that while the party in power is able to dish out favours and get large donations from businessmen from multi-nationals and other enterprises, the JSP found itself unable to field candidates in some constituencies because of the financial burden involved. So long as an election continues to give more weight to those candidates who have more money, the JSP will be handicapped and will have very little chance of winning more seats.

The JSP is also unrealistic in its approach to several matters relating to Japan's practical problems. For instance, it has closer relations with Communist countries like North Korea and People's Republic of China than with South Korea and Taiwan. It has maintained close relations with North Korea while adopting a hostile attitude towards South Korea. It follows this distorted idea because it adheres to the formalistic Marxist Leninist theory that a Communist regime is democratic and non-Communist government undemocratic. It refused to recognise the Communist government as undemocratic. It refuses to recognise the Japanese Self-Defence Force as a constitutional body and thus has been boycotting invitations by SDF to attend their functions. It also does not recognise "Kimigayo" as a legal national anthem of Japan and even the "hinomaru" as Japan's national flag. The JSP also boycotted all functions organised by Emperor Hirohito. Whenever I attended the Emperor's functions, the absence of JSP representative was always conspicuous. The Japan Communist Party also take a similar attitude towards the Japanese anthem, national flag and attending the Emperor's functions.

On 8 September 1986, the JSP elected a woman as its president. She was Takako Doi, then 57, a spinster and once a senior lecturer in a privately

Takako Doi, Speaker of the Parliament, who led the Japan Socialist Party.

endowed Doshisha University law school. In her acceptance speech, Doi appealed to members to make a fresh start with the "new declaration" which the party had adopted. She made a stumping tour to various parts of the country, attending fund raising parties for her party and being interviewed by the media. She even made an appearance on several "quiz shows" and similar entertainment programs on TV and radio as a guest. Indeed, a new "star" had been born in national politics for the first time in years. And the media called it "the Doi boom". For a moment, she seemed to have great potential to become a unique "communicator" between the increasingly apolitical Japanese public and the world of politics in general and the JSP in particular. The JSP issued telephone cards featuring a portrait and autograph of Doi for the purpose of fund-raising which sold well, and she was chosen by a national association of pachinko (Japanese style pinball game) parlour owners and operators as one of the first winners of the "Pachinko Cultural Award". Doi was one of the best pachinko players in Japan. Her favourite catch-phrase "Yarukkya-nai" (you have got no choice but carry on) became the winner of a special award by a publisher of an encyclopaedic almanac which selects the "word of the year". Doi was so superb in her public relations work that the press was comparing her to the Conservative British Prime Minister Margaret Thatcher.

One morning, she suddenly arranged for a discussion at the Parliament Building with Asean Ambassadors stationed in Japan. She wanted to know how Asean Ambassador felt about the general fear of Japan's rearmament in Asia. When it came to my turn to speak, I told her of my experience of hiding from Japanese Kempetai in a Malaysian jungle for three years, and that naturally I did not welcome Japan's military return to Asia. This took my Asean colleagues by surprise. The Brunei Ambassador, Pengirang Idris, said, "You are really very blunt and frank. I never expected you to say those things." I replied, "This is what I am. I never hide the facts of life although I may be an Ambassador."

Doi's enjoyment of her limelight did not last long. Although she spent a great deal of time and energy trying to sell the JSP, she failed to persuade other more radical leaders to discard the old shackles of ideological dogmas heavily influenced by Marxist Leninism.

The collapse of the Soviet Union and Eastern Europe has made an impact on the JSP. Under the leadership of Tomiichi Murayama, the party changed its traditional Cold War doctrine and became practical and realistic. The Murayama-led JSP saw the futility of remaining as opposition in Japan and decided to go in for power. In the strategy of political convenience, they agreed with the LDP faction led by Yohei Kono to run Japan as an alliance under the Prime Ministership of Murayama, who became the second socialist Prime Minister Japan has known since World War II. Murayama changed JSP's previous stand on objecting to the Japan–US Security Peace treaty and other basic policies such as opposing to the formation of Japan's Self-Defence Force and recognising Japan's national flag and national anthem.

If the JSP could attune its policy more realistically to suit the prevailing circumstances in Japan, it would have a better future.

Democratic Socialist Party (DSP)

The DSP was formed in 1960 by defectors from the JSP and was founded by Domei, the umbrella organisation of private sector unions. The defectors were dissatisfied with JSP's Marxist Leninist policies and founded the DSP to espouse social democracy. Originally, the DSP advocated revision and not abrogation of the Security Treaty and the expansion of the welfare state. Today, the DSP is more rightwing than some sections of the LDP.

I came to know the former President of DSP, Kasuga, when he visited the Peoples Action Party headquarters in Singpore in 1965 when I was the Organising Secretary of PAP. DSP always regarded the PAP as a fraternal party as both the parties believe in democratic socialism. He was short, slightly bald at the front, with big eyes and a low voice. He came with Watanabe, then the Director of International Affairs. They got in touch with the PAP because we also believed in democratic socialism. When I was sent to Japan as Ambassador, I contacted these old friends and they were useful in my contact with the political world. Kasuga, who died in 1988, was old-timer in politics and got on well with LDP leaders. He played an important role in behind the scene negotiations between LDP leaders and opposition parties.

In 1985, the DSP worked out a draft action programme that kept the door open for its coalition with the ruling LDP. One of the ambitions of DSP was to form a coalition government with the LDP.

With 51 seats in both Houses of the Diet, the DSP is the nation's No. 3 opposition group, after the JSP and Komeito. The new program does not rule out the possibility of a coalition with the conservative LDP, saying that the party would not oppose formation of a coalition so long as its own policies were reflected in the administration.

In December 1984, DSP chairman Sazaki was involved with supporting LDP Secretary General Nikaido's move to oust Nakasone from office and replace him as Prime Minister. This move misfired because it did not get the approval of Tanaka. As a result of this unsuccessful manipulation, Sasaki had to resign as chairman of the DSP.

At various times, DSP suggested an alliance with Komeito, the JSP and the anti-mainstream LDP factions to form the government. With an unabashed yearning for power, the DSP has been following the pragmatic principles of its founder Suehniro Nishio, who once said, "A cat that does not catch mice is no cat."

The Komeito (The Clean Government Party)

The Komeito was established in 1964 as the Soka Gakkai's political arm. When founding the party, its leaders stated that the purpose was the promotion of Buddhism in national politics, a dubious notion dividing religion and government. In the late 1960s, Komeito's close relationship with the religious organisation began to generate bad publicity. A book was written entitled *I Denounce Soka Gakkai* alleging brainwashing and electoral manipulation. Despite behind the scene support from Tanaka to suppress the publication, the book became a bestseller.

In 1970, the Komeito was re-established as an independent political party, dedicated to the advancement of "humanitarian socialism". Although legally speaking it has severed its relations with Soka Gakkai, it receives the support from Soka Gakkai members.

In electoral terms, the Komeito has been easily the most successful opposition party, attracting between 9 percent to 10 percent of the popular vote. Komeito has 59 seats in Lower House and 27 seats in the 255-seat Upper House. It is the second strongest opposition party in Japan. The party has 3,000 local Assemblymen affiliated to the party. It has also become the ruling party of 60 percent of Japan's prefectures. The supporters belong to the less educated obedient masses of the lower income strata in urban areas. They are shoppers, owners of small factories, restaurant owners, blue collar workers who do not belong to unions, taxi drivers and the less educated masses. Of course, many of its leaders are also lawyers, medical doctors and executives of big business. These obedient and hardworking ordinary people are not so much affected by the revolutionary changes brought about by the World War II. The older members, who were released from the military services after the war, resumed their previous jobs or businesses as though nothing had happened. They hate war and would like to live in peace.

They were forgotten by the bureaucracy, which kept its organisation intact, and the trade unionists who had expanded under the guidance of the Allied Occupation Forces. Just as the LDP receives its support from big business and the farmers and the JSP gets its support from the left-wing trade unions, the Komeito draws its support from this group of the ordinary citizens and small businessmen. Soka Gakkai provided these ordinary citizens with a sense of belonging and they feel that they have a voice in the Parliament through the Komeito.

I met the Komeito chairman in December 1984 when I first arrived in Japan. The then 59-year-old chairman, Yoshikatsu Takeiri, was elected to the Lower House seven times. The Komeito has a small but comfortable headquarters which the chairman described as "small". Takeiri started life as a mechanic and then later joined the National Railways, resigning to contest election 29 years ago. He was humble and unassuming and spent one and a quarter hour with me offering cakes and fruits.

I asked Takeiri about the relationship between Komeito and Soka Gakkai. He said the Komeito was originally formed by the Soka Gakkai's former president, Ikeka, who had now become a symbol of the party. Later, it was discovered that it ran against Japan's constitution which prohibited religious bodies from forming political party and was later legally separated from Soka Gakkai. Soka Gakkai and the Komeito however belong to the same organisation.

At the beginning, most of the Komeito Dietmen were also leaders of the Soka Gakkai. Events have proved that Soka Gakkai leaders were not necessarily good politicians. As leader of the party, Takeiri had to announce that there should be an age limit to Komeito Dietmen, fixing it at 66. His purpose was to signal to the Soka Gakkai Dietmen that they could not go beyond 66.

Takeiri said, "The situation now is different. We do not need to nominate Soka members and we have better quality dietmen. But I have made the proposal, I have to take the lead to resign when I am 66." Takeiri said that one of these days, Komeito might need experienced people to take over the government and limiting the age of 66 might be a great handicap. In Japan, 66 is considered relatively young for a politician. To be a Minister, one must at least be over 60.

Takeiri explained that the Soka Gakkai has no hand in picking election candidates and does not interfere very much with the party policy. But, the leaders of Soka Gakkai and the Komeito are in frequent contact. I told Takeiri that the fact that Komeito got its support from Soka Gakkai might create an impression that Komeito was trying to create a Buddhist society. He said that Komeito is a non-religious party which aims at creating a free democratic society with religious freedom granted to all religions according to the constitution. I asked him whether the Komeito has any Christian dietmen. He scratched his head and asked his Director of International Affairs, Senator Akira Kuroyangi, who sat in at the interview for an answer. Akira said he was not aware of any. But he added that there were several dietmen who were not members of the Soka Gakkai.

How does the party get its funds? Takeiri said the Komeito would not accept any donation from big business for it does not want any interference from big business. The party got its funds from Soka Gakkai members and its supporters, and through their publications. Has Komeito any ambition to form the government and if it should succeed what type of government and society would Komeito want? Takeiri said that Komeito has reached a stage where it can think of a coalition government. It is friendly with the Democratic Socialist Party as well as with some of the LDP leaders.

"One of these days, we might form a coalition government with the DSP and some of the LDP factions," said Takeiri. I chipped in, "Without Nakasone?" Takeiri laughed and said, "We do not like Nakasone because he is too close to Reagan. He wants to rearm Japan and make it a military power again. We are also against his intention to raise taxes."

With the growing Russian threat to Japan, did he not think it was better for Japan to build up military to defend itself instead of depending on the United States?

Takeiri said that however much Japan might expand militarily, it would not be able to defend against a Russian attack. In fact, he added, Japan could hold on to Hokkaido for only five days should there be a Russian attack. He added, "Sometime ago, a survey was made to study the reaction of our young generation to a possible foreign attack on Japan. About 40 percent of your youths said they would run away if an attack should come." Having watched the youths of Japan for the past four years, I tend to agree with Takeiri.

Takeiri emphasised to me that the Komeito had four main principles in its party policy: 1) There would be no change in the present constitution; 2) The defence budget must be limited to 1 percent GNP; 3) There should be clean and honest politics without interference from the Zaikai (meaning the multi-national financial power), and 4) Democracy and freedom would be ensured for all religions.

The last principle is important as Soka Gakkai leaders have a constant fear that the clock may be turned back to the day when State Shintoism will be the country's dominant religion. Soka Gakkai leaders were detained in the early part of its history by government leaders who were pro-Shintoism.

Is there factionalism in the Komeito? Takeiri said, "Outwardly, there is no factionalism in our party", hinting that there is also certain amount of factionalism within the Komeito. Factionalism seems to be in the blood of all Japanese. Generally speaking, the Japanese are loyal to their leaders and less so to an idea. Even in the Communist and Socialist Parties, there is factionalism.

Japan Communist Party (JCP)

The Japan Communist Party is probably the best organised party in Japan. It has 400,000 members, more than five times the strength of the JSP. It receives its funds from membership dues and sales of the party paper "Akahata" which claims a circulation of 3.5 millions. Founded in 1922 under the direction of the Comintern, the JCP began its existence as an underground organisation subject to stiff repression by the government. In pre-war years, development in China made Japanese leaders worried about the existence of the JCP. By the mid-30s, all the main JCP activists were in prison and exiled. As a result, right up until the 80s, the party was controlled by a generation of politicians whose knowledge of the revolutionary struggle was theoretical rather than realistic.

For example, the Communists originally hailed the occupation forces as an army of liberation, but as soon as the cold war intensified, shifted back to the advocacy of violent revolution. The authorities responded with the purge on the reds in 1950, in which thousands of suspected communists were barred from political activity and dismissed from their jobs. In 1952 during the Korean war, the JCP staged a terrorist campaign but failed to stimulate popular uprising. They lost all 35 of their Lower House seats.

In 1972, JCP achieved some electoral success with some anti-LDP voters. In 1976, the phrase "dictatorship of the proletariat" was dropped from the party's platform and "scientific socialism" replaced Marxism Leninism. It advocated parliamentary democracy and denied the need for "dictatorship" as practised in the Soviet Union.

Although the JCP had opposed the United States–Japan Security Treaty and took part in the two biggest campaigns against its revival, in 1960 and 1970, it was criticised by left-wing student group for not being militant enough. By 1980 it had modified its opposition to the existence of the Self Defence Force and, with the end of the Vietnam War, became less critical of the United States. It only called for the nationalisation of big businesses and comprehensive social welfare.

After the debacle in 1952, the JCP gradually recovered and constantly held a handful of seats in the Lower House of the Diet. Its most dramatic gains came in the 1969 elections, when it won over three million votes for the first time and increased its membership in the Lower House from 5 to 14. It won over 10 percent of the vote in 1972, 1976 and 1979 elections and dropped slightly to 9.8 percent in 1980, but the number of Diet members varied a lot.

The JCP broke with the Russian Communist Party in 1963–64 and broke ranks with the Chinese Communist Party in 1966–67. It adopted an independent and nationalist stance and thus increased its popularity and respectability at home. It emphasised traditional Japanese folk culture and has been outspoken in its demands for the return to Japan of the Soviet-occupied islands north of Hokkaido. Because of China's antipathy towards it, the JCP was the only party that played cool to the normalisation of relations with PRC in 1972 when Prime Minister Tanaka went to China to sign the China–Japan Peace and Friendship Treaty in 1978. The party, however, has close relations with the Communists in Italy, France and other Western states.

The JCP had missed its chance in the early period of post-war Japan when the people were poor and hungry. As a party which was championing the cause of the proletariat, the JCP became a legal political party and should have made special effort to lay a foundation for their party. But events took place too fast for the JCP. The Korean War, which made the Americans fall back on the Japanese for assistance, had helped Japan rapidly develop economically. The quick change in the world situation had also benefited Japan's economic development. Within a short period of 40 years, Japan has caught up with the world and has become an economic giant. The pragmatic and realistic Japanese people, who are not fond of ideology and empty dogmas, favoured capitalism more than Marxist Leninism or socialism. It is human nature to want a better living standard and better life. The Japanese, particularly, are no exception. With economic progress, left-wing parties lost favour and could not capture the imagination of the Japanese.

The Hosokawa Administration

With the complete collapse of the Soviet Union and Communism in Eastern Europe, the chances of the JCP and JSP entering the corridors of power have become dimmer than ever. With the present world trend and the mood of the times, the chances of a Socialist Japan, not to mention a Communist Japan, are very remote indeed. But with the break up of the LDP into splinter parties, the Socialist Party found an opportunity to be a partner of the Coalition government under the leadership of Moihiro Hosokawa, head of the Japan New Party, following the August 1993 general elections which ended LDP's 48 years monopoly of power.

Hosokawa's coalition government consisted of seven partners: the Japan New Party led by Hosokawa, the Shinseito led by the Deputy Prime Minister Tsutomu Hatta who broke away from the LDP, the Sakigake, another group of ten junior LDP dietmen led by Masayoshi Takemura who also broke away from the LDP, the Democratic Socialist Party, the Japan Socialist Party and the United Social Democratic Party. Hosokawa and leaders of these parties found common ground in wanting an immediate political reform in the Japanese political system and they wanted to do away with Japan's money politics and the country's corrupted politics.

The 55-year-old leader of the Japan New Party is known as a strong advocate of administrative reform and deregulation. He once belonged to the LDP faction led by former Prime Minister Kakuei Tanaka. During his eight-year governorship in Kumanoto — where his ancestors had ruled as feudal lords from the early 17th century to 1868 — Hosokawa vigorously promoted deregulation and decentralisation, and implemented various policies and events for the benefit of the prefecture.

I met Hosokawa in 1985 when he was still Governor of Kumanoto, when I visited the prefecture. He talked about the clean politics of Singapore and expressed his great admiration for our then Prime Minister Lee Kuan Yew. He gave me the impression of a good leader and appeared to me rather ambitious.

Born in January 1938 in Tokyo, Hosokawa graduated from Sophia University, the same university where my two daughters had graduated. In 1963, he joined one of Japan's largest daily newspapers, the Asahi Shimbun, as a journlist. Hosokawa comes from an aristocratic lineage that has produced several leaders. His grandfather served as Prime Minster in 1937–1939 and his father, Morisada Hosokawa, was a duke in pre-war days. His younger brother, Takateru Konoe, married the daughter of Prince Mikasa, the brother of Emperor Hirohito.

Morihiro Hosokawa (1993–1993), the first non-LDP Prime Minister who formed a coalition government to take over from the LDP administration.

Seventeen years ago, when Hosokawa was Vice-Minister of Finance, Yohei Kono, presently President of LDP but then Chief Cabinet Secretary who quit the LDP, had asked him to join when the latter founded the New Liberal Club. Both Kono and Hosokawa were fed up with the LDP because the party was embroiled in a crisis of confidence over the Lockheed payoff scandal involving Tanaka.

Explaining why he had refused to join Kono's New Liberal Club, Hosokawa said, after he became Prime Minister: "In those days, both talented and ambitious men like Takeo Fukuda, the late Masayoshi Ohira, Yasuhiro Nakasone and Noboru Takeshita were waiting in the wings to take power, and the LDP's framework was thought still firm enough to survive the scandal.

"This time, I was convinced that the established parties of the right and left alike were incapable of reforming national politics and were not able to cope adequately with rapidly changing situations at home and abroad, and I thought that the LDP was so rotten that it could fall at the slightest push.

"Many people told me that I was too hasty and impatient. However, soon after we acted, the Sagawa Kyubin scandal leapt into the headlines, followed by the Kanemaru affair. The timing was right."

The Hosokawa government's proposed reform of the electoral system was expected to trigger off fundamental changes in the nation's political landscape, obliging parties to seek new groupings or even mergers for survival in the next general election.

Nakasone predicted that the Hosokawa regime would not last one year. His reason was that the new government had very few members who had past experience of ruling a country.

When Hosokawa became Japan's Prime Minister in the summer of 1993, ending 38 years of unbroken rule by the LDP, he identified reform of the country's corrupt and antiquated political system as his coalition's principal task. Through the influence of Tanaka, Japan has been ruled by money politics. Hosokawa's reform bill had the potential to make Japanese politics cleaner and more transparent by replacing the current multi-seat constituency system. His government introduced a system of mixing the present proportional representation with single seat districts. Hosokawa got the bill through the Lower House in November 1993, but when it came to the Upper House, it was defeated. Hosokawa's failure to get his bill passed by the Upper House at the end of January 1994 reflected the complex nature of his seven-party coalition and in particular the imposition of its largest component, the Socialist Democratic Party, 17 of whose members crossed the floor to vote with the opposition LDP. Ironically, the only party which could assure him of a majority to salvage at least part of his plan was the LDP.

Unless the problem was swiftly resolved, economic confidence would take a further battering. Hosokawa faced the most serious economic recession since World War II, and the US was mounting pressure on Japan's trade surplus. Vital decisions on stimulating and deregulating the economy were being held hostage by the political reform. Failure to reach an agreement on political reform would only prolong the political and economic agony and aggravate Japan's relations with the US — its most important partner.

After many nights of political "nemawasi" (consultation) with LDP leaders, Hosokawa finally achieved what was without doubt his greatest achievement so far as Prime Minister, on 29 January, 1994. He reached an eleventh hour accord with the LDP President Yohei Kono and paved the way for the approval of the package of four reform-related Bills by both Houses of Parliament. It is noteworthy that 17 years ago, both Hosokawa and Kono quit the LDP and the latter had asked Hosokawa to join his New Liberal

Club but the former had refused. And Kono became the President of LDP and Hosokawa the Prime Minister of a coalition government.

Hosokawa's reform success raised his stature in the international community, not least in Washington where he met with US President Bill Clinton in early February 1994. His triumph, plus the high support rating which he continued to enjoy among the Japanese people, had helped him to tackle other pricking issues such as a controversial proposal to raise Japan's sales tax and completing a third supplementary budget for 1994–95 beginning in April. Settling these economic problems had been delayed while Hosokawa struggled to pass political reform.

Critics had given Hosokawa's fragile coalition little chance of bringing about the reforms. The reform package was essentially a compromise between Hosokawa and the LDP, which authorised the Hosokawa administration to transform the electoral system for the Lower House. It did this by replacing existing multi-seat wards with a mixed system of single-seat constituencies and proportional representation, and by modifying official controls over political donations. Although many of the measures have been watered down, the reforms will do much to discourage the influence-peddling that has toppled several recent goverments. Replacing the current system of multi-seat Lower house districts with 300 single-seat districts, for instance, will discourage candidates of the same party from competing against each other by peddling favours to constituents. It was this sort of competition that brought about money politics. The aim of the single seat wards proposed for the Lower House was to shift the focus of election campaigns from factional politics to national politics; whereas before, politicians from the same party ran as candidates from rival factions and depended heavily on their factions campaign support groups, now politicians would be able to run on partywide platforms that superseded factional differences and were supported by all local campaign groups.

This electoral system is also expected to change the nature of political parties. The LDP organisation was long characterised by the formation of factions and by the ceaseless feuds and alliances among them. The factions were an outgrowth of the multi-seat constituency system, under which the LDP ran two or more candidates for each electoral district, or two to six seats. These candidates generally came from different factions of the party, and their success depended on the strength of their factional backing. The single-seat constituency system makes factional support no longer necessary, and in fact since the approval of the system, LDP factional activity has rapidly ebbed.

While most commentators commended the Hosokawa administration for its reform efforts, almost all were not so sure that the proposed changes to the political system would be effective in cleaning up Japanese politics.

What were the reasons that had brought about Hosokawa's reform success? Several LDP elder politicians wanted to see the collapse of the Hosokawa's regime. What had caused the LDP to change its mind to support Hosokawa? To my mind, the average Japanese, politicians included, had always had at heart the interest of the country. Japan could not afford to drag her feet on political reform and allow the country to go down the drain economically. Time was too precious and pressing for a decision to be made to boost Japan's economy, which was suffering from a serious recession. Unemployment was already mounting. However much some of the older LDP leaders might want to see the fall of Hosokawa, they could not ignore the fact that if Hosokawa could not deliver his promise to bring about political reform, the LDP would be blamed and for that they would lose the support of voters in future elections.

Would the Hosokawa's political reform bring about a change in the nature of Japanese politics? Would money politics disappear from the political scene? Could he succeed as the first and only Prime Minister to do away with money politics? Would there be cleaner politics after the political reform? Could the new ruling change the nature of the Japanese people?

These questions were uppermost in the minds of those who were interested in Japanese politics. Many thought that at long last Japan would see cleaner politics and Prime Minister Hosogawa would go down in history as the "hero" who brought about dramatic change from money politics into cleaner politics? He did his very best, but the LDP old guards and supporters of money politics would not allow that to happen.

The Hatta Government

An opportunity came when they discovered that the fragile coalition of Hosogawa's administration was beginning to show signs of weakening. They begin to dig into Hosogawa's personal financial past. After the political reform bills were passed, the division between the pro-Ozawa and anti-Ozawa groups deepened. Hosogawa's success was engineered by Ichiro Ozawa, a protege of Kakuei Tanaka and Kanemaru, a genius in political strategy and who in fact was the "king-maker" of the Hosogawa regime. Like his former boss, Tanaka, he pulled strings from behind the scene. The time was not ripe for him to take over power because within the Hosogawa's lost coalition were many who were scared of Ozawa because of his political background. It was the common desire not to allow the LDP to return to power and it was their shared objective for political reform that glued them together.

But Ozawa had over-exposed his keen desire to bring about his dream of a two-party political system to replace the multi-party system and was suggesting that the parties of the coalition government should merge as soon as possible. This angered the anti-Ozawa group who did not want to lose their identities and were afraid of being dominated by Ozawa, whose political maneuvers were known to them. Ozawa's style was different from Japan's traditional method of slow consensus building. On many issues they were never consulted and this made them increasingly dissatisfied with Ozawa. However, Hosogawa was increasingly dependent on Ozawa's help to maintain his position.

After the political reform bills were passed, the division between the pro-Ozawa and anti-Ozawa groups widened. It was then that allegations of Hosogawa's personal financial scandals emerged. It was alleged that Hosogawa was misusing a 1982 loan of 100 million yen that he had received from the now notorious Sugawa Kyubin, a parcel delivery company. Sugawa, which spread enormous amounts of money around to politicians during the roaring 80s, was at the heart of the scandal that toppled LDP king-maker Shin Kanemaru in 1992. Hosokawa had long maintained that he used the money to rebuild one of his family's ancestral homes, and that he fully repaid the loan. But he conceded that he paid no interest, and could not — or would not — provide documentation that proved how he used the money. Nor would he allow a key aide to testify in his defence. The LDP, for its part, had claimed that he had used the money to finance one of his political campaigns in the early 1980s and was now covering it up. The LDP refused to allow the introduction of Japan's new budget until Hosokawa's former secretary submitted to formal questioning in the Diet. The stalling tactics was especially painful because the budget contained new spending that was central to the government's plan to pump some life into Japan's supine economy.

Driven into a corner, Hosogawa announced his decision to step down as Prime Minister on 14th April 1994.

Hosokawa's sudden leap to the prime minstership allowed Japan to shake off almost four decades of conservative stagnation. His brief tenure as Prime Minister will be remembered abroad as well as at home, for the expectations it raised and then failed to meet. For a short while, it seemed like this could have been Japan's "Camelot". Now that moment was lost, frittered away both by Hosokawa himself and by his implacable political enemies.

Hosokawa lacked both the will and the ability to put Japan on a radically new course. After he became leader of his Japan New Party, many of his best friends were dismayed by the haphazard way he had selected his party candidates. In his eagerness to defeat the ruling LDP, he had hurriedly accepted the support from rebel LDP power brokers discredited by exposes of past LDP corruption. As Prime Minister, he had to cope with trade and economic problems created by past LDP mismanagement, with little help from the volatile mass media and electorate. Most of all, he had to cope with amorphous bureaucracy determined to hold on to power.

As for the alleged financial wrongdoings that were supposed to be the immediate cause of his downfall, it was Japan and not Hosokawa that was to blame. In Japan's apolitical society, only the communists and the religious-backed parties can rely on funds donated by individuals. Precisely because it was so apolitical, the same society demanded that politicians spend enormous sums to win votes. The result was a dilemma that cut right through to the heart of Japanese politics.

Japan has no shortage of worthwhile politicians. Hosokawa was one of them. But, unless they had inherited wealth, like the current LDP head Yohei Kono, they have to take enormous risks in raising the funds needed to prevail against the uglier and more corrupt members of their own profession. Japanese politicians have already refined their fundraising game into a fine art. Post-war Japanese politics has already seen several such victims — Hosokawa was one of the more tragic ones.

Whatever Hosokawa might have done, he had helped trigger the earthquake that rocked Japan's politics. He promised to clean out the Japanese political sewer, open up Tokyo's markets, tear down regulations and in general give Japan's long-suffering urban consumers a break. In retrospect, Japan needed both the rise and fall of Hosokawa to bring home a point: Japan needs cleaner politics and the way he has paved may see a clearer political division, one in which the worthy compete directly against the ugly and win.

Would Hosokawa's successor be able to bring about the political reform which most Japanese had hoped for?

After a frantic search and behind-the-scenes negotiations, the deputy Prime Minister Tsutomu Hatta, the Foreign Minister, was elected to take over as Prime Minister. Hatta has earned a reputation for being "clean" despite having been a protégé — together with Ozawa — of the late former premier Kakuei Tanaka, the politician who epitomised Japan's scandalous money politics. Hatta was also a close aide of former premier Noboru Takeshista, who was implicated in several political scandals, until he led an exodus from the LDP and formed the Shinseito (Japan Renewal Party). Compared

Tsutomu Hatta (1993–1994), who was forced to the position of Prime Minister because of political bickering.

to the aristocratic Hosokawa, Hatta was every inch "the people's Prime Minisiter". Hatta is the complete opposite of his chief backer, the brash and influential power broker Ozawa. During last year's election campaign, Hatta talked of his relationship with Ozawa. He said, "I am the actor and Ozawa is the scenario writer. It is a division of labour. I think this is what politics is all about."

Seen widely as an ordinary and unpretentious man whose greatest assets are a mellow character and a balanced outlook, Hatta rarely displays his short temper. When he was young, he served a bus company for ten years including stints as a bus conductor. An economic graduate of Seijo University in Tokyo, a school noted more for its extra-curricular activities than its academic standards, Hatta has ties with many prominent Japanese in business, academia and the arts, including world-renowned conductor Seiji Ozawa, his classmate in high school. A mild smoker, the politician enjoys eating out — noodles are a favourite — and an occasional game of golf. A lover of theatre and classical music, he conducted an orchestra recently for a charitable cause.

Hatta had never expressed much interest in the post of Prime Minister. He always declared that he was better at helping others than directing them. There is no doubt that he has the calibre of a Prime Minister, having served as both Finance and Foreign Ministers and holding the agricultural portfolio twice. However, apart from the passion he shows when speaking about political reforms, little is known of his political vision and philosophy.

The Socialist–LDP Coalition

The Hatta regime lasted only a few months and he was forced to resign because of internal squabbles. The coalition parties that took over from Hatta were the strange combination of conservative politics and radical leftwingism. It was an unexpected "honeymoon" between the LDP and the Socialist Democratic Party of Japan (SDPJ), under the Prime Ministership of the chairman of SDPJ, Tomiichi Murayama. It shook Japan's political circles. For the second time in the history of post-war Japan, the SDPJ had come into power with its chairman as the Prime Minister. The SDPJ is a minority partner in the SDPJ–LDP coalition government and it is widely known that Murayama is only a frontman manipulated by the Deputy Prime Minister Yohei Kono. But, Murayama is prepared to head the government even though he knows that he is not the real power.

In Japanese politics, as I have mentioned before, status and position is more important than power. Japanese political parties have fought and held power for decades on the basis of personal trade-off and personal contacts between party and faction leaders, rather than shared ideas or common ideologies. It has been the politics of expediency. This coalition of SDPJ–LDP is the politics of expediency taken to new lengths.

Murayama became Prime Minister on June 29 1994, when 261 members of the 511 strong lower house of the Diet voted for him in a run-off ballot for the leadership. He defeated the former Prime Minister and LDP member, Toshiki Kaifu, who ran as the candidate of the outgoing coalition headed by Hatta. Murayama, the son of a fisherman and a former labour union organiser, now heads the strangest cabinet in post-war Japan — 13 LDP politicians, 5 socialists and 2 members of Sakigake, a party that formerly supported both Hosokawa's and Hatta's coalition governments.

The LDP and the SDPJ are linked by a common dislike of Ichiro Ozawa, the reformist politician who started the turmoil in Japanese politics when he founded the Japan Renewal Party with a group of LDP rebels in the

Murayama (1994–), the first Socialist Prime Minister, who leads a government backed by LDP.

summer of 1993. But, there is little sign that the two parties agree on any of the major issues facing Japan. The composition of the Murayama Cabinet, which gave a majority to the numerically larger LDP, may have exaggerated the policy rift between the two parties. In a Parliament session held in July 1994, Prime Minister Murayama announced that the SDPJ has now recognised the legality of Japan's Self-Defence Force, reversing the old policy of non-recognition. The SDPJ has also reversed its stand on the National flag and National anthem and also started to respect the Japanese Imperial functions.

The LDP, which voters heaved out of office last summer after 48 increasingly corrupt years, has now returned as the dominant partner in government, without the inconvenience of having to fight an election. What happened was a breathtaking triumph for the polities of vengeance. The LDP old guards have succeeded in thwarting the man they believe betrayed them by engineering the political revolt which toppled the LDP. That man was Ichiro Ozawa. They threw what few principles they had left to the wind and allied themselves with their old adversaries, the Socialist Party, just for the sake of gaining power.

The most significant point of the coalition is that the LDP's party president, Yohei Kono, who was a key figure in realizing the new government, has something in common with both Murayama and Masayoshi Takemura, the representative of the Shinto Sakegake, a minor partner of the coalition. All three are liberals and "peace-loving". Kono was known as a dove even during the Cold War years. He once deserted the LDP to form a liberal, dovish party of his own. After he returned to the party, he kept his liberal stance, favouring the preservation of the peace constitution though his ideas were outside the party's mainstream. This shows that the LDP was far from being monolithic. In fact, one of the LDP's strengths was that it had such a reserve of people to use as the need demanded.

The former Prime Minister Yasuhito Nakasone was a good example. He filled the party's top post when Japan had to demonstrate to the US Government that the two nations were allies. Right now, Kono is an appropriate party representative to deal with the world as a post-Cold War politician who is suited to present world situation. The LDP, under Kono's leadership since August 1993, faced a new task — the elimination of members with a Cold War mentality. Kono and his supporters opted to make it clear that the LDP wanted to shift its basic policies away from Cold War thinking and applied a litmus test to each of its Diet members. The litmus test was the tie-up with the SDP. This link up with the Socialist was the last straw for some members who could not agree with the idea.

Similarly, the SDP also faced the same task of eliminating members who held traditional Cold War doctrine. Again the test was its decision to form a coalition government with the LDP. The arrangement with the LDP was a convenient one. The Socialists left the cabinet posts of finance, trade and foreign affairs to the LDP because the socialist traditional ideas would be incompatible with the party's new directive in these three areas, which meant there was no room of conflict with the coalition partners. This strategy would help Murayama and others to realise a soft landing in the post-Cold War era without dividing their party. In the past, the LDP and SDP seemed to confront each other often over crucial issues such as security and foreign affairs relations.

One other partner in the LDP–SDPJ coalition is the Sakigake Party, which holds two seats in the 20 member cabinet. This small party could, in theory, act as a bridge between the LDP and the Socialists. The Sakigake leader, Masayoshi Takemura, holds the post of Finance Minister.

In politics, today's friends may become enemies tomorrow and yesterdays' enemies may become friends today. The LDP and the Socialist Party had been enemies for decades and today they are more than friends. The total collapse of communism and socialism in the Soviet Union and Eastern Europe has made a great impact in the world of politics. The Berlin Wall is torn down, and the two Germanies are now united. Today even Russia has been accepted as a member of the NATO Alliance. It is not at all surprising that the Japan Socialist Party has also taken a reorientation of their policies and become more realistic.

What will happen to Japanese politics? Will Prime Minister Murayama stay long in the coalition with LDP? Will the Murayama regime be able to implement what the Parliament have passed on political reforms? Will his government be able to overcome some of the major problems facing Japan?

Japanese politics is difficult to fathom, particularly for foreigners. Nothing can be judged from the surface. One has to dig deep into the roots of Japanese character to understand Japanese politics.

Human nature does not change so easily. Money politics is already in the blood of most Japanese politicians. Political analysts do not believe that money politics will disappear from the corridors of power. Japanese politicians will always need a king-maker who can provide political financing as Japanese politics always need money. Most dietmen are followers who follow the leader who can provide the financing. In Japanese politics today, two leaders now manipulate political currents, one the man who controls the LDP, and for that matter the present coalition between LDP and the Socialist party. The other is Ichiro Ozawa, the man who was the real power behind the Hosokawa and Hatta administrations. Both of them were prodigies of the late Kakuei Tanaka. Takashita split out of the Tanaka faction and formed his own faction, whereas Ozawa was the blue-eyed boy of Kanemaru, who was a king-maker after the fall of Tanaka and who is related to Takeshita. Takeshita and Ozawa are now opposite camps but both are skillful in money politics. Both of them are behind the struggle of the two leading political groupings that are contending for power in Japan. In this struggle for supremacy, Ozawa has the support of the Komeito backed by the Soka Gakkai, whose main boss is Daizaku Ikeda. Ozawa and Daizaku are close friends. Soka Gakkai's political wing is the Komeito which has 50 seats in the Parliament.

Political observers should watch the movement of these two politicians carefully if they wish to understand the future trend of Japanese politics.

CHAPTER 9

Japan's Defence and Rearmament

Japan's first peacekeeping mission abroad set sail for Cambodia on 16 September 1992 from the western port of Kure, amid both hearty send-offs from well wishers and bitter protests by hundreds of demonstrators. Security was tight as three vessels carrying the 34 member contingent departed, with the Maritime Safety Agency deploying 47 patrol boats against dozens of protesters on more than 20 vessels.

A contingent of 683 Japanese soldiers and policemen had flown into Phnom Penh to join the U.N. peacekeeping effort in Cambodia, an operation headed by Yasuhi Akashi, a U.N. diplomat from Japan. The dispatch — the first since World War II — was authorised by a controversial U.N. Peacekeeping Co-Operation Law, which went into effect on 3 August after being passed by Parliament in June 1992.

Who could have imagined that Japanese "heitai-san" (soldiers), once the conquerors of Southeast Asia, would so soon return to the countries they had conquered but this time as "peacemakers". After 47 years of inaction, the Japanese have made a breakthrough after being defeated in World War II.

The breakthrough was a slow but steady process. After World War II, the defence of Japan was under the umbrella of the United States after the signing of a peace treaty in 1951 in San Francisco. The Constitution declared that Japan should be a peaceful nation and should not be rearmed. By 1970, the Security Treaty with the US was renewed with little opposition and defence was no longer a major political issue in the early 1970s. In 1976 the Miki Government decided to limit expenditure on arms to a maximum of 1 percent of the GNP (Gross National Product). This figure remained the basis of policy until January 1987, when the Nakasone government topped the 1 percent. The abandonment of this limit reflected American pressure for Japan to play a larger role in East Asian defence.

Japan's Defence Agency budget (US$33.5 million in 1992) is the largest in the world after those of the US and the former Soviet Union. The Agency has asked for a 5.4 percent increase in defence spending to pay for 28 locally made tanks, nine warships, 11 F-15 fighters, 10 patriot ground-to-air missile systems and other weapons. Japan's Self-Defence Force has 246,000 troops, including a 170-ship navy (Maritime Self-Defence Force) which has 17 submarines, six destroyers and 60 frigates. Then, there is a 10-fighter squadron Air Self-Defence Force and a quick-reaction Ground Self-Defence Force, including 45,000 US troops, half of them Marines.

Japan faced a tough time convincing the Diet (Lower House of Parliament) to get the Peace-Keeping Operations (PKO) Bill passed by the ruling Liberal Democratic Party in June 1992. The opposition Japan Socialist Party had used the ox-walk delay tactic in an attempt to prevent the bill from being passed. The filibuster technique of "ox walking" meant that JSP Dietmen inched their way to the podium to vote, sometimes taking up to 30 minutes to cover the 20 metre distance. One ox-walk session took a record breaking 13 hours to complete. Several elderly members felt ill and many slumped asleep on their desks. The Speaker had to adjust House rules to allow dietmen to go to the toilet. The delaying tactics, however, failed to prevent the bill from getting a rough passage, because the Speaker had the right to limit voting time. When the bill was passed, JSP and Japan Communist Party members gathered around the vice-speakers chair to protest against his ruling but soon dispersed while LDP members raised their fists in the traditional "banzai" cheers.

The bill was designed to allow about 2,000 Japanese soldiers to be deployed as U.N. peace-keepers to trouble spots such as Cambodia. While Prime Minister Kiichi Miyazawa said the time was ripe for Japan to contribute personnel as well as cash towards settling regional conflicts, the bill triggered unease in Asian countries which have suffered invasion and harsh occupation by the Japanese Imperial Army. Protests were particularly fierce in North and South Korea, both colonised by Japan between 1910 and 1945. China, too, warned of the danger of rearming Japan. The Chinese are worried that Japan might be rearmed again and become once again a military power.

The Problems Facing Jieitai

The birth of the Jieitai (Self-Defence Force) was clothed in secrecy. The Japanese Government acted clandestinely on the Jieitai because the Japanese people on the whole are opposed to the rise of a full-fledged armed force so soon after the most disastrous and miserable war in Japan's history, when the country was completely devastated.

The Japanese have ample reason to abhor war. Almost two million soldiers were killed in the battlefields. The remains of tens of thousands of them still lie in foreign lands and subtropical islands. I once visited West Irian in Indonesia and saw hundreds of skulls and bones of Japanese war dead lying here and there near a big tunnel. When I was Ambassador in Japan, I met Rear Admiral Itoh at the National Day party organised by Papua New Guinea in a Tokyo restaurant in May 1985. He told me that he would soon lead a 660 crew of two Japanese warships which would sail to 13 countries in Asia Pacific to hold ceremonies to commemorate the "unknown" soldiers who died during World War II. Admiral Itoh said, "We will bring the ashes of these unknown soldiers to the ship and perform the ceremony on the sea. We will all line up and bow to the dead and fire three shots in the air. We will have a minute of silence for the dead to remember their deeds." He said there was a move by those who survived the war to dig out the graves of these "unknown soldiers" and bring them back to Japan to rebury them.

This action alone proves that the Japanese have not learnt from the lessons of history. Many Japanese, especially in military circles, do not consider the sending of troops down south during World War II as a mistake.

The Japanese Constitution was changed, with a clause inserted saying that armed forces may exist although it was considered an illegitimate child. One industrialist once said to me, "The baby was born despite the 'no, no'." The word Jieitai reveals Japan's guilty consciousness, as the authorities would not admit that Japan had armed forces. The naming of the military has been a recurring problem. At first it was National Police Reserve (1950), then it was changed into National Safety Force (1952) and now National Self-Defence Force. It may be changed again in future. It was incidentally the Korean War and the departure of US soldiers stationed in Japan for the Korean battlefields that led to the establishment of a National Police Reserve which was the forerunner of the Self-Defence Force.

The Japanese Constitution says nothing about a Self-Defence Force or any force. Many Japanese still retain unpleasant memories of the Kempatei, the "thought control police" of pre-war and wartime days. The Constitution does not mention Japan sending its so-called Self-Defence Force abroad as peacemakers.

At the beginning, the new officer corps came from the ranks of the purged, the many thousands whose military career had abruptly halted with

Japan's defeat. Many were jobless and were glad to put on uniform again and receive regular paychecks. Before being allowed to command troops, they were put on orientation courses in democracy so that they were in touch with Japan's post-war reality. It was meant to be a force unlike the old, imperial force.

After Japan's defeat in 1945, many of the former militarists and ultranationalists went into hibernation for a few years, only to emerge after the US Occupation ended. Then one thing happened in the mid 1960s that strengthened the might of the ultras — the tie-up between the most notorious underworld gangs with the major rightist groups into one big family called Kantokai. The man who initiated the alliance was Yoshio Kodama, the most foremost rightist theorist in Japan. A fund raiser and political manipulator, he operated the Kodama Organ in China during the war which helped obtain an uninterrupted flow of supplies of food and materials to the Imperial Navy. Kodama later played a key role in manipulating the Liberal Democratic Party during the time of Prime Minister Kishi, who was also a war criminal, released at almost the same time as Kodama.

Ever since Japan regained its sovereignty, many key politicians in the country have been the very same persons who appeared in the wartime cabinets or who held other important wartime posts in government and industry.

The image which the Jieitan tries to project is one of a peaceful, democratic and harmless self-defence unit without much teeth. The Jieitai looks very different from the defunct Imperial forces. The uniforms look more democratic and more plebian. During my stay in Japan, I seldom saw a soldier in uniform. The Japanese generally hate uniforms. Those in the Jieitai have difficulty getting a life partner. An article in the Mainichi Daily News appeared in January 1986 which reads: "Last November, 3,000 military men were engaged in an exercise at the foot of Mount Fuji. Outside the exercise grounds' barbed wired periphery was an unusual sign, contingents of riot police standing guard to protect the very people supposedly doing their job of defending Japan."

The article said that half of the soldiers carrying out the exercise were Americans and the other half were Japanese. The immediate enemy were not hypothetical invaders from the Soviet Union, but far-left domestic extremists who have been waging a continuous campaign against "militarism". There were 2,450 policemen to keep troublemakers away.

The unflattering reality was that the Americans felt funny that Japanese soldiers required the protection of ordinary policemen. Said one of the the Jieitai officers, "We have trouble explaining to our American friends why we need policemen to protect us."

Masaki Higashi, the officer-in-charge of training of the Eastern Army, said in a press interview in Tokyo that it is difficult when the soldiers do not know the terrains they are expected to defend. Even the size of the training grounds is shrinking all the time, nibbled away by private developers who claim back their land. Where tanks once rumbled and soldiers charged, now golfers tee off on links reclaimed from the Jieitai. Some developers are now talking of building a ski resort on the Mt. Fuji slopes which were previously training grounds.

Today, Japan's howitzers can score hits at a range of 30 kilometres, while at Higashifuji, the ground forces of Jieitai are allowed to lob the cannon shells to a maximum of 3 kilometres and no more. Higashi said, "Deference to local wishes are such that the Jieitai breaks off cannon fire for two hours in the evening 'in order to avoid disturbing the milking of the cows.'"

Under the training doctrine, personal safety and accountability come first and foremost with the Jieitai. In rifle shooting practice, for instance, the Jieitai assigns one training officer to each shooter, whereas the US Army has only one officer for the whole platoon. Apart from the safety officer, the Jiaitai also assigns another officer each for recovering the spent cartridges. "We have got to count all the cartridges in order to account for the number of cartridges shot," said Higashi, who explained the stiff Japanese laws on firearms.

Personal safety concerns have also made the Jieitai look less than professional in military manoeuvres. Commanders, for example, are forbidden to move their troops on the ground beneath cannon trajectories. "There is fear that shells could blow up in mid air with the soldiers below getting injured by the falling shrapnel," said Higashi.

Higashi said that helicopter-borne soldiers in manoeuvre are not allowed to jump before their crafts touch the ground as in other armies. Instead, they are told to wait until the helicopters land properly.

"It's a paper tiger," remarked one Jieitai officer, who said he was disappointed with the way the Jieitai is being sacrificed for political expediency.

With the lack of a strong leadership and with the influence of left-wing politicians and trade unionists who are against rearming Japan, it is almost impossible to introduce compulsory military training.

The discipline of the youths of Japan is fast eroding, as they are influenced by Western films on sex and crime depicted by a flood of TV channels, newspapers and magazines. When the youths are asked what they would do if the Russians should attack Japan, they say, "Of course, I will run away."

Yet, when one visits Jieitai bases, one is sometimes startled to see a display or two that invokes the blood and iron of the war years. At the navy's officer training school at Etajima, near Hiroshima, I saw preserved momentos of youthful kamikaze suicide pilots who went on one-way missions against the enemy. Among the memorabilia is a bloodstained letter of a young officer who risked his life. Battle flags and photographs of the heroic pilots are exhibited.

The Japanese generally admire courage and heroism. Lieutenant Onoda Hiroo, who waged a "one-man war" in the jungles of the Lubang islands after the Japanese defeat in World War II, received a hero's welcome when he returned to Japan. His refusal to accept defeat unless commanded to do so by an immediate superior strikes most of us as a rather absurd military principle. Yet that is precisely what Onoda did. Sustained by the spirit of the Meiji era Imperial Precepts to soldiers and sailors and the regulations governing combat operations, he persisted in fighting for three decades. The unabashed national admiration for the peculiar tenacity that he displayed, the glorification of this living fossil of pre-war militarism as a "model soldier", suggests that the ghosts of militarism have not yet been laid to rest.

Although the authorities try to project the image of the Jieitai as a "lovable Jieitai", a "people's self-defence force", members of the Jieitai are subject to the discipline of the army which calls on everyone to obey "all commands willingly and responsibly" in a framework of "mutual affection for our comrades in arms, in order to create a new Jieitai spirit". Like its predecessor — the Imperial Army — the Jieitai sees itself as military force that exists for the purpose of winning wars. Captain Nagataomo Saizo of the air defence force left no room for doubt about this fact when, several years ago, he wrote, "The prime responsibility of the Jieitai is to engage in battle. Its essential military nature is in no way different from that of the pre-war army when it comes to the basic principles involved in warfare."

Today's self-defence forces clearly constitute an "army" in terms of equipment and war potential. The only thing they lack is actual battlefield experience.

The Vanguard of Japanese Rearmament

One thing the Japanese do not lack is the capacity to produce arms. Armaments production plays a vital role in Japan's super economy. The Japanese zaibatsu have been producing some of the world's biggest battleships, submarines and Zero fighters. Mitsubishi Heavy Industries (MHI) together with other zaibutsu, such as Kawasaki Heavy Industries and Fuji Heavy

Industries, reckoned on defence contracts through 1976 big enough for them to triple their aircraft sales. At its Nagoya aircraft workshops, Mitsubishi has been developing supersonic jet trainers for the Defence Agency. Fuji Heavy Industries, Nissan Motors and Tokyo Shibaura Electric (Toshiba) have also been manufacturing ship-to-ship missiles. The Mitsubishi group of over 40 corporations controls a third of Japan's defence industry, producing warships, tanks and missiles as well as jet aircraft for military use.

The Japan Atomic Industrial Council predicted that the nation would produce more than 280 nuclear-driven ships before the end of the 20th century. Japan completed two nuclear powered merchant ships in 1980, built 50 to 60 more by 1990 and aims to produce more than 280 by the year 2000.

The President of Mitsubishi Trading Company, Chujiro Fujino, appealing to racial feelings, once said, "Now is the right time for us coloured Asian races to unite again. I believe the concept of the pre-war Great East-Asia Co-Prosperity Sphere was right. We must look to the interests of just our own country."

It was General MacArthur's policy to dissolve the zaibatsu because of their role in helping to promote militarism in Japan. But, the zaibatsu's influence has by no means declined. They are now stronger than before, revolving around big banks such as Fuji, Mitsubishi, Mitsui, Sumitomo, Dai-ichi Kangyo and Sanwa, becoming richer by producing arms for sale to neighbouring countries. Perhaps the only difference between the old zaibatsu and the new is a change in leadership. Before, they were run by huge monopolies and now they have a more national atmosphere.

The Defence Agency made an important announcement in 1971 which had far-reaching consequences for big business and the nation. It informally asked the zaibatsu to employ the ten thousand military men discharged from service each year. This established a technological tie up between the military and industry. Japan's military personnel have already gained a foothold in industry.

Between 1960 and 1970, about 420 Japanese generals, admirals and hundreds of other high-ranking officers were given jobs in Japan's defence industries after their retirement. Mitsubishi Heavy Industries, for instance, had a number of prominent retired military men on its staff. They included people such as Ichiro Sugita, former Chief of Staff of the Ground Self-Defence Forces, and Mitsugi Ihara, former Chief of Staff of the Maritime Self-Defence Forces.

Japanese companies are sending their employees to Jieitai training camps to gain some discipline. They want their employees to take orders without question, like a soldier take orders from their superiors.

Japanese zaibutsu had in the past ganged up with military leaders to enhance Japan's economic and territorial interests. General MacArthur's headquarters reported that during the war, the zaibutsu had given cash, stocks and property to Premier Tojo to help conquer and plunder foreign land. Overseas adventures were often rationalised by patriotic and nationalistic slogans. The zaibutsu and the military leaders also influenced political leaders into doing things their way. There had also been a marriage of convenience among the three groups to further strengthen their unity. The three groups had one thing in common: to conquer Asia and Southeast Asia under the pretext of bringing prosperity to the region under the banner of the "South Asia Co-Prosperity Sphere".

After the war in 1947, Japan's Constitution prohibited any form of military force under the article which renounced war. When the Defence Agency was set up in 1954, there was strong criticism from the Japan Socialist Party and the general public that its existence was a violation of the constitution. However, in contrast to the freedom accorded the army and navy under the Meiji Constitution, the Jieitai has been placed under strict civilian control, a civilian who presides over the Jieitai under the supervision of the Prime Minister.

The Director General of the Defence Agency is assisted by internal bureaus of the agency, staffed mainly by civilians to control the ground, maritime and air Self Defence forces. The Joint Staff Council, consisting of a chairman and the three chiefs of staff, assists the director general in coordinating plans and operations conducted jointly by two or more of the Jieitai. In addition, the director general of the Defence Agency is a member of the National Defence Council, which is set up in the Cabinet and consists of the Prime Minister, the Ministers of Finance and Foreign Affairs, and the Directors-General of the Defence Agency and the Economic Planning Agency. This council is responsible for the formation of national defence policy.

The Defence Agency also operates several institutes and schools, including the National Defence College, the National Defence Academy, the National Defence Medical College and the Technical Research and Development Institute.

As befits its role in an economic superpower, the Defence Agency is spending a great deal of money on defence equipment. Japan may soon have the world's most expensive tank. The Nippon Steel, the world's largest steel maker, has been asked to provide the steel for the tank and Mitsubishi Electric and Nippon Electric will probably provide the electronics for Japan's elite tanks, planned for completion during the fifth defence build up. Japan also has equiped itself with the latest production techniques and facilities for manufacturing modern warplanes. Mitsubishi built about 200 Phantom jets in the mid 1970s.

When I was in Japan, Yoshistaro Inayama, President of Nippon Steel Corporation, was chairman of Keidanren. He told me that there were strong voices among the zaikai calling for Japan to go nuclear so that Japan would not be used as a whipping boy by the other economic powers.

For some years, Japan was not officially in the arms export business. The constitution prevents her from doing so. The anti-war population is against it. Presently, the Japanese government says that weapons may be exported only if they are weapons for defence. The sale of weapons has been banned in three areas: Communist nations, nations involved in conflicts and nations to which a United Nations resolution has prohibited arms sales. These principles however have not been rigidly followed. From 1970s onwards, the Japan Weapons Industry Association was raising its voice, asking the government to relax its three principles. In fact, Japan has been exporting arms quietly to the Thai police force under the pretext that they are "hunting equipment". Small consignments of arms have also been exported to Singapore and Malaysia with "samples" stamped on the shipping crates. If the opposition parties had got wind of what was going on, the government would have been put in an awkward and embarrassing position.

In 1967, Japan gave the Philippines an ammunition plant worth $5 million with an annual capacity of 15 million rounds as part of war reparations. The shipment, sent in secrecy, was labelled "metal processing machinery". In 1974, Kawasaki Heavy Industries agreed to sell Sweden some antisubmarine helicopters. It is said that Japan has received requests for munitions including aircraft and warships from nearly every country which is having quarrels with its neighbours. Military sources say such requests also came from the Middle East imbroglio but they have gone unfulfilled. Japan is very discreet in such matters and such news was seldom leaked out.

Japan's Lucky Stars

Fifty years ago, Japan was a defeated nation. She had lost everything and was poor and devastated. But within a short period of time, she has become one of the powers to be reckoned with. Militarily, she has been under the umbrella of American protection. But she has become so strong that she is sending 2,000 troops under the United Nations' supervision to Cambodia as a "peace force". I have explained the reasons behind the miracle of Japan's economic recovery in a separate chapter. One important factor in Japan's recovery was that she has been lucky throughout history in her dealings with foreign countries.

Mongolia twice attempted to invade Japan but on these two occasions, they were driven away by unusual thunderstorms described by the Japanese as "kamikaze". That was the first event that made the Japanese believe that they were a divine and unbeatable race.

In the late 1880s, when the Ching dynasty was weak and crumbling, Japan defeated China in a Sino-Japanese battle. The corrupt and weak kingdom would have collapsed by itself because it was too rotten.

Japan engaged Russia in a war in 1904 when the Russian Empire was about to crumble because it was decadent, corrupt and militarily weak.

In the case of the Sino-Japanese and Russia-Japan wars, it was not so much that the Japanese were superior but due to the fact that China and Russia were both becoming decadent and on the verge of complete collapse. These two wars with their big neighbours somehow convinced the Japanese that they were strong and invincible. Thus, it stirred up the ambitions of Japanese militarists to invade China and Southeast Asia, and later even take on the Americans by bombing the Pearl Harbour.

The Japanese do not know when to stop when they advance. Generally speaking, most Japanese are followers and few have the time to do analytical thinking. When the mechanism is switched on, few know when to switch off.

It was not only after the atom bombs were dropped in Nagasaki and Hiroshima that the Japanese realised how weak they were. Historically speaking, Japanese policies were often changed by foreign interference. The Japanese did not know that they were weak until Commodore Perry pounded their cannons and they were forced to open the door to the outside world after 300 years of isolation. Similarly, they did not know that they were weak until the atom bombs were dropped on them. Emperor Hirohito had to decide to call off the war and surrendered because he could not bear to see so many Japanese suffer and perish at the stroke of a gigantic bomb which was beyond their imagination.

After World War II, the Japanese became so poor and devastated that they could hardly survive. Again, fate was on their side when the Korean War started. The Americans needed Japan to help win the war. Japan became a military base and the Americans needed the Japanese to rearm. It was incidentally the Korean War and the departure of US soldiers stationed in Japan for the Korean battlefields which led to establishment of a National Police Reserve, the forerunner of the Self-Defence forces. It was generally believed that if South Korea was communised, Japan would soon be caught in the same net. The southern city of Korea, Pusan, is only 120 miles from Japan. At the time of the greatest advance by the Communists during the Korean War, Pusan remained within the small perimeter of land that was not overrun by the enemy.

Throughout history, Japan has been lucky. In times of adversity, something always came along to help the country and its people. That is why most Japanese think that God is on their side. They become over-confident and subjective. They are by nature forgetful. Therefore, they want the younger generation to forget the past. The right-wing elements within the Education Ministry did not want the younger generation of Japanese to know the atrocities their ancestors had committed during World War II. Japanese textbooks describe the Nanking massacre as an "incident", omitting the facts that at least 200,000 civilians were massacred in cold blood. Most inflammatory of all, the Japanese textbooks said the annexation of Korea in 1910 was as much the fault of the Koreans as of anyone else.

The worst scenario happened sometime in August 1985 when I was still Ambassador to Japan. The Minister for Education Masayuki Fujio made a startling statement which shook the world, particularly China and Korea. Fujio's statement openly defended Japan's annexation of Korea and he went to the extent of saying that the Nanking massacre was more in the imagination, and that it was overplayed. This happened two months after Prime Minister Nakasone had visited Korea and had apologised to the Koreans for what Japan had done. There was strong protest from China and Korea in reaction to Fujio's statement. There were even demonstrations against Japan in the two countries. Nakasone had to dismiss Fujio to pacify the Chinese and Koreans.

Fujio, known in LDP as a "wild samurai", had always believed in "making a decision fast and carrying it out once decided". He must have thought that Japan had not done wrong both in the annexation of Korea and in the Nanking massacre, and he chose to make public his feelings when he was Minister of Education. Fujio belonged to the Fukuda faction and was in fact climbing the political ladder when he was appointed chairman of the LDP Policy and Research Affairs Council, which was in charge of all budget and financial matters related to government spending. All expenditures relating to government spending have to be approved by the chairman of the Policy and Research Affairs Council before they to the Diet Committee of the Diet for final approval.

Fujio wanted to visit Asean countries with a view of ascertaining the actual requirements of the respective governments. Before his departure to the

Asean countries, he met the six Asean Ambassadors to Japan in his office. He struck me as someone who was as bold as a samurai. He mentioned an important point which other LDP leaders did not dare say. He said that the 21st century would see Americans and Europeans losing their influence in world affairs and that it was an era for the Asian — meaning of course that that Japan would lead the world, particularly in the Asia Pacific region.

Fujio was ambitious. He was aiming to be the Secretary General of the LDP in the next party reshuffle that autumn, although he knew that he could not attain the Prime Ministership.

What made Fujio make the controversial and disturbing statement which brought about his fall from power? I think it is the neo-nationalistic feeling which is growing among the right-wing Japanese. There is a general feeling among the Japanese — Dietmen, business leaders, professors, as well as ordinary people — that Japan should become a major political power as well as a major economic power. It was this neo-nationalistic feeling that inspired Fujio to make the bold statement justifying Japan's colonisation of Korea and the Nanking massacre. It was also this feeling that led to Prime Minister Nakasone making a slip of the tongue when he antagonised the minorities of America. He said America could not progress fast enough because of the existence of the minority race. It was this same feeling that brought three young Dietmen to see the South Korean Ambassador to Japan, Rhee Kyu-ho, in the early 1990s, threatening that Japan might go to war with Korea and China if they continued to interfere with Japan's internal affairs.

The three Dietmen, led by Shizaka Kamei, a Dietman elected from Hiroshima Prefecture, went to see the Ambassador on the pretext of asking him to arrange a visit to Seoul "to promote closer understanding between the two countries". Kamei was quoted by the Japanese press as having told the Ambassador:

"Japan and South Korea are not in a state of war at present because Japan has the security treaty with the United States, and the United States has another treaty with South Korea. But, we are not sure if these security arrangements will last 10 or 20 years. Who can guarantee that there will be no war between Japan and South Korea caused by Japanese frustration if South Korea and China interfere in problems like (the screening system) of Japanese school textbooks and Nakasone's visit to Yasukuni shrine in Tokyo as they are doing right now?"

What Kamei meant was that whether Japan should revise textbooks for their children and whether Japanese politicians should pay respect at the Yasukuni shrine were matters to be decided by the Japanese, and that both the Chinese and Koreans had no right to interfere. Both Korea and China were victims of Japanese atrocities during World War II. How could Kamei say Koreans and Chinese have no right to comment when the Japanese are deliberately distorting history?

Textbooks and the Yasukuni Shrine

Is the Nanking massacre a reality or an illusion? This incident has been the topic of discussion for a long time among historians. In November 1984, a few months after my arrival at Japan, Chuo Koron, a leading Japanese magazine, published the diary of General Kesago Nakajima, who was the 16th division commander responsible for the Nanking massacre. During the Sino-Japanese War, the 16th division commanded by Nakajima moved from one place to another in China and took a main role in the Nanking massacre. Nakajima's family had been preserving five notebooks of his diary since his death in 1945. A professor at Aoyama Gakuin University learned about the diary and asked for the family's permission to study them. According to Chuo Koron, the diary disclosed details of the plan to massacre not only war prisoners but all civilians. The diary also described the manner in which victims were massacred.

More and more evidence has come to light during the last few years as consciences were pricking those who took part in the massacre. I read a book *I Killed The Chinese* written by 100 Japanese soldiers who took part in the killing. They lamented the incident and apologised for what they had done to the Chinese people.

How could Fujio, holding the position of Minister of Education, have denied historical facts and described the Nanking massacre as just "imagination and illusion"? How can the Japanese right-wing complain when the Chinese and Koreans protest against the distortion of historical facts written in Japanese textbooks? How can they say this is interference in the internal affairs of Japan?

But, this was exactly what the three-men delegation led by Kamei had done when they requested to see the Korean Ambassador to Japan, Rhee Kyu-ho, who happened to be the Foreign Minister when I presented credentials to Korea. I met Rhee quite often in Tokyo and he told me that the Kamei delegation had been rather rude and arrogant.

The South Koreans reacted sharply to Kamei's remarks and the spokesman of the ruling Democratic Justice Party (DJP) described Kamei's statement as a "threat" to South Korea and warned that such remarks would seriously damage Seoul-Tokyo relations. The Hankook Ilbo (韓國日報) newspaper headlined the remarks "Words of Abuse to South Korean Envoy" in a front-page splash. Another major daily, The Chosen Ilbo (朝鮮日報), printed a five column article about the incident. The Government-owned Korea Broadcasting System made the remarks one of the major news items of the day. Koreans generally were angry with the Japanese threat.

The Korean Foreign Minister, Choi Kwang-Soo, called up the Japanese Ambassador to Korea, Kiyoshisa Mikansagi, and asked him to explain the "threat".

The man who made the threat, Kamei, 54, is now chairman of the LDP economic affairs bureau. He has been elected to the Diet five times and is on his way to becoming a full-fledged minister. Who knows, one of these days he may even become the Prime Minster.

This group of young Dietmen, led by Kamei, belong to a group called Kokka Kihon Mondai Soshikai (Society of National Fundamental Issues) which is an association for neo-nationalists in the LDP. This group was formed soon after the landslide victory by young Dietmen from the various factions. Their leader was Kamei. There were ten from the Abe faction (the majority right-wing, having inherited the right-wing policies of Kishi, the former Prime Minister who was a die-hard rightist supporting Chiang Kai-shek and who had gone to jail as a war criminal), six from the Miyazawa faction, four from the Tanaka faction, two from Komoto faction, one from the Nakasone faction and two from non-factional groups. The purpose of this group was to discuss the nation's basic problems including diplomacy, defence, education and other delicate issues. They made proposals from time to time to the Nakasone Cabinet on these matters. This hawkish group considered the amendment of the constitution their ultimate aim. They felt that the constitution was out of date and was hindering the development of Japan as a major political power.

A former newspaper correspondent of Nihon Keisai Shimbun, Shiro Saito, told me during a lunch in Tokyo in November 1986 that these young Dietmen knew very little of Japan's contemporary history, particularly the atrocities that Japanese soldiers had committed during World War II. Saito, who was well-versed in Japanese politics, said these younger generations of politicians were getting rather frustrated when they saw the older generation leaders like Nakasone bowing to Japan's immediate neighbours. They could not understand why Nakasone should have been so humble to South Korea and China, as they think that Japan has become the strongest economic power on earth.

Saito said that a day might yet come when these young Dietmen take over political power and they might then demand a change in the constitution to enable Japan to flex its muscles. They might easily gang up with the military leaders and bring Japan back to militarism.

The younger generation of Japanese are not taught the cruel things their ancestors did in the past, particularly during World War II. The right-wing intellectuals think that the younger generation will have a permanent guilty conscience if they are made to realise how cruel their ancestors were. They therefore screen off all the cruel aspects of Japanese militarism in the school textbooks, leaving only the skeleton of contemporary history. The present generation are thus ignorant of the realities of the last war. They only know how cruel the Americans were by dropping atom bombs on Hiroshima and Nagasaki, without understanding why the bombs had to be dropped.

The leader of the right-wing group, Shizaka Kamei, was born in 1936 in Hiroshima where the atom bomb was dropped. When he graduated from Tokyo University, he entered the police force and served in the Policy Agency until 1979. He was Chief of Research Division, Metropolitan Police Secretariat. He was elected to the Lower Houses in 1979 and re-elected five times, fit to be nominated as a Cabinet Minister. During the double election in July 1986, he got more votes than Miyazawa, now the Prime Minister. Both of them competed in the same constituency. Kamei came up top because he made fiery speeches stirring the feeling of the Japanese nationalism.

Diet members who campaigned in the twin elections in July 1986 pointed out that among Japanese people, there is both a growing feeling that Japan is a great power and a concomitant rise in what may be described as neo-nationalism. According to Shiro Saito, who covered the general election, Nakasone's campaign speeches received the most response and applause from the audience when he stated that, "I will speak for Japan and negotiate on an equal footing with President Reagan and Gorbachev", a comment that seemed to stimulate a feeling of nationalism among Japanese. The impression is that the Japanese themselves want to perceive their country as a major political power.

According to Saito, over the past ten years most of the Japanese public have come to feel that even although Japan has gained for itself a position as a major international economic power, it still has not become a major political power, a view long held by the Japanese media as well. In fact, economically, Japan ranks second in the free world in terms of GNP. Its business activities have become completely internationalised and its influence in international economic organisations has grown substantially. However, in international politics and on issues of defence and peace, Japan's information, analytical skills, viewpoints and influence appear far inferior to other major powers, thus giving the impression to the Japanese people that the country still lags far behind the leading powers in terms of political acumen. Because of this, Japanese politicians, particularly the leaders of the ruling LDP, have been longing to join with those who influence world politics, such as the leaders of US, Russian and European nations. They dream of becoming a major political power as well as a major economic power.

This is also true of Japanese circles. Until the spring of 1985, Japan's largest industrial organisation, Keidanren, was under the chairmanship of Yoshihiro Inayama, known as an advocate of the "the philosophy of patience". He was the president of Nippon Steel — thin, a little bald-headed, spoke with high-pitched voice and was a real Japanese gentleman. I met him occasionally at Keidanren meetings. He was an expert on China and visited China frequently. He argued that patience was a form of repayment for the help that Japan has received from the US since the war and that in today's society it is impossible to achieve complete *laissez faire.* He further promoted the necessity of maintaining a free world system — a concept that might sometimes require Japan's self-imposed restrictions on exports.

However, in May 1986, the chairmanship of Keidanren was handed over to Eichiro Saito, chairman of the Nippon Steel Corporation — a change in the attitude held by industrial leaders concerning the Japan–US trade friction issue. Upon assuming the chairmanship, Saito stated that he would continue Inayama's policy, but with regard to the issue of trade friction with the US, he questioned the practise of passively listening to US arguments and felt the necessity for speaking out more clearly and firmly the Japanese point of view. He demonstrated this new stance by emphasising trade friction does not rest only with Japan, but with America as well.

Beyond political and business circles, there is a growing number of people in economic circles who support Saito's nationalistic policies.

In July 1986, leading members of the Keidanren held a meeting in preparation for the 23rd Japan US Businessmen's Conference in Tokyo. This meeting became a forum for the expression of this new mood with such statements as "selling inexpensive, good quality products is beneficial to American consumers", "the main cause of trade imbalance lies largely with Americans," and "Japan should demand more effort on the part of the US". And in his keynote address, Saito himself took the strongest stance ever against the US.

During the past years, there have been a number of essays and comments which give theoretical support to the arguments of the aforementioned business world leaders. Among these essays are papers presented by Osmu Shimomura, a well-known economist, and Professor Ryutaro Kimiya of Tokyo University. Kimiya said: "The reasons for the imbalance in US–Japan trade lie on the US side. If the imbalance is to be corrected, it is first necessary for the US to find a means to decrease its national debt."

The Bank of Japan recently released a report stating that the cause of the growing US trade deficit lies in the characteristics of America's economic system, a remark which understandably angered the US treasury.

My friend Saito said if the major concept of power and feelings of neo-nationalism which are rapidly emerging in Japan lead to a narrowminded sense of racial superiority, an extremely dangerous situation may arise.

The Chief Secretary of the Nakasone Cabinet, Masaharu Gotoda, who was referred to as a man of wisdom in the LDP and who once belonged to the Tanaka faction, was said to have told his close colleagues, "One of the major problems confronting Japanese politics is now to regulate pressure from the right-wingers and the trend towards conservatism." In the transition stage from being a major economic power to a major political power, it is important to see what kind of national principle is established. If the clannish, self-complacent and neo-nationalism tendency takes over, then Japan may indeed face a potentially volatile situation.

The most significant shift in Japanese tendency towards neo-nationalism was revealed in Prime Minister Nakasone's official visit to the Yasukuni shrine in August 1985, when I was Ambassador in Japan. On 15th August that year, Nakasone led 20 members of his Cabinet to pay respect to the dead war "heroes" enshrined in the Yasukuni shrine. It was the 40th anniversary of the end of the Pacific War. The shrine kept the ashes of the 2,400,000 Japanese killed in action since 1853, two million of them in the Second World War. "See you at Yasukuni" was the parting phrase of the kamikaze pilots when they clambered into their Zeros. Hundreds of members of the Nippon Izokokai (Japan Association of Bereaved Families of War Dead) congregated at the Shinto shrine and clapped their hands as Nakasone, accompanied by his Cabinet, gathered there to mourn the war dead.

The official visit was made in accordance with new formalities set by the Chief Secretary in consultation with the Bereaved Families Association, whereby the Prime Minister took one bow in front of the main shrine, instead of two bows, two claps of hands and one bow in the shinto rituals. The government also paid about ¥30,000 for fresh flowers displayed at the shrine in the name of the Prime Minister. The new ritual was considered as the official way of respecting the dead.

The Yasukuni shrine where Japanese heroes, including war-time Prime Minister Tojo, were enshrined.

General Hidejo Tojo, Prime Minister in 1944, was sentenced and hanged as a war criminal.

Following the visit, Nakasone told reporters, "I have just made the visit in my official capacity, and I am convinced that the overwhelming majority of the people support the official visit." There were strong protests from China and Korea about Nakasone's official visit. Nakasone merely said he would try to clarify the true intention of visiting the shrine to China and Korea.

Immediately outside the shrine compound, a score of members from the delegation of Christians, Buddhists and adherents to some other religions were shouting anti-Nakasone slogans. Some of them tried to hand over protest notes to Nakasone. A police picket line, however, prevented them from approaching the Prime Minister's party. I attended the function as diplomats were invited to observe the occasion.

The Yasukuni shrine is situated on Kudan hill in Tokyo, not far from the buildings of War Ministry. Many Japanese walked silently beneath its cool trees to worship before the black and gold lettered tablets inside the sanctuary. The spirits of the honoured dead soldiers, including that of General Tojo, the Prime Minister who was responsible for World War II and who was hanged as a war criminal, were enshrined there. So were the spirits of a great number of Class A war criminals collectively enshrined. Class A criminals were criminals of the highest order.

Yasukuni is not an old shrine. It was founded on the present site in 1869 by the Meiji government, as a memorial to the Imperial soldiers killed during the civil wars of the Restoration. Gradually, the shrine gained in importance, especially after the Russo-Japanese War, when the ashes of those who fought in the war were enshrined.

Yasukuni was the heaven-on-earth of the Shinto religion backed by the militarists. Its gaunt wooden gates were symbols to recruit millions of soldiers into battle in China. Shinto taught the Japanese that whoever died in battle calling the name of the Emperor would automatically be enshrined in Yasukuni and received the Emperor's blessing. The Emperor's war was a holy war and those who sacrificed themselves for the Emperor would be remembered.

On 19 October, 1938, a cool Monday evening in Tokyo, Emperor Hirohito drove to Yasukuni to pay respect to the 10,334 officers and men who died in the China incident. The old Shinto rites were conducted in darkness and in utter silence. Although the widows and families of those who died in the China incident were present, there was complete silence during the ceremony. Only the voice of the Shinto priests reciting the the Shinto verses and the rustling of dead leaves by the autumn breeze could be heard.

Similarly, Nakasone tried to revive this spirit of paying respect to those who had died for the nation, despite the fact that they were war criminals.

For several years following the war's end, the Yasukuni shrine was almost completely forgotten by the starving people. It was just like another park where children would play baseball during the day and American GIs dated their Japanese girlfriends after dark. However, bereaved families of the war dead began to throng the shrine in the mid 1950s to worship the souls of the dead on one day each year — the anniversary of the war's end. In due course, those bereaved families who made yearly visits to the shrine — mostly from rural areas — began to put pressure on the Dietmen to lead or follow them on their regular visits to the shrine. It did not take long before they began to demand that the Prime Minister make visits to the shrine on behalf of the people. The Nippon Izokokai first voiced their demand, which was then followed by the Eirei ni Kotaseru Giin Kyogi-kai (Dietmen's Council to Respond to the War Dead). But it took more than a decade for any Prime Minister to visit the shrine. Prime Minister Miki was the first Prime Minister to go to worship at the shrine, on the anniversary of the war's end in 1975. He made the visit strictly in a private capacity. He used his private car, signed his name without the title of Prime Minister, and paid the fee for the "sacred branches" out of his own pocket. This precedent was followed by two of his immediate successors, Fukuda and Ohira. Ohira made his visit to the shrine in 1979 despite his faith in non-denominational Christianity, disappointing the Christians. Prime Minster Suzuki also visited the shrine without making it clear whether the visits were made in an official or private capacity.

Nakasone visited the shrine in 1983 and 1984 in his private capacity but registered himself as "Prime Minister of Japan". This raised hopes among the bereaved families that he would eventually make official visits, whilst raising suspicion among their opponents.

In 1984, Nakasone formed a panel of 15 advisers to study the whole controversial issue and requested that it complete its study in time for the forthcoming 40th anniversary of the war's end. The panel, chaired by Keizo Hayashi, President of the Japanese Red Cross, came up with a report which paves the way towards official visits to the shrine by the Prime Minister and his Cabinet members.

There are still many Japanese who resist visits to the shrine because war criminals are enshrined there. There is also widespread resentment of the enshrinement of only military personnel there, despite the fact that hundreds of thousands of civilians fell victim in the last war. Soon after the war, the Japanese government announced its estimate that 1,440,000 army men and officers, 420,000 Navy personnel and 660,000 civilians had been killed in the war. However, these figures are generally believed to be unreasonably underestimated.

It was once suggested that a new non-religious mausoleum for all the war victims be built on the basis of a consensus of the people. However, there is no evidence that Nakasone ever paid any attention to this suggestion. He seemed to have been concerned only with the Yasukuni shrine.

Nakasone's special concern with the Yasukuni shrine and his talk about creating a "Japanese identity" through the educational system was a clear sign that he was trying to turn the clock backwards. If Nakasone was serious in wanting to establish a "Japanese identity" he had to place emphasis on what makes Japan different from the rest of the world. He had found Shintoism and the existence of the Emperor. Only in Japan can one find Shintoism and he wanted the Japanese people, particularly the young, to pay respect to the Emperor as their forefathers had done before the war.

This was why opposition parties and intellectuals were afraid that Nakasone wished to turn the clock backward to build an economically powerful, militarily stronger Japan, marked by a clearer identity based on Shintoism worshipped by the Imperial family — the goal set by Japan in 1968 when the country restored the Emperor's rule and opened its contact with the rest of the world.

Nakasone saw the danger of Japan going soft, with the younger generation of Japanese only interested in pleasure, the young in schools not saluting to their national flag and singing the national anthem and the young not undergoing military training. Nakasone wanted to turn the tide away from softness. For this, he needed to gradually cultivate the Japanese respect for a figurehead in the person of the Emperor and thus revive the old spirit of samurai.

Nakasone was a right-winger all along. Born in 1918, he has been elected to the National Diet since 1947. He held important posts in the ruling party and the government, including that of Director General of the Defence Agency. It was under his tenure as civilian chief of the Agency that the first post-war Defence White Paper was issued, an event which was important in the sense that it gave de facto legality to the Self-Defence Forces. I was Ambassador to Japan when Nakasone was the Prime Minister. This man, who is a zealous believer in military build-up, is a suave, articulate, fluent in English adriot, ambitious and pro-imperialist. He once ran a private school which looked more like a small private army — similar to Yokio Mishima's Society of Shields — than a conventional school. It was reported that Nakasone's school had 800 young men enrolled to be indoctrinated with anti-Communism and patriotism. Their motto was: "Let us sacrifice ourselves for the Showa Restoration." This appeal for a restoration of the Emperor system has been the theme of many ultranationalist groups. In pre-war days, it was considered an honour to die for the Emperor. An Emperor system means allowing the Emperor to make national decisions and giving him the power to rule the country.

Nakasone was the first Prime Minister who successfully increased Japan's defence spending to greater than one percent of GNP. He was the first Prime Minister to pay respect at Yasukuni shrine as the "Prime Minister". He became so confident, being the longest reigning Prime Minister, serving three terms, that his speech became rather racist. In 1986, he made a slip of the tongue. He talked about America's inability to make much progress because of her multi-racial society, having a minority of coloured people of "blacks, Puerto Ricans, and Mexicans", unlike Japan which has a homogeneous people. What he was trying to say was that Japan could progress so fast because the population consists of a homogeneous society belonging to the same race and speaking the same language. The American blacks took strong offence to this statement and demanded an apology from the Prime Minister. Under pressure, Nakasone did make an apology and explained exactly what he meant.

This slip of the tongue, and his forced decision to dismiss his Education Minister, left a big blot on Nakasone's otherwise outstanding record as one of the most effective Prime Ministers in post-war Japan. On closer scrutiny, these incidents reflect a growing preoccupation among the ruling elite to seek a national identity for the nation and define Japan's role in the world.

The Japanese are once again beginning to show considerable pride in their accomplishments and are conscious of their potential. They are beginning to ask the question: What is a Japanese? Is it merely being an "economic animal", ever in pursuit of greater economic might? Apart from the Toyotas, the Panasonics and the Canons, what can the Japanese show to the world of their Japaneseness? Is the stereotyped image of a camera-toting, bespectacled group travelling the real image of the Japanese? No one in Japan seems quite certain of his own image and identity.

An author and former director-general of the government's Cultural Affairs Agency, Shumon Miura, once said, "The young people today have lost their own sense of belonging. They behave as if they are simply temporary residents in their own country."

"The Japanese these days have everything. They drive beautiful cars, stuff their houses with lots of electronic gadgets, wear brand-name clothes and can afford to eat the best the world offers. Yet, when they are on their own, they start to think what does being a Japanese mean," observes another author Akiyuki Nosaka.

Economic success is not everything. The Japanese want more than economic success. They want Japan to be No. 1 in everything — a political and, if possible, military presence in the world. I would like to quote the opening sentence of an article which appeared a few years ago in the magazine Jitsugyo no Seikai (World of Business): "One of the best traits of the Japanese is that they are a superior race." Nakasone must have been under the influence of this feeling of pride and arrogance when he allowed himself to lapse into nationalistic expressionsim. Some years ago, commenting on the excellence of Japan economic and industrial brains and the merits of the Japanese Zero fighter plane of World War II, Nakasone said, "Japan must truly be a superior nation."

Ishihara's Ultra Nationalistic Views

In 1989, Shintaro Ishihara, a right-wing Dietman belonging to the Abe faction who ran for LDP Presidency and lost to Kaifu, wrote a book entitled *The Japan That Can Say No* which revealed the ultra right-wing thinking of the Japanese. The book, which became a bestseller in Japan, asserts that as Japan moves toward economic and technological supremacy, it will no longer be content to play second fiddle to the United States. Ishihara talks of Japan's new role as a major world power and the potential repercussions for the United States.

Ishihara joined the LDP in 1968 and received the largest number of votes of any candidate. Except for one brief period after he was defeated in his race for governor of Tokyo, he has remained in the Diet. He was former Minister for Communication and was a close associate of Akio Morita, chairman of Sony.

In his book Ishihara said, "Japan now has a decisive technological advantage. I believe that Ronald Reagan, Mikhail Gorbachev and their advisers realised the absurdity of the situation — that the accuracy of their nuclear arsenal depended on Japanese chips — and agreed to call off the arms race." He said a Pentagon report corroborated his belief that Japan held the trump card in the nuclear arms race. A report from the Defence Science Board's task force on semiconductor dependency, he said, revealed US apprehension about Japanese technology, especially in the field of semiconductors.

Shintaro Ishihara, who wrote "The Japan That Can Say No", the extreme right-wing LDP politician who thinks of changing Japan's constitution.

He observed that the (Pentagon) report accurately notes US weaknesses and Japanese superiority in microchips, adding "that if the situation were to continue the United States would be at Japan's beck and call." Ishihara claims that the US semiconductor industry lags more than five years behind Japan's and is falling further back. According to him, Japan is ahead of the Germans, both theoretically and in actual test performances in superconducting magnets. He also claims that Kissinger once told him that although it was a remote possibility, Japan might become a military superpower.

The book describes how Americans felt that they could not trust the Japanese. "In World War II, for example, the United States bombed German cities and killed many civilians but did not use atomic bombs on the Germans."

Ishihara believes that "US planes dropped the atom bombs on the Japanese because of their race. Every American I mention this to denies that race was the reason, but the fact remains that nuclear bombs were dropped on Hiroshima and Nagasaki. We should never forget this. The same virulent racism underlines trade friction with the United States."

Ishihara said that former Prime Minister Nakasone's decision to codevelop with Mitsubishi Heavy Industries (MHI) and produce the FSX was a "sell out". He said MHI produced the world's best ground-to-air missiles and that when The Pentagon saw Japan's FSX blueprints it panicked, and he continues, "No other fighter around will be able to hold a candle to the MHI aircraft. It can easily shoot down the F-15 and F-16. Astounded at the prospect, US Secretary of Defence Caspar Weinberger frantically tried to stop MHI from developing the FSX." Ishihara believes that Japan should withdraw from joint developments with the US.

He added, "We have not maximized our advantage in the high stakes game of international politics. It is beyond me why, when our technology gives us leverage in certain key areas, our leaders do not act more confidently."

Ishihara feels that the US nuclear umbrella is an illusion and that the security treaty is no longer indispensable, saying, "We have sufficient resources to maintain the present level of defence capability on our own... like it no not, before long we will have to reassess the pact and make a decision."

Ishihara also condemns Japan's foreign policy of bowing to the United States and other Asian countries. He feels strongly that Japan should say "No" when it is necessary for the good of Japan. He quoted the instance of Gaimusho's (Ministry of Foreign Affairs) treatment of the Japanese claim for compensation for students killed in China in February 1987. The book said:

"In February 1987, a group of high school students from Kochi Prefecture, on a school trip, were involved in a train accident near Shanghai and more than 30 teenagers were killed. The Japanese parents had asked for a solatium of about US$210,000 and the Chinese offered only US$2,100. Former Prime Minster Takeshita was about to visit China and Ishihara had asked the lawyer who headed the parents' claim to raise the issue. And this was what Premier Li Peng had said, 'I am concerned about the negotiations. Japan is so much richer than China that the requested amount is far out of line with what we can afford.' In fact, Li appealed to Takeshita to have the parents reduce their claim."

Commenting on the incident, Ishihara said that the attitude of the Gaimusho was incomprehensible. He said Gaimusho officials were more worried about the reaction of other governments than about what Japan should do and that "A country must clearly articulate what it wants. The Foreign Ministry is such a weak spokesman for Japan that the Tokyo handlers in Washington, Beijing and elsewhere take advantage of this deferential unassertiveness."

There is not the slightest shadow of doubt that right-wing elements like Ishihara are thinking of changing Japan's Constitution and doing away with the security treaty with the United States. What would have happened if Ishihara had been elected as the new President of LDP and therefore became Prime Minister of Japan?

Japan is becoming more and more right-wing. One would have thought that Nakasone was moving towards the right. Ishihara has gone further than Nakasone. The fact that he is gaining popularity shows that the people are beginning to think that they are a superior race.

Racial Discrimination

Racial discrimination certainly exists in Japan. This prejudice involves minorities, mainly Koreans and Chinese, but especially the Koreans who constitute the biggest minority in Japan. Many Koreans and those of mixed blood often hide their ancestry in order to advance in Japanese society because the Japanese people are insular, clannish and homogeneous.

More than two million Koreans came to Japan before and during World War II. Many of them were forced to work in mines, factories and Japanese farms. About 300,000 were conscripted into the military service. Many of the soldiers I saw during the first wave of invaders into Malaya were Koreans. They were more brutal than the Japanese. With the ending of the war, a large number were repatriated, but many decided to remain behind because of better living standards and more opportunities. Many were already married to Japanese and becoming used to living in Japan.

Today in Japan there is a population of about 850,000 foreigners, 650,000 of them Koreans. These Koreans have to be fingerprinted every five years when their residence certificates are renewed. More than 1,300 Koreans in Japan have refused to be fingerprinted, calling the requirements a human rights violation. They have staged many protests — hunger strikes, rallies, petitions to the United nation and the Japanese Government. They formed themselves into an organisation called Mindan which claims that it has 450,000 members. This organisation receives US$4,000,000 annually from the South Korean government.

A Japanese critic and columnist for The Japan Times, Miss Tsugi Shiraishi, once wrote in her column, "Naturalised Koreans usually have Japanese names, but as soon as the employers find out about the ancestry of the job applicants, excuses are made to reject the Korean job seekers." She said that employment at big industrial plants is virtually closed to Koreans, not because they are inferior to Japanese in skills but because they are of Korean parentage.

The Japanese discriminate against the Koreans by using a method called Koseki-shohon (the secret dossier file). This is an official notarised transcript of the individual's complete vital-statistics dossier, kept permanently on file in a local government office somewhere in Japan. This dossier is an accumulative record of every detail concerning the life of an individual. It begins with the official record of birth, including names and birthplaces of both parents, followed by a complete listing of all changes in residence, any changes of name, marriages, adoptions, births of children and so on. When a transcript of this record is submitted, as by law and customs it must be, together with an application for a job or for admission to an educational institution, it unquestionably identifies the individual in question along racial lines. A person may be Korean and act Japanese, and yet he or she will be identified as Korean the moment the official transcript of this Koseki-shohon is submitted. The same applies to other races.

Before 1st July 1985, all non-Japanese residents were fingerprinted like all other criminals, with their fingers and thumbs imprinted with black. Since Nakasone's visit to Seoul in 1985, the Japanese government revised the fingerprinting procedure from July 1985 with a new method which employes colourless ink and involves only pressing the finger tips down. This new procedure is described as "flat fingerprinting" or "clean fingerprinting". When the government introduced this new system, they hoped that it would reduce the psychological pressure felt by Korean residents. The Koreans, however, were not impressed by the new system and the change did not solve the crux of the matter.

Nakasone must have used this relaxation of the fingerprinting regulations as a political tool to ease the relations between Japan and Korea, damaged by Minister of Education Fujio's remarks about China and Korea. The deterioration of the relationship between Japan, Korea and especially China might hamper Japan's overall defence plan with the United States and the Western Allies. Nakasone saw Japan playing the mediating role in maintaining peace in the international community and therefore could not afford to hurt the feelings of its neighbours.

Burakumin — The Outcasts

One class of people who are really being discriminated against in Japan are the burakumin, which literally means "village people". They are truly a downtrodden people, who are frequently called "eta", a word which has a religious connotation of "unclean". In other words, they are the "untouchables", like the pariahs in India. Some critics refer to them as "Japan's negro problem". The problem is, however, more economic than social in origin. Even those who harbour prejudice against them acknowledge that they are of the Japanese race.

During the feudal days of Japan, the burakumin, now totalling more than 1 million, performed what was considered to be the most menial work: slaughtering animals, burying the dead, making animal glue and cleaning the rubbish in the streets and so on. They were forbidden to marry into the upper classes and were required to live in special ghettos. About a hundred years ago, a decree was issued which, in theory, emancipated the burakumin. But in actual fact, a good deal of prejudice still exists among the average Japanese towards the burakumin.

Even today, the burakumin community, found mostly in western Japan. suffer indignities such as discrimination in jobs, housing and marriage. A large percentage of them are unemployed and many others have lowly jobs. The most difficult hurdle for a burakumin is the document of lineage which everyone has to show to get a job or marry. With this document it is easy to find out who were their ancestors were. It is most difficult to escape the accident of birth. Only very few have become successful in politics and the business world.

The Danger of Rightist Fanatism

Racial discrimination in Japan is not a serious problem that can affect its relations with the international community. It is an internal problem, which the government is making every effort to solve. The real problem facing Japan is the rising tide of rightist fanaticism which believes in the revival of the samurai spirit and the imperial system of administration.

In the 1970s, Japanese society was showing signs of decadence and corruption. An author by the name of Mishima who had an eye cocked for the Nobel Prize, a stylist who could display charm and wit in English or Japanese, committed harakiri (suicide) on the balcony of the Eastern Army headquarters of Japan's Self-Defence Forces. That was on 25th November 1970. His dramatic suicide failed to rouse patriotic feelings. All he got was shocked ridicule from the young military who watched him doing the harakiri with great amusement.

Mishima was a militaristic superpatriot who hated democracy, which to him meant flabiness and femininity. He also hated the peace constitution and worshipped the Emperor. He wanted to see Japan militarised. In 1967, he secretly spent a month training with the Self-Defence Forces and in 1968 formed a private army of 100 men, the Tate no Kai (Shield Society) which was sworn to defend the Emperor. Being a successful author, he was quite rich and spent ¥20 million on running this small army.

To Mishima, the post-war democratic reforms were a sinister influence on the young people, who were getting soft. He thought the democratic system was robbing the young of their virility. He had a lust for uniforms, swords and the martial arts.

As a boy, Mishima, whose ancestors were samurai, showed little interest in the young officers who had staged coups in the 1930s against the ruling class. But he admired their beautiful, undiscriminating patriotism. In his work *The Voice of the Heroic Dead* (Eirei no kaze), he revealed his inner feelings for the Emperor when he said "If the Emperor was not a god, the death of kamize's pilots would had been meaningless."

Before he committed harakiri, he harangued the soldiers assembled below him to revolt and overthrow the government, returning the Emperor and Japan to their rightful places in the Heavens. Baring his abdomen, he made the obligatory horizontal cut of the suicide ritual that had fascinated him for so long, then signalled to his kaishaku to cut off his head. The kaishaku had no experience in lopping off human heads and it took him three cuts to completely separate Mishima into two pieces, badly knicking the blade in the process.

Although Mishima may have been cheered by young military officers in 1970, today his suicide has made an impact on the population. His suicide has made many Japanese think about their duty and the role they should play in society. A movement called "The New Right" has propounded an ideology that lurks in the hearts of the more conservative elder Japanese. Spokesmen for the New Right claim they are concerned with national apathy and materialism, and the flood of comic books. They charge that Japanese youth these days are weak-kneed, fainthearted and apt to commit suicide at the first sign of personal setback.

Yukio Mishima, who committed harakiri in front of the Defence Ministry in November 1970 to arouse patriotic feelings among the Japanese.

Mishima did not die in vain. His statue can be seen in the Tokyo Wax Museum which depicts not a man of books but a naked warrior holding a long sword. It is just as he wished to be remembered. On the first anniversary of his death, there were demonstrations of kendo and karate instead of readings of his literary works.

In one of his suicide notes, Mishima wanted a life-size bronze statue of himself erected at a place where Mt. Fuji and the sea could be seen. His family had a life-sized nude statue of Mishima made by a Tokyo sculptor and placed it in the desired place.

It is often said that Mishima had found the purest expression of Japan's spirit among the defence forces. When he was training his private army, he was given special permission to do the training at military campsites.

To commemorate Mishima's death, the nationalistic minded author and critic, Fusao Yahashi, together with a right-wing student group helped found the Mishima Research Institute. A part of the new institute's prospectus said that: "Japanese history has been shunted to the sidelines, the traditions neglected and warrior spirit lost. In these modern times of unprecedented degeneration, the Japanese nation has at last burst out of the years that had bottled up its real anger."

The prospectus went on to say that the institute will do all it can to stir up patriotic fervour and will "defend against revolution against the Emperor... and make a national army out of the Self-Defence Forces, in keeping with the basic principle of founding an army, and will enhance the glorious spirit of the Japanese nation."

Mishima had often spoke critically of the Japanese society. He once wrote: "The Japanese people began to decline in morality in 1876, with the decree abolishing the wearing of swords for men... Unless everyone comes to have the spirit of being ready to take a rifle and stand up in case of emergency, Japan will come to a sad predicament in the future." He believed that post-war society had become perverted because "it has lost uniforms". In the streets of Tokyo, I seldom saw a soldier in uniform, for military uniforms have become unpopular and much hated by the ordinary Japanese.

He had a poor opinion of modern literature. He once wrote, "Japanese modern literature is a paradise of insomniacs, neurotics, impotents, ugly masses of fat, cancer and stomach disease patients, sentimentalists and semilunatics. Those who can fight are few."

Mishima was familiar with the literature on Bushido and in 1967 wrote an essay entitled *The Code of Hagakure and I.* He said, "Japanese sword once unsheathed must not be replaced until it has cut through something or someone", almost paraphrasing what was said several centuries ago by leading samurai. He knew the samurai ethics by heart. He strongly believed in Bushido, which taught people how to die.

The Hagakure's (Hidden behind the Leaves) most gripping sentence says something along the line of "When one is forced between life and death, it is important to choose death without hesitation". Words like these goaded Mishima into action and formed part of his basic psychology. He often exhorted his fellow citizens to lay down their lives to recapture the lost glory of the Japanese Empire and to kill the post-war Japanese constitution.

Perhaps the most striking side effect of the Mishima incident was that it revealed a deep vein of antimodernism among many Japanese who have a fondness for heroic action and tradition. Some of the adjectives that were used to describe Mishima's harakiri included "sublime", "aesthetic", "beautiful" and "pure".

Mishima's action was actually in step with a rising opinion among zaibatse and ruling party leaders like Nakasone, who feel that it is essential for Japan to possess nuclear weapons and to be strong militarily again so that the country will not be inferior to the superpowers.

Mishima did not die in vain. His self-sacrifice kindled in the minds of many Japanese the desire to make Japan strong again. His suicide reminded the youth not to be softened by decadent Western democracy. His death has had far-reaching repercussion in reviving the nationalistic spirit of the people.

If Mishima could see from his grave what the Japanese have done to rearm itself to become a military power to be reckoned with in the international family of nations, and to send a so-called "Peace keeping" troup to Cambodia, he would have been happy. His death would have been worthwhile.

This was what most Japanese would think.

The National Council to Defend Japan

The Mishima incident was just the beginning of Japan's swing towards right-wing nationalism. In 1981, a group of concerned Japanese patriots, including scholars, artists, ex-government officials and Shinto priests, among others, formed a new citizens' organisation, small in number but increasingly vocal: The National Council To Defend Japan. The organisation's titular chairman is the 83-year-old Toshikazu Kase, Japan's first Ambassador to the United Nations and a member of the Japanese surrender delegation aboard the battleship Missouri. Sponsoring members include such well-known names as Masaru Ibuka, honorary chairman of Sony, and Nobutaka Shikanai, publisher of the Sankei Shimbun daily newspaper. But the man who furnishes the fire power is composer Toshiro Mayuzumi, head of the steering committee.

The debonair Mayuzumi, whose energy belies his 57 years except for some graying at the temples, sat on the edge of his chair and leant forward, the light of commitment in his eyes, as he explained to the council: "We are profoundly concerned by two important facts. One, most Japanese are not proud to be Japanese. And two, Japan has no emergency law wherewith to defend itself.

"Few people know, for instance, that tanks charging down the roads and highways of Japan to meet an invading enemy would have to obey the traffic lights. Few people are aware that no Japanese Self-Defence Force can dig a foxhole on privately-owned land. Thus, one of our major objectives is to effect laws that would allow our forces to defend Japan in actuality, not merely in name."

What does the National Council to Defend Japan stand for? According to a pamphlet, it concentrates on four major projects:

1) To establish the Emperor as head of state. Publicity efforts in this direction include an eight-minute motion picture of the Emperor. The film has been shown in 1,500 locations, and the council wants to show it in all Japan's 3,300 cities, towns and villages. The showing of the film is linked with cultural activities, aimed at reinforcing the concept of the Emperor's "Imperial virtue".

2) Defence of Japan's peace and safety. At no time has Japan needed defensive power more. The issue of defence must be squarely faced. The people must be educated and the Self-Defence Law must be changed.

3) Revision of Japan's peace constitution. Since the war, fractures have appeared in the fibre of every field of endeavour — government, business and everyday society. The Council vows to hold rallies, give speeches, develop seminars and study groups and other activities that will promote the revision of the present constitution.

4) Normalisation of education. The council will work to revises texts, lobby the Ministry of Education, promote reverence of the flag and national anthem, and reverse the leftist trends of post-war education. Thus, love of home and country will gradually be planted in the hearts of Japan's youth.

The council first gained prominence when a major newspaper claimed that a council-revised textbook had changed the word "invade" to "advance" when speaking of Japan's actions in Korea and China prior to The Second World War. The article provoked anger in both countries and controversy raged for weeks.

Mayuzumi, commenting on the textbook affair, said: "The whole thing was a fabrication. The newspaper ran an apology — very small — but people will equate us with that lie. There was no revision of the word "invade". The entire affair was the result of the overactive imagination of a newspaper reporter.

"Why are we presenting a re-edited high school history text? Because the 17 textbooks presently authorised for high school use all show Japan as a "bad" country. Japan is not a bad country. Nothing in pre-war Japan was done without a reason. The Great East Asia Co-Prosperity Sphere was established for a reason. We even went into a war we knew we could not win because we had no other choice."

In an interview with the Asahi Shimbun, Mayuzumi aired his views on revising Japan's constitution: "Present interpretations of the constitution are studies in artful dodgery. Take defence, for example. Even the Japan Socialist Party, which makes a big thing of saying the Self-Defence Forces are unconstitutional, in practice recognises its existence. But there are no clear constitutional grounds for the Self-Defence Forces. In other words, the spirit and the letter of the law are much too far apart. And that is unhealthy for the government, society, philosophy and culture of Japan.

"Our constitution was foisted on us by the Allied forces. Its preamble is obviously translated from English, as are other sections. The train of thought is often unclear. These sections need to be rewritten into clear, understandable Japanese."

Mayuzumi said that the most important part of the consitutional revision concerned the position of the Emperor, whom he thought should not be only symbolic. He said he should be given the clear right to defend the country.

The National Council to Defend Japan is gaining strength. There are chapters in every prefecture and metropolitan area. Their normalisation of wartime activities is gaining considerable acceptance. Their re-edited version of Japanese history will be on the roster of accepted textbooks for the new school year. Some 30 high schools have already decided to use the book.

Anyone who is interested in the rising tide of Japan's right-wing nationalism should follow this organisation called the National Council to Defend Japan, as it is exerting tremendous influence on government policies in education, defence and other matters involved with the reviving Japan's samurai spirit. It appears that the National Council to Defend Japan is the think tank of the ruling LDP Government. How far the Council will go and how effective its activities are will affect Japan's future trends.

The Japanese live on fragile islands, crowded, treacherous but beautiful. The earth beneath them shakes and their mountains coughs, the seas smash onto their chipped coast, the wild winds tear the leaves from their bent trees. Their life is mortgaged to the uncertainties of cruel nature and crammed by the smallness of nature's products. They do not feel a sense of brotherhood among nations. Their strength lies in discipline and the collectiveness of their community. They have to struggle in order to live. Their goal is not fixed and only life's necessity drives them on to accept the challenge of the time. The Japanese follow the leader who is able to wield power and tells them what to do, but have no knowledge where he will lead them. The National Council to Defend Japan will directly and indirectly guide the masses into a definite direction. Will the Council provide the leadership necessary for a passive society like Japan? Will the Council's influence take root? The future is worth watching.

The present scenario in Japan is very precarious. Politicians are corrupt, the youth soft, society is rotten and discipline among the population slacking. As the Council and ultra right-wing nationalists get stronger in line with the growing influence of the military, there is no guarantee that there might not be a "gang up" to clean up Japan's society "for the good of the divine country". History may repeat itself. Who knows, a new Ikki Kita may emerge in present-day Japan?

In October 1931, Ikki Kita, Japan's military firebrand, led the Brocade Flag Revolution involving 120 officers and their troops, planning to assassinate ministers, government servants and court officials. Someone within the group turned informer and the plot was uncovered. The rebels then assembled in front of the Imperial Palace and by way of apologising to the Emperor committed harakiri.

Once again the trials of the rebels provided the Japanese citizens with melodrama and propaganda. The assassin in Japanese history had often been a more sympathetic figure than the victim. Was there not some lack of virtue in a man who got himself involved as a target of assassination and was not an assassin who murdered for lofty purposes merely trying to defend the common people against tyranny? Overwhelming evidence of guilt notwithstanding, the two killers were not executed but given life sentences, from which it was obvious they would be paroled in a few years. It was the old story — amnesty for any actual violence if it was done for the glory of the nation.

In the early 1930s, the radical nationalists within the army took the law into their own hands and turned to assassination as a means of achieving power. Each member of the Blood Brotherhood was pledged to kill at least one "corrupt" political, financial leader or government official.

In May 1932, nine navy and army officers took taxis and forced their way into the residence of Prime Minister Tsuyushi Inukai, a diminutive man of 75 with a goatee. The old man calmly led the would-be assassins to a Japanese style room, where they politely removed their shoes and sat down. At that moment, a comrade who had got lost in the corridors entered, dagger in hand and cried out, "No use talking. Fire." Everyone began shooting at the courageous little Prime Minister who had opposed the conquest of Manchuria and steadfastly refused to recognise the puppet government of Manchuria, now under the name of "Manchukuo" (State of Manchu). The assassins later surrendered after throwing bombs at the Bank of Japan and scattering handbills in the streets.

The establishment of Manchukuo was in fact inspired by two military leaders, Ishihara and Itagaki, who were in charge of the invasion of the Chinese territories. When they invaded Manchuria, they invested one billion dollars into the bandit-infested, sparsely populated territory and maintained such law and order along the railroads that hundreds of thousands of Japanese, Chinese and Korean traders arrived. Settlers started flooding the area. It was this mass influx that inspired Ishihara and Itagaki to envision a Manchuria free of its Chinese war-lord rulers. Ishihara dreamed of making it an autonomous state, a haven for all of its ethnic groups — Japanese Chinese, Manchurians, Koreans and White Russians. Here, genuine democracy would be practised and a buffer would be set up against Soviet Russia. But, both the Emperor and the War Ministry had refused to sanction such a plan. Undeterred, Ishihara and Itagaki acted on their own — in Japanese it is called "gekokujo". The military leaders eliminated the Chinese war-lord Marshall Chang Tso-lin (the old Marshal) and took over Manchuria, defying orders from Tokyo. After the abortive Brocade Flag Revolution, progress in the Manchurian adventure was assured.

The coup led by Ikki Kita, commonly known as May 15th Incident, had fizzled out and it brought forward even more sensational trials. The people were in sympathy with the assassins. Feelings ran high and 110,000 petitions for clemancy, signed or written entirely in blood, inundated officials of the trial.

The Kuromaku of The Yakuza-Rightist Underworld

Ikki Kita was only a frontman who received his support from his "kuromaku" (the black curtain) of the yakuza right-wing underworld, or "the godfather", who operated behind the scene. The kuromaku has, since the 19th century, been a pivotal figure of Japanese politics. In the Japanese political arena, the kuromaku (also known as the "godfather" or "king-maker") has always been exerting the power behind the scene. In Japan, kuromaku more often than not refers to the ultra right-wing elements supported by yakuza. The word "kuromaku" originated in classical Kabuki theatre, in which an unseen wire puller controls the stage by manipulating a black curtain. Today, it connotes a powerful godfather or fixer who operates from behind the scene. The kuromaku serves as a bridge between the yakuza-rightist underworld and the legitimate world of business and mainstream politics.

Ikki Kita's Godfather was Mitsuru Toyama, founder of the Genyosha or Dark Ocean Society which had its origin in 1881. The name Dark Ocean suggested the dark narrow passage of water separating Japan from Korea and China, which the organisation wanted very much to conquer. Toyama had founded the society as a paramilitary force to realise his dream of tapping the sentiment among the ex-samurai for expansion abroad and establishing an authoritarian rule at home. The society's charter was vague: to revere the Emperor, love and respect the nation and defend the people's rights.

Using the Dark Ocean Society as a weapon, Toyama carried out a campaign of terror, blackmail and assassination to exert influence over members of the military corps, government bureaucracy and to bring Japan into East Asia and declare war with the United States. The society's agents were sent to China, Korea and Manchuria as spies. They operated schools where an entire generation of ultranationalists were trained in martial arts, foreign languages and spying techniques. These trained spies created the basis for the sophisticated intelligence network serving Japan before World War II.

In 1895, a squad of Genyosha agents, trained in the martial arts of Ninja, infiltrated the Korean Imperial Palace and murdered the queen. That act precipitated Japan's invasion of Korea and occupation for 50 years.

The successor of Genyosha, the Kokuryu-kai (the Amur River Society or The Black Dragon Society), founded in 1901 by Toyama's righthand man, Ryohei Uchida, did spying work in China just as the Dark Ocean Society was doing in Korea. The name suggested that the Society had the ambition of expanding to Amur River, which is the boundary between Manchuria and Russia. For 30 years, the Black Dragon Society helped create conditions advantageous for a Japanese invasion of China. The yakuza groups, working hand in hand with the militarists, occupied Manchuria and carried out "land development" programmes. Among the lucrative businesses they carried out was the Manchurian Government's Opium Monopoly Bureau, which had a dual objective of making money and weakening the Chinese fighting spirit by fostering drug addiction. Japan's narcotisation policy in China earned Japan about US$300 million a year, which was spent on the industrial development of the occupied lands.

The ultimate aim of the Black Dragon Society was the domination of Asia, with the slogan "Hakko-ichi-u" (the eight corners of the world under one roof). The roof was that of the Emperor of Japan, descended from the Sun God in an unbroken line.

Toyama continued to rise through the tumultuous 1930s and became Japan's hero. He was the one who was asked to lead the three cheers for the Emperor at the Imperial Palace during dinner functions. In Japan, he was the kuromaku — the Godfather, who possessed wealth and prestige, handpicked cabinet members, as well as arranged for assassinations of those who were against their ambitions to march into Manchuria. Toyama died in 1944, at 89, before seeing his beloved Japan conquer much of Asia and the Pacific. After his death, his portrait adorned the walls of nearly all rightist offices and many yakuza organisations. He was lucky that he did not have to experience Japan's disastrous defeat.

There were three well-known kuromakus of post-war Japanese politics. All of them were ultra right-wingers with connections with the yakuza underworld. They were Yoshio Kodama, Ryoichi Sasakawa and Nobusuke Kishi. All of them had exerted considerable influence over the Liberal Democratic Party: The three of them were well-known pre-war leaders involved with World War II. They were tried as Class A war criminals and went to Sugamo Prison but were released by the American Allied Forces because the Korean War necessitated Japanese help in fighting the Communists in the Korean peninsular. After their release, they became prominent post-war leaders: Kodama became the Godfather and financier of LDP which he helped to put into power; Kishi, who was vice-minister in Tojo's wartime cabinet, made the world's biggest political comeback and emerged as Prime Minister of Japan in March 1957; and Sasakawa became the leader of the right-wing extremists and a multi-millionaire, dishing out support for right-wing movements. The trio was the bulwark of the right-wing movement which was anti-Communist, advocated loyalty to the Emperor and backed Japan's rearmament.

Kodama, the fifth son of Nihonmatsu city folk who were financially handicapped, started life in 1911. At the age of eight, he lived with a distant relative in Korea and suffered isolation and hardship. He understood the plight of labourers. At the beginning, he turned to socialism but later became an ultra-nationalist. He was not very good on theory but gifted in organisation, had a knack for gaining quick profit and would use whatever method to achieve it, including violence.

Kodama started off as an apprentice to the infamous Mitsuru Toyama, the Godfather of the ultra-nationalist underworld who was founder of the Dark Ocean Society. As an apprentice, and a worshipper of the Emperor, he tried to hand over a letter to him appealing for increased patriotism. He was arrested by the police in a motorcade before he could hand over the letter and was put in jail for six months. After his release, he participated in an abortive attempt to assassinate cabinet ministers, including Prime Minister Admiral Saito. For all the crimes he had committed, he served a total of six years in prison. During his six years in jail he wrote a book entitled *I Was Defeated.*

After his experience in violent activities, he become interested in the world of foreign policies and entered the Foreign Ministry's information bureau. He later joined the expeditionary force to China and the East Indies, and was attached to Navy, Air Force and Ministry of the Interior. Kodama's talents were recognised, and in 1939 he was sent to spy for the government in China. He set up a network of Manchurian spies and collaborators all over China. When Japan attacked Pearl Harbour, he started his Kodama Kikan (Kodama Agency) which had an exclusive right to supply strategic materials needed for the war effort to the Navy and Air Force. Kodama dealt in tungsten, guns, radium, cobalt, nickel and copper. He obtained the materials from China and Manchuria at cheap prices, forcing the Chinese at gunpoint and sold them at lucrative prices. Kodama Kikan became a financial giant with a working capital of US$175 million in industrial diamonds, platinum and banknotes.

Kodama used "self-sacrificing youths" to work for him, thus reducing his cost. Besides doing business, he continued to handle intelligence work and financed the Kempei Tai, the Japanese Secret Police. By the end of the war, Kodama was fabulously rich. He returned to Japan at 34 years old and became adviser to the Prime Minister Prince Higashikuni. He tried to help the Americans accept Japan's surrender with less violence, but the Americans did not trust him. Then, in early 1946, together with other high ranking pre-war politicians and business leaders, he was arrested and put in Sugamo Prison. However, he was not even tried nor charged.

It seems that Kodama's release was a result of a secret deal he struck with the Americans G-2 officials who were then obsessed with the rise of Communism in Korea and China. He cooperated with the CIA after his release.

Being easily one of the richest man among the 644 suspected war criminals, Kodama supported the LDP which became the ruling party in Japan for 37 years. He was the most powerful single individual within the LDP and in 1954 helped engineer the election of Hatoyama to the Prime Ministership. He owned a real estate firm and several national distributed sports (gambling) newspapers, a baseball team and a shipping line. He also owned part of the Ginza nightclub empire that was controlled by his strikebreaking partner, Korean gang boss Hisayuki Machii.

In 1981, Kodama was sentenced to three-and-a-half years imprisonment and a fine of US$3 million for his involvement with Prime Minister Tanaka's Lockheed corruption case. The sentence was postponed because of his worsening ill health. It seems that roughly US$7 million, most of it in yen bills packed in a cardboard boxes, had been covertly sent to Kodama, who was the Lockheed's secret sales agent.

On the evening of 17 January 1984, the 72-year-old Kodama suffered another stroke and silently passed away. At his funeral, leading businessmen, rightists, gangsters and entertainers turned up. Curiously, however, his close political allies over the years who had received money from him felt shy and thought it unwise to publicly honour the man whom they owed so much.

The story of Kishi, who was Japan's Prime Minister in 1957, is the most remarkable of the three. He began his political career as a follower of Ikki Kita, the engineer of the Imperial Palace coup. Kishi's real power base was Manchukuo, Japan's puppet state in conquered Manchuria. From 1936 to 1939, he was officially the second highest ranking civilian in Manchukuo; some people referred to him as the ruler of the province. With the help of rightists and gangsters, he developed Manchukuo. After his return from Manchuria, he was appointed Minster of Trade and Industry and Vice Munitions minister in Tojo's wartime cabinet.

When Japan was defeated, Kishi was detained as a Class A war criminal. Then, in December 1948, he, Kodama and Sasagawa were released in mysterious circumstances. In 1952, he re-entered politics and made the world's greatest political comeback. In 1955, he became LDP's secretary general and became deputy Prime Minster under Prime Minister Yoshida. In 1957, backed by Kodama's financial resources, Kishi became Prime Minister.

Kishi had never been personally popular as Prime Minister, but he continued to work behind the scenes after his retirement. He remained influential until the years when I was Ambassador to Japan. By giving the coalition of rightist and yakuza the official imprimatur of the government, Kishi reinstated a tradition dating back to the dark days of ultra-nationalism. His actions legitimised the post-war ties between the government and the underworld, and ushered in a period of gangster-rightist cooperation. In 1971, Kishi, together with other former LDP ministers, stunned many Japanese when he guaranteed bail for a Yamaguchi-gumi boss convicted of murder. In 1974, he was among scores of prominent guests invited by Yamaguchi godfather Kazuo Taoka to the lavish wedding of his son. Unable to attend, Kishi made sure the family received a congratulatory telegram, as did Sasakawa.

Sometime in 1986, when Kishi died, I attended a commemoration ceremony held for him at a stadium. It was a grand affair and the whole Japanese cabinet was present.

The Kishi faction was taken over by Fukuda and then later by Shintaro Abe, the son-in-law of Kishi. Abe was groomed to be Prime Minister after Takeshita unfortunately died of cancer. Many leaders within the Abe faction are rightist.

The only prominent pre-war rightist leader left — the last of the trio who emerged from the Sugamo prison — is Ryoichi Sasakawa. He took a slightly different route to fame from that of Kodama and Kishi, although all of them came from the same roots. Someone told me that expenses for Tokyo's right-wing ultras, who chant slogans almost everyday in the streets from mobile vans against Russian occupation of the Northern territories and against the Communist visitors, are being financed by Sasakawa.

Sasakawa was not merely an ultra-nationalist before the war, he was also an open admirer of Mussolini and ordered his private militia to don block shirts, imitating the Italian Fascists. It was at the Sugamo prison that he met Kodama and they became friends and "comrades".

Sasakawa made his fortune from his involvement in China during the war. It was in connection with the custodian of Chinese (enemy) properties which he was asked to handle. After the war, he built up a gambling empire from motor racing. He founded the Japan Motorboat Racing Association, which sets up the race course, operates the stands and the boats, pays the drivers, and deals with all aspects connected with motor racing. He bragged publicly that he was a drinking partner of Japan's leading godfather, the Chief of Yamaguchi-gumi, Kazuo Taoka, and served as mediator between feuding yakuza gangs.

I met Sasakawa when he visited Singapore in 1983, when he presented 40 racing boats to the People's Association of which I was Deputy chairman. We had dinner at the home of Akiko Aw, wife of Aw It Haw, son of millionaire Aw Boon Haw. He gave me the impression of a man who was fond of publicity. He bought up huge blocks of television airtime to exhort youngsters to honour their parents and to keep the earth clean. His face appeared almost every night on Japan's TV advertisements showing him giving away gifts to underdeveloped countries. He embarked on a career of self-aggrandisement, running hundreds of print and television ads bearing his smiling face and reminding Japan of his beneficence.

In an interview with the Time magazine in 1974, Sasakawa said: "Formerly I had Yoshio Kodama and many other roughnecks around me. I was their leader. So some may call me a rightist. I am not a rightist. I am a humanitarian. I am the world's wealthiest fascist."

Tyoichi Sasakawa, the ultra-nationalist and admirer of Mussolini.

The names of Kodama, Kishi and Sasakawa have become synonymous in Japan with the dark side of the nation's politics. All of them exerted enormous influence over the LDP. They have had close connections with the yakuza who clamour for a rapid buildup of Japan's armed forces. Historically, the yakuza have been active supporters of a potent military Japan. They formed ultra-nationalists groups in the 1920s and 1930s, pushing the country into World War II. They also participated in "land development" programing to settle occupied Manchuria and after the war they organised paramilitary units, designed to help police and military battle leftist groups. Today, the yakuza back the rightists call for a repeal of Article IX of Japan's post-war constitution, an antiwar clause that in effect limits the country to a small, defensive military force. Nowadays, these rightist gangs, often staffed by yakuza, are a common sight in Japan's major cities. I often saw these gangs clad in helmets, battle fatigues and sunglasses, darting around town in steel-plated trucks sporting military banners and flags adorned with the Rising Sun. Atop the vehicles stood huge loudspeakers blaring martial music in all directions, with breaks in the score to call for strident anti-Soviet measures, repeal of the constitution, an immediate buildup of Japan's military strength and restoration of the dignity of "the Japanese race". Some groups even call for the nuclear arming of Japan. It is estimated that there are about 120,000 of these neo-Fascist characters, split into some 840 groups nationwide.

Other worrying signs in Japan today are the revisionist changes in the Japanese view of World War II. Recently, a glorified movie of the life of Hidejo Tojo, the war criminal who served as wartime Prime Minister, became one of the best sellers in Tokyo. Tojo began to gain huge popularity. History textbooks were changed to soften the description of wartime atrocities such as the 1937 Nanking massacre. Some prominent politicians even openly said the Nanking massacre was "just an imagination" and that there was no truth in it.

There are indications that the ultra right-wing forces in Japan have gained strength. The way Prime Minister Miyazawa handled the impending visit of Emperor Akihito to China clearly showed that the ultra right-wing in Japan were not happy with his visit. They were also pressurising the Emperor not to apologise to the Chinese leaders as the ultra right-wingers believed that Japan had done no wrong to China and needed to give no apology.

Emperor Akihito visited China in October 1992. He was given a red carpet treatment by the Chinese with several hundreds of school children waving paper Japanese flags. It was the first time a Japanese monarch had set foot on Chinese soil in 2,000 years — a compelling signal of Tokyo's determination to forge a new relationship with a budding superpower and traditional rival. But, curiously the tone of the visit was low key. Emperor Akihito did not "apologise" for Japan's wrongdoing in World War II. He merely deplored the suffering caused by the Imperial troops during the war saying:

"In the long history of the relationship between our two countries, there was an unfortunate period in which my country inflicted great sufferings on the people of China. I deeply deplore this. When the war came to an end, the Japanese people, believing with a sense of deep reproach that such a war should never be repeated, firmly resolved to tread the road of a peaceful nation."

The absence of a formal apology for the estimated 10 million deaths caused by Japan's Imperial troops during their brutal occupation of much of China was a grave disappointment to many Chinese people. But, they did no harm to the Emperor during his visit and the Communist authorities too did not embarrass the visitor by pressing any demands. The Chinese were eager to regain international prestige after the 1989 Tiananmen Square crackdown and easily agreed that no apology was necessary. It seemed that the right-wing group in Japan had again strengthened their credibility.

Another disturbing factor in recent events was that Miyazawa, normally a moderate and pro-US, was pressurised to visit the Yasukuni shrine as Prime Minister. Although he did not join the other right-wing cabinet ministers when they visited the shrine in 1992 to pay respect to war dead including Tojo, he did promise to go some other day.

The ultra right-wing pressure group is extremely strong. Miyazawa, who was previously against Japan's rearmament, had to support rearmament and spoke of Japan's international duty to send troops abroad as U.N. peace keeping forces to Cambodia.

In March 1995, when the Socialist-backed proposal for a "war-renouncing" parliamentary resolution to mark the 50th anniversary of the end of World War II was debated in the Diet, a group of right-wing supporters calling themselves the "People's Council for the 50th anniversary of the End of the War" protested against the resolution. This group collected signatures from more than 270 parliamentarians, or about a third of the total number of members in both houses of the Japanese Parliament. They held a meeting in Tokyo attended by politicians from the LDP and the opposition New Frontier Party. Although the LDP is a member of Japan's three-party coalition government, more than 150 of its Dietmen earlier banded together to form a league opposing the passage of any parliamentary resolution apologising for Japan's Wars of aggression in Asia and declaring that Japan would never go to war again. League members include several top LDP executives, among them Party Secretary General Yoshiro Mori, Trade Minister Ryotaro Hishimoto, two former Lower Houses speakers and even half a dozen former foreign ministers.

However, the Socialists and the small Sakigake, the two other members of the coalition, support a "no war" resolution containing a form of apology, which they said was agreed to in a pact reached last year among the coalition parties. But, many LDP members are against Japan saying sorry to its Asian neighbours over its past military conduct.

Seisuke Okuno, a former Justice Minister and head of the LDP league, recently criticised the Socialists for trying to push for a "no war" resolution.

He said, "Japan did not fight with Asia. The Americans and the British were the ones who fought a war of aggression. Japan was also the victim of atrocities in Manchuria and elsewhere."

Several other Liberal Democrats, as well as opposition politicians who once belonged to the LDP, had in the past denied that Japanese military aggression or the Nanking Massacre had ever taken place.

Meanwhile, as the rest of the world prepares to celebrate the 50th anniversary of the end of World War II, the Japanese have been remembering the event in their own inimitable way. Scores of new books are appearing on the shelves of Japan's railway kiosks, telling a history of the war that is very different from the one the rest of the world knows.

In lurid paperbacks, dozens of hacks have been making fortunes titillating readers with roaring yarns of how Japan won the war and defeated, even colonised, America. Their heroes are idealistic, selfless Japanese soldiers, sailors and airmen who liberated Southeast Asia from the colonial yoke of Western thuggery and brought a new and superior cilivisation to their emancipated Asian brothers.

The authors are not pretending that this is anything other than fiction. For many Japanese, however, the stories bear a striking resemblance to their own warped understanding of Japan's war role.

In Japan, the post-war generations are ignorant of what Japan did during World War II and the atrocities Japanese soldiers committed in China and Southeast Asia. School history books have been purged of all but the barest details of the embarrassing period in Japan's history. Often no mention is made of the attack on Pearl Harbour or the torture and massacre of countless civilians and prisons of war. Although in recent years the Monbujsho (Japan's Education Ministry) has begun to permit slightly longer accounts of the war in school textbooks, Japan is still portrayed as virtually blameless. Japanese War memorials, particularly at Hiroshima, imply that the Americans were the real criminals.

In recent years, leading Japanese officials, including Prime Ministers, have apologised for Japan's wrong doings. But no official apology has been made by the Diet, Japan's parliament, and many Asians fear that without a full acknowledgement of responsibility for the wartime atrocities, most Japanese will remain ignorant of them and are likely to blunder into another war.

Who can guarantee that history may not repeat itself if the younger generation is not aware of what went wrong in the contemporary history of Japan and what led to the dropping of the atom bomb in Hiroshima? The ultra-military leaders that led them to war have caused disaster to themselves and the nation. The younger generation who do not know where they went wrong are likely to follow the leader and make another mistake. In my observation of the Japanese during my stay, I find that the Japanese act more than they think. They prefer someone else to think for them. At present, it seems that the National Council to Defend Japan is doing the thinking. The leaders of the ultra right-wing nationalists, backed by the yakuza, exert pressure on the political thinkers. They want Japan to revive the glory of pre-war "achievements".

Once activated, the Japanese go on doing, and do not know when to stop until something from outside shakes them to their senses. Commodore Perry shook Japan, which had been in self-isolation for 200 years, into realising that they were weak after all. The atom bomb made the Japanese realise that they were not strong enough after all to conquer Asia.

Since the end of the World War II, Japan has turned her people to accept the philosophy of "saving, scrimping and exporting" as a virtue and in the past fifty years the whole nation acquired this habit. In between, no leader told the Japanese to change their course. They kept exporting, amassing huge fortunes for Japan and this is hurting most countries, including America which is providing them with security. It takes the cry of American protectionism to wake the Japanese up to the fact that they have to change their course.

The Japanese are generally good followers. They conform. As individuals they do not make up their own minds and have to be told by their leaders what to do. They never learn from the lessons of history. The younger generation only knows that the cruel Americans dropped the atom bomb which killed millions of Japanese in Hiroshima. They are not aware of the atrocities their ancestors committed during Word War II and accept the simplistic statement at face value because they have not been taught the subtleties of the situation.

The Japanese have been dangerous and may be dangerous again. In the intensity to compete with the world for supremacy, they have no knowledge of where they are being led and and how it will all end up.

The Japanese have never felt secure while riding on someone else's tails. American protection is never a good answer to satisfy their sense of security. They have built up enough military power to be self-supporting. With the collapse of Russian Communism, they may be toying with the idea of telling the Americans that they can look after themselves and even challenging America in the sales of arms to developing countries which are fested with rivalries. They will not step aside to see China getting the benefit of selling arms to developing countries. The National Council to Defend Japan and the right-wing ultra-nationalists may press for the change of constitution to enable Japan to re-arm in full swing.

With America's encouragement, they will first of all do their basic role of keeping sea lanes relatively clear of enemy submarines and build up enough fighters to provide an interceptor network around the four vulnerable islands. They are now encouraged to send troops to Cambodia. What next? Nobody knows.

The Japanese move step by step. Sometimes they do not know what the next step will be, and the next step may be darkness. The problem with the Japanese is that they do not know when to stop.

Index